#MeToo

This edited collection on #MeToo activism challenges the overwhelming whiteness and straightness of #MeToo discourse and coverage. Using intersectional and decolonial frameworks and historical, archival, organizational and legal methods, these essays offer a rich exploration of #MeToo to understand how activism around sexualized violence reproduce and harm a wide variety of people.

The swift and powerful arrival of #MeToo as a compilation of complaints about sexual misconduct (especially in the workplace) has created pressure to dive deeper into the history of sexual assault and abuse in the United States. *#MeToo: A Rhetorical Zeitgeist* answers the call for more complicated analyses of systemic sexual harassment and abuse with essays that are deeply concerned with the whiteness and heterosexuality of #MeToo coverage and media framing to understand how and why #MeToo began to capture the public's attention in 2017 against the backdrop of Donald J. Trump's presidential administration.

These essays offer the first comprehensive study of the rhetorical politics of #MeToo. They tackle the complexities of sexual harassment, sexual violence and rape beyond white celebrity discourse to understand: how both violence and #MeToo activism affect transgender people; how #MeToo fails Black male victims of assault and rape; how Indian-American masculinity and comedy skirt sexual accountability; how the legal and affective precedent in the Supreme Court during the Kavanaugh hearings amplified concerns about sexual assault and rape; decolonial approaches to resisting sexualized violence from indigenous peoples; and narratives about assault from within the higher education community.

The chapters in this book were originally published as a special issue of *Women's Studies in Communication*.

Lisa M. Corrigan is Professor of Communication and Director of the Gender Studies Program at the University of Arkansas, USA. She is the author of: *Prison Power: How Prison Influenced the Movement for Black Liberation* (2016) and *Black Feelings: Race and Affect in the Long Sixties* (2020). She also co-hosts a popular podcast with Laura Weiderhaft called *Lean Back: Critical Feminist Conversations*.

#MeToo
A Rhetorical Zeitgeist

Edited by
Lisa M. Corrigan

NEW YORK AND LONDON

First published 2022
by Routledge
605 Third Avenue, New York, NY 10158

and by Routledge
2 Park Square, Milton Park, Abingdon, Oxon OX14 4RN

Routledge is an imprint of the Taylor & Francis Group, an informa business

© 2022 The Organization for Research on Women and Communication

All rights reserved. No part of this book may be reprinted or reproduced or utilised in any form or by any electronic, mechanical, or other means, now known or hereafter invented, including photocopying and recording, or in any information storage or retrieval system, without permission in writing from the publishers.

Trademark notice: Product or corporate names may be trademarks or registered trademarks, and are used only for identification and explanation without intent to infringe.

Library of Congress Cataloging-in-Publication Data
A catalog record for this title has been requested

ISBN: 978-1-032-01816-4 (hbk)
ISBN: 978-1-032-01819-5 (pbk)
ISBN: 978-1-003-18020-3 (ebk)

DOI: 10.4324/9781003180203

Typeset in Minion Pro
by Newgen Publishing UK

Publisher's Note
The publisher accepts responsibility for any inconsistencies that may have arisen during the conversion of this book from journal articles to book chapters, namely the inclusion of journal terminology.

Disclaimer
Every effort has been made to contact copyright holders for their permission to reprint material in this book. The publishers would be grateful to hear from any copyright holder who is not here acknowledged and will undertake to rectify any errors or omissions in future editions of this book.

Contents

Citation Information		vi
Notes on Contributors		viii
	Introduction: The #MeToo Moment—A Rhetorical Zeitgeist Lisa M. Corrigan	1
1	(Trans)forming #MeToo: Toward a Networked Response to Gender Violence V. Jo Hsu	6
2	Expendables for Whom: Terry Crews and the Erasure of Black Male Victims of Sexual Assault and Rape Tommy J. Curry	24
3	#AzizAnsariToo?: Desi Masculinity in America and Performing Funny Cute Ali Na	45
4	Anger's Volumes: Rhetorics of Amplification and Aggregation in #MeToo Emily Winderman	64
5	"Our Bodies Are Not *Terra Nullius*": Building a Decolonial Feminist Resistance to Gendered Violence Ashley Noel Mack and Tiara R. Na'puti	84
6	Isolating Structures of Sexual Harassment in Crowdsourced Data on Higher Education Tiffany A. Dykstra-DeVette and Carlos Tarin	108
	Index	131

Citation Information

The chapters in this book were originally published in *Women's Studies in Communication*, volume 42, issue 3 (2019). When citing this material, please use the original page numbering for each article, as follows:

Introduction
The #MeToo Moment: A Rhetorical Zeitgeist
Lisa M. Corrigan
Women's Studies in Communication, volume 42, issue 3 (2019), pp. 264–268

Chapter 1
(Trans)forming #MeToo: Toward a Networked Response to Gender Violence
V. Jo Hsu
Women's Studies in Communication, volume 42, issue 3 (2019), pp. 269–286

Chapter 2
Expendables for Whom: Terry Crews and the Erasure of Black Male Victims of Sexual Assault and Rape
Tommy J. Curry
Women's Studies in Communication, volume 42, issue 3 (2019), pp. 287–307

Chapter 3
#AzizAnsariToo?: Desi Masculinity in America and Performing Funny Cute
Ali Na
Women's Studies in Communication, volume 42, issue 3 (2019), pp. 308–326

Chapter 4
Anger's Volumes: Rhetorics of Amplification and Aggregation in #MeToo
Emily Winderman
Women's Studies in Communication, volume 42, issue 3 (2019), pp. 327–346

Chapter 5
"Our Bodies Are Not Terra Nullius": Building a Decolonial Feminist Resistance to Gendered Violence
Ashley Noel Mack and Tiara R. Na'puti
Women's Studies in Communication, volume 42, issue 3 (2019), pp. 347–370

Chapter 6
Isolating Structures of Sexual Harassment in Crowdsourced Data on Higher Education
Tiffany A. Dykstra-DeVette and Carlos Tarin
Women's Studies in Communication, volume 42, issue 3 (2019), pp. 371–393

For any permission-related enquiries please visit:
www.tandfonline.com/page/help/permissions

Notes on Contributors

Lisa M. Corrigan, Department of Communication, University of Arkansas, Fayetteville, Arkansas, USA.

Tommy J. Curry, School of Philosophy, Psychology, and Language Sciences, University of Edinburgh, Edinburgh, Scotland, UK.

Tiffany A. Dykstra-DeVette, School of Communication, San Diego State University, San Diego, California, USA.

V. Jo Hsu, Department of Rhetoric and Writing at the University of Texas at Austin.

Ashley Noel Mack, Department of Communication Studies, Louisiana State University, Baton Rouge, Louisiana, USA.

Ali Na, The Department of Film and Media, Queen's University, Kingston, Ontario, Canada.

Tiara R. Na'puti, Department of Global & International Studies at University of California, Irvine.

Carlos Tarin, Department of Communication, University of Texas at El Paso, El Paso, Texas, USA.

Emily Winderman, Department of Communication, University of Minnesota Twin Cities, Minneapolis, Minnesota, USA.

INTRODUCTION

The #MeToo Moment—A Rhetorical Zeitgeist

Lisa M. Corrigan

When editor Kristen Hoerl approached me to help edit this special issue on #MeToo, I told her that we would need to have a lengthy phone chat because my perspective on the #MeToo moment was far less jubilant than many other feminists. Indeed, while I was generally glad for the public outcry over sexual harassment and sexual violence and thought that hashtagging experiences was good to both amplify the frequency of sexual harassment and violence and to provide community for survivors, I was also concerned about white women hijacking a hashtag started by a black woman (Tarana Burke, an advocate for victims of sexual violence and *Time*'s 2017 Person of the Year along with women the magazine named "the silence breakers"), celebrity whitewashing (on Twitter and at the 2018 Oscars), the erasure of male victims, the lack of nuance about bidirectional violence, and disregard of sexual violence against LGBTQ people but especially trans women of color. Given the high profile and rampant murders in the last several years of trans women of color ("Violence Against the Transgender Community in 2019") and indigenous women ("How The Treatment of Indigenous Women in the U.S. Compares to Canada"; McLean and Weisfeldt), thinking about harassment without attention to lethal brutality seemed egregious in the larger conversation about #MeToo.

Additionally, I voiced serious concerns with how sexual consent was centered in conversations around #MeToo after actress Alyssa Milano started using it in connection to revelations about (now-former) film producer Harvey Weinstein. Consent, especially sexual consent, implies that people are peers. And in a capitalist culture, peers are recognized through their ownership of property. Since women, people of color, children, and LGBTQ people are often thought of *as property* because they are *propertyless*, I am reticent to talk about sexual violence through the lens of consent rather than property, and, by extension, whiteness (see Harris; Mills). This is particularly true because consent language cannot remove coercion from sex; the coercion is central to hierarchies of power centered on property. Rather than focusing on consent, which is one-way and always already implies the ultimate (heterosexual) power of one partner over the other, I am far more interested in futurist imaginings that start with two partners being socially equal. Consequently, it seems to me that this kind of speculative politics requires class justice to precede sexual justice. So while consent language is certainly better than nothing, the overreliance on consent to ameliorate problems that fundamentally begin with property ownership as the foundation of compulsory heterosexuality seems insufficient. In cultures where there is no comprehensive sexual education, consent language as a lone intervention seems unsatisfactory and may even function as a diversion to real political solutions to sexual violence. Consent also implies that sexual violence is not intentional, which strikes me as a very odd rhetorical intervention given the murders of transgender women and indigenous women alone.

I also wondered publicly about ways in which #MeToo functioned as a post-truth technology for white women. While the slogan "Trust Women" has circulated for years, particularly in the reproductive justice community where I spend so much of my time, it has seemed somewhat disingenuous when applied to sexualized violence. On the reproductive justice front, "Trust Women" makes sense as an assertion of autonomy over their reproductive health, particularly the right to a wide range of health care services, including abortion. This is especially true in this moment where the revocation of abortion rights has gained traction in the circuit courts and states. But given the massive violence against boys and men *by women* (white women, in particular), it seems that the blanket call to "Trust Women" in the context of #MeToo is a problem when even just a bit of intersectional analysis and quite a bit of empirical data are applied. In this framework, trusting women (or rather, trusting *white cis-hetero* women) seems quite harmful. I often wonder, for example, about what Emmett Till would say about trusting (white) women. And, given my activism and political work in Little Rock, I can say with certainty that white women were not to be trusted during the desegregation of Central High School in 1957 (Anderson). Furthermore, with 53% of white women voting for Donald Trump, I find the blanket call to "Trust Women" in the context of narratives of violence to be perplexing. Consider as well the many false accusations, rape myths, controlling images, and stereotypes that have served as justifications for violence toward black men.

Rather than thinking through the details and complexities of sexual encounters, the call to "Trust Women"—particularly as Betsy DeVos's Department of Education seeks to dismantle Title IX—dismisses specificity of experience, which is a de facto privileging of whiteness, heterosexuality, and able-bodiedness. The slogan works to circumvent the same kind of accountability that, rather ironically, feminists called for during the confirmation hearing of Supreme Court justice Brett Kavanaugh in September 2018. As an irony of liberal feminism, and perhaps as a feature of toxic white femininity, "Trust Women" works to detach sexual violence from non-white, non-heterosexual, non-female victims and survivors as well as from white, female, heterosexual perpetrators. This rhetorical consequence has the possibility of undermining any productive inquiry (or legal protection) for women and for everyone else as well.

As I thought about what kind of issue I'd like to curate in both content and form, it was clear that the erasures produced by the whiteness of the tweet threads, the sexual consent frame, and those that emerged as intentional and unintentional consequences of the combination of #MeToo and #TrustWomen would need to be front and center. I wanted to showcase perspectives by interlocutors who were marked by subject positions that did *not* fit the white framework that celebrity culture brought to Tarana Burke's work. And even within celebrity culture, I wanted more nuanced examinations of contemporary claims of #MeToo issues that were not apparent in popular media's hot takes.

Unsurprisingly, I also wanted to curate an issue that was predominantly written by people of color, including LGBTQ folx and indigenous authors. In a field grappling with #COMMSoWhite and "An Open Letter on Diversity in the Communication Discipline," it was paramount for me to seek out authors who could speak to the lacunae on this political moment with clarity and depth (see Paula Chakravarrty et al.; "An Open Letter on Diversity to the Communication Discipline"). The issue begins with Jo Hsu's excellent appraisal of the exclusionary rhetorics that have emerged as a constitutive force of #MeToo. Hsu explains, "Attempts to address how gender is lived differently by people of color, transgender people, immigrants, poor people, and/or disabled folks move primarily along a 'horizontal' axis, gesturing to similarities and difference without mapping the cultural arrangements through which these differences are (re)formed" (272–73).

Likewise, Tommy Curry's essay examines the case of former National Football League player and actor Terry Crews, who sued Hollywood executive Adam Venit for assault after a being groped by Venit at a party. Crews's case is interesting because in presenting himself as a victim, he both subverts the image of the white female victim of assault and confirms his appropriateness as a victim through white feminist appeals. Curry argues "that Crews's acceptance by #MeToo is rooted in his confirmation of the dominant feminist view that men are primarily the perpetrators of sexual violence and women are almost solely victims, a position that is actually at odds with the views of Tarana Burke—the original founder to #MeToo" (289). This is interesting given Curry's own empirical and historical work on the persistent sexual violence and rape of Black men and boys.

Next, Ali Na's essay surveys the landscape surrounding accusations of comedian Aziz Ansari's potentially inappropriate sexual habits. Na introduces the concepts of "Desi masculinity" and "performing funny cute" to understand the "cultural response to Ansari as simultaneously desexualized as sexually undesirable *and* sexually deviant in his noncompliance with white normative masculinity" (308). Demonstrating how white masculinity is the litmus test against which Ansari is considered, Na's essay highlights how hegemonic white masculinity shapes the terms of debate around consent and sexual practice.

Emily Winderman's essay considers the (gendered but also racialized) double bind of performing public anger that is both a "laudable part of #MeToo" but one that "has been a restricted emotional resource for those whom the original movement was designed to serve" (329) to understand how anger—particularly *volume* as it amplified and diminished anger after #MeToo—became a global phenomenon. Especially for white women, anger has been a slippery emotional and political vector that complicates its use here.

Tiara Na'puti and Ashley Mack provide the next essay on decolonizing #MeToo by offering readings of Missing and Murdered Indigenous Women and the coalitional initiative Violence on the Land, Violence on Our Bodies. They "suggest that witnessing is one heuristic for approaching decolonial feminist critique that works to build deep coalitions by radically de-centering our voice as authors in favor of centering the voices of Indigenous communities" (349). This case study helps us understand the role of sexual violence for settler colonialism and to understand the important indigenous rhetorical appeals necessary to resist such violence.

Finally, the issue concludes with an extremely important essay by Tiffany Dykstra-DeVette and Carlos Tarin who "identify several salient structurating processes that (re)produce harassment via *networking and professionalization* and *estrangement from agency*, which draw on resources, rules and norms, and agency in particular ways" (372). In thinking through the structures that create the leaky pipelines of faculty of color and women away from successful careers, they identify features of organizations that undermine sexual harassment responses, even as the Department of Education continues to erode Title IX protections.

These essays offer provocations about how the communication discipline should understand the #MeToo moment from a historical and intersectional framework as well as from within the structure of higher education. As the communication discipline grapples with its own history of racism, sexism, heterosexism, and ableism, scholars need to reimagine how we talk about sexual harassment and violence as well as how we respond in our communities. In my mind, the only path towards a more just and equitable community is a decolonial path that acknowledges the brutal and sexualized history of settler colonialism, the use of black boys and men in the plantation economy, the lethal violence against the LGBTQ community that sustains white heteropatriarchy, the deft moves made by men of color as they navigate accusations of harassment and violence, the scant rhetorical tools for describing violence against men of color, and the ways in which the organization of higher education replicates sexualized violence as a feature of its relationship to capital and resource extraction. Thanks so much to Kristen Hoerl and the Organization for Research on Women and Communication for the opportunity to curate this issue.

Works cited

"An Open Letter on Diversity in the Communication Discipline," 2019, https://bit.ly/2XJCzxr. Accessed 22 July 2019.

Anderson, Karen. *Little Rock: Race and Resistance at Central High School.* Princeton UP, 2010.

Chakravarrty, Paula, Rachel Kuo, Victoria Grubbs, and Charlton McIlwain. "#CommunicationSoWhite." *Journal of Communication*, vol. 68, no. 2, 2018, pp. 254–66.

Curry, Tommy J. "Expendables for Whom: Terry Crews and the Erasure of Black Male Victims of Sexual Assault and Rape." *Women's Studies in Communication*, vol. 42, no. 3, 2019, pp. 287–307. doi:10.1080/07491409.2019.1641874.

Dykstra-DeVette, Tiffany A., and Carlos Tarin. "Isolating Structures of Sexual Harrassment in Crowdsourced Data on Higher Education." *Women's Studies in Communication*, vol. 42, no. 3, 2019, pp. 371–93. doi:10.1080/07491409.2019.1641873.

Harris, Cheryl L. "Whiteness as Property." *Harvard Law Review*, vol. 106, no. 8, 1993, pp. 1707–91.

Hsu, V. Jo. "(Trans)forming #MeToo: Toward a Networked Response to Gender Violence." *Women's Studies in Communication*, vol. 42, no. 3, 2019, pp. 269–86. doi:10.1080/07491409.2019.1630697.

Mack, Ashley Noel, and Tiara R. Na'puti. "'Our Bodies Are Not *Terra Nullius*': Building a Decolonial Feminist Resistance to Gendered Violence." *Women's Studies in Communication*, vol. 42, no. 3, 2019, pp. 347–70. doi:10.1080/07491409.2019.1637803.

McLean Scott and Sarah Weisfeldt, "Why Do So Many Native American Women Go Missing? Congress Aiming to Find Out," 9 Apr. 2019, https://www.cnn.com/2019/04/09/us/native-american-murdered-missing-women/index.html. Accessed 22 July 2019.

Mills, Charles. *The Racial Contract.* Cornell UP, 1997.

Na, Ali. "#AzizAnsariToo?: Desi Masculinity in America and Performing Funny Cute." *Women's Studies in Communication*, vol. 42, no. 3, 2019, pp. 308–26. doi:10.1080/07491409.2019.1639573.

"Violence Against the Transgender Community in 2019." Human Rights Campaign, https://www.hrc.org/resources/violence-against-the-transgender-community-in-2019. Accessed 22 July 2019.

Winderman, Emily. "Anger's Volumes: Rhetorics of Amplification and Aggregation in #MeToo." *Women's Studies in Communication*, vol. 42, no. 3, 2019, pp. 327–46. doi:10.1080/07491409.2019.1632234.

(Trans)forming #MeToo: Toward a Networked Response to Gender Violence

V. Jo Hsu

ABSTRACT
Drawing from critical trans theory's methods of systemic analysis, this article examines how #MeToo's carceral politics have reinforced the exclusion and ongoing abuse of those most vulnerable to gender and state violence. The stories of many people of color, queer, transgender, poor, and/or disabled folks remain inarticulable within a retributive system that requires survivors to narrate themselves as "perfect victims." Adopting critical trans theory's emphasis on administrative violence, I connect the transformative visions of penal abolition with discourses on sexual violence. Focusing on the rhetorical strategies of incarcerated survivors and their defense committees, I demonstrate how these rhetors model forms of Rebecca Dingo's "networked arguments." In doing so, they offer a promising vision of how organizers and advocates can address the particularities of individual experience while also responding to and working collaboratively against oppressive social and state institutions.

As long as we are going to have prisons we are going to have sexual abuse in prisons. That's the reality. That's what happens.

—Gerard Bryant, New York City Board of Correction

Gerard Bryant—a former warden for a federal prison[1]–made this statement in 2016 amid public scrutiny about Rikers Island's "culture of brutality" (Malinowski). Since then, multiple investigations into the New York jail have revealed the ongoing torture of inmates, the targeting and endangerment of transgender prisoners (Stahl), and a "scourge of racism on the part of correction officers" (Foderaro). Bryant's almost flippant response assumes the inevitability of prison violence. These are institutions designed for isolation, surveillance, and control. When compounded with the disproportionate criminalization of people of color, poor people, trans and gender-nonconforming people, and all others who live beyond the bounds of White, middle-class respectability, prison becomes a mechanism through which social inequities are enforced—and through which sexual abuse becomes a means of that enforcement.

While articles featuring the primarily affluent women at the center of #MeToo often acknowledge how "others" are disproportionately targeted by gender violence, few discussions actually explore the mechanisms through which that vulnerability is created. For instance, *TIME* magazine's article "The Silence Breakers," which featured #MeToo as their 90th annual Person of the Year, acknowledged that "47% of transgender people report being sexually assaulted at some point in their lives" (Zacharek et al.). That single statistic is the only sentence to even mention trans people. In actuality, those numbers are even higher for trans folks who are American Indian (65%), multiracial (59%), Middle Eastern (58%), and Black (53%) (Grant et al.),[2] and the cultural architectures that undergird these numbers require deeper and more thorough explanations.

The precarity of trans lives is not simply an amplification of the experiences of cisgender women but a product of myriad policies and practices that severely constrain trans people's access to fundamental resources. As critical trans scholars have demonstrated, trans lives are actively truncated by state and social apparatuses that circumscribe "everyone's field of action, existence, and self-understanding" (Nichols 43). Trans people experience three times the rate of unemployment and four times the rate of homelessness compared with the cisgender population (James et al.; Grant et al.). Relatedly, trans folks are also much more likely to experience employment and housing discrimination. Combined with the disproportionate rates of poverty among people of color—with the ways that property has been denied and stolen from Black, Latinx, Asian, and Native communities—trans people of color may find that abusive situations are their only options for survival. Even within the narrow range of life choices they are given, any survival strategies they take are far more likely to be criminalized and prosecuted.

It should come as no surprise, though, that the experiences of trans and incarcerated survivors (and particularly those of trans incarcerated survivors) have received minimal attention from #MeToo. While #MeToo has ruptured a pervasive silence around sexual assault, it has also done so largely through a vocabulary of criminalization and carceral punishment. This limited vision of justice has left many—specifically those most vulnerable to gender violence—beyond the purview of #MeToo. The few stories that acknowledge the existence and susceptibility of trans survivors mostly omit the fact that trans people are far more often targeted by police discrimination. In fact, trans people are incarcerated at six times the rate of the cisgender population and are far more likely to experience abuse of all kinds in prison.[3] In an attempt to channel the energies of #MeToo toward more inclusive solutions, this article shifts focus away from casting rooms and boardrooms. Instead, I begin with the presumed endpoint of many prominent #MeToo narratives: the prison cell.

Bryant's statement highlights a reality that has gone mostly untroubled amid the #MeToo uproar: Sexual violence is an integral component of the prison system, and the people most vulnerable to sexual violence are also most frequently targeted by policing and criminalization. In the United States, nearly one in six trans people and almost half of Black trans folks have been imprisoned (Grant et al.; Bierria et al.; James et al.). In 2015 alone, 65% of trans people who interacted with law enforcement experienced some form of mistreatment—from verbal and physical assault to being forced by officers to engage in sexual activity to avoid arrest (James et al.).[4] In addition to the racial inequities amplified by all experiences of transphobia, rates of violence also skyrocket for homeless trans folks, who are much more likely to experience police harassment (78%), as well as for unemployed trans people (75%) and those with disabilities (68%). In the broader trans population, those who have experienced homelessness are also more likely to have been sexually assaulted (65%); the same goes for those with disabilities (61%). This tight networking of abuses reveals the ongoing need for more intersectional vocabularies. Without the ability to articulate and address these interrelated harms, any singular approach to systemic disenfranchisement inevitably reproduces other oppressions.

While intersectional theories and activisms are hardly new, as with conversations about sexual violence, advocates must continually struggle against their erasure. More recently, critical trans scholars have (re)turned to a systemic focus, intervening in the rights-based framework of mainstream "LGBTQ"[5] politics.[6] The antidiscrimination and hate crime laws at the center of LGBTQ activism do little to address the ways that legal and social apparatuses reproduce structural vulnerabilities.[7] These campaigns also rarely account for how anti-queer and anti-trans violence is amplified on bodies of color, disabled bodies, and bodies that cannot find secure housing or jobs—the same bodies targeted for sexual abuse both inside and outside of prisons. Instead of pursuing legal protections against individual harms, critical trans theorists and activists have turned toward the "processes of gendered racialization ... congealed in violent institutions" (Nichols 43; see also Enke; Spade; Stryker; Snorton; H. Davis), and they have channeled their efforts toward transforming these institutions.

In alliance with such efforts, this article explores interconnections among transformative justice movements, transgender theory, and intersectional feminism, and the ways they can inform liberatory responses to gender-based violence. I propose a trans-ing of the #MeToo moment that addresses the entanglement of gender violence and carceral politics. Adopting critical trans theory's emphasis on administrative violence, I connect the transformative visions of penal abolition with the current "revolution" (Zacharek et al.) against sexual violence. What emerges is a rhetorical strategy that can attend to the ubiquity of sexual violence while also addressing how that violence is enmeshed in other forms of state and social control that specifically compound the subjection of people of color, immigrants, transgender individuals, those with disabilities, and others who find themselves entangled in the criminal legal system.

In the sections that follow, I begin with a trans reading of the #MeToo moment and the limitations of popular framings as exemplified by *TIME* magazine's "The Silence Breakers." I then consider potential (trans)formative directions via the networked rhetorics of incarcerated survivor defense campaigns. Through an analysis of *#SurvivedAndPunished*, a guidebook designed by and for supporters of incarcerated survivors, I demonstrate how critical trans theory and politics can help channel the #MeToo fervor toward the material conditions that structure vulnerabilities to gender violence—and, for that matter, to most forms of social violence. Combining systemic analysis with intersectional feminism's "bottom-up" approach to justice, I argue that both thinking *about* trans experiences and thinking *with* trans theory enables intersectional discussions that account for uneven circulations of power. In attuning to the networked insights of stories from the margins, proponents of #MeToo might envision responses to gender violence that do not rely on similar forms of cruelty.

Thinking trans

I draw my understanding of "trans" from the foundational work of Susan Stryker, Paisley Currah, and Lisa Jean Moore. In "Trans-, Trans, or Transgender?" they define trans as movement among the "macro- and micro-political registers through which the lives of bodies become enmeshed in the lives of nations, states, and capital-formations" (14). In this conceptualization, trans moves along a vertical axis rather a horizontal one. Instead of focusing on the lateral transitions of gender identity (from male to female or anywhere in between), trans analysis shifts from the embodied experience of gender to the "set of practices through which a potential biopower is cultivated, harnessed, or transformed" (14). Trans-ing thus becomes an analytical practice through which to understand how identities, classifications, and administrative policies conspire in the uneven distribution of life chances. Such a perspective can illuminate not only the biopolitical mechanisms of gender but also those pertaining to race, class, nationality, and other sites where identity is cultivated.

This systemic approach to trans-ing facilitates yet another form of trans-theorizing: Rebecca Dingo's "networking arguments." Dingo advances "networking" as a transnational feminist approach to rhetorical analysis that connects "individual lives, stories, and sufferings to wider systems of historical, cultural, and material local- and geo-politics" ("Networking the Macro and Micro" 532). In "Networking the Macro and Micro," she demonstrates how transnational feminist literacies can encourage more holistic conversations about women's pain. Rather than comparing or contrasting individual accounts of suffering, transnational feminist literacies imagine and map relational matrices among peoples, nations, economies, and texts. Such rhetorical practices encourage systemic responses to marginal accounts, focusing on "*how* and *why* people become disenfranchised" (543) rather than single-issue solutions. While my focus here is the U.S. prison system, which is overwhelmingly the largest in the world, this nation's prisons are built upon—and sustain—violences enacted by European emigration, by technological advancement and deindustrialization, and by a shifting global economic order. A transnational feminist approach to trans theory thus reveals how even domestic institutions are inevitably bound up with global flows.

In exploring how trans theory can produce networked rhetorics, I envision the "vertical" movement of trans theory as a method of situating individual voices within state and global configurations of power *and* of locating counterhegemonic alliances within those configurations. Integral to this conception of trans is the centrality of trans experience—a respect for the insights that border crossers have into strategies of containment. When examining the conditions of gender violence, then, it is imperative to consider those whose embodiments of gender are read as inherently transgressive. In the United States, that population includes many people of color, poor people, disabled people, trans, queer, and gender-nonconforming people, and others who violate the strictures of white, middle-class respectability.

While the most prominent #MeToo cases have effectively tacked out from individual experiences of sexual violence to—in Alyssa Milano's words—"give people a sense of the magnitude of the problem," conversations have focused largely on cisgender, heterosexual, middle- and upper-class white women. Attempts to address how gender is lived differently by people of color, trans people, immigrants, poor people, and/or disabled folks move primarily along a "horizontal" axis, gesturing to similarities and differences without mapping the cultural arrangements through which these differences are (re)formed. This cursory recognition is perhaps most effectively illustrated by *TIME*'s "The Silence Breakers," which helped repackage Tarana Burke's long-standing campaign for mainstream audiences. Whereas the phrase "me too" began as words of solidarity within Burke's healing circles for marginalized communities, the hashtag attributed to Alyssa Milano's viral tweet has recentered the stories of affluent women. In the year since *TIME*'s watershed text, Burke has voiced many concerns about #MeToo's trajectory, focusing on how its prevailing iteration neglects marginalized survivors as well as structural responses to those survivors' needs (Burke; Adetiba; Rowley). These critiques reflect shortcomings not only of #MeToo but also of many major feminist and other social movements, positioning #MeToo as a generative study for how exclusionary rhetorics emerge regardless of inclusive intentions.

"The Silence Breakers" and single-axis politics

In December 2017, *TIME* magazine's "The Silence Breakers" declared #MeToo their collective Person of the Year, adding #MeToo to a nearly century-long roster of worldwide influencers. *The New York Times* described *TIME*'s issue-length feature as a gesture that "crystallized the #MeToo moment" (Bennett, "The #MeToo Moment"). As authors Stephanie Zacharek, Eliana Dockterman, and Haley Sweetland Edwards stress throughout the profile, one of the driving forces of #MeToo has been the convergence of many storytellers—among which disparities in status and privilege vary "not by degree but by universe." What has resulted, however, is not a democratic commingling of stories but a vocal configuration that replicates extant social hierarchies. "The Silence Breakers" maps a sort of trickle-down justice through which "[w]hen a movie star says #MeToo, it becomes easier to believe the cook who's been quietly enduring for years" (Zacharek et al.). Faithfully tracing the series of events that brought #MeToo to more public spaces, Zacharek et al. begin with the untouchable glamour of movie stars, describing exquisite wardrobes and luxurious homes. Despite all this opulence, "it turns out, in the most painful and personal ways—movie stars are more like you and me than we ever knew." This line of reasoning suggests that celebrities are "like us" in that they also experience sexual assault and are threatened or gaslit into silence. When they break that silence, the rest of us are supposedly also empowered to speak.

"The Silence Breakers" returns to that hopeful vision at the end of the article. Bringing together an eclectic array of stories—from those of beloved celebrities to that of an anonymous woman identified only as a "former office assistant"—Zacharek et al. conclude: "The women and men who have broken their silence span all races, all income classes, all occupations and virtually all corners of the globe... . They're part of a movement that has no formal name. But now they have a voice." This singular voice belongs primarily to the social elite. It pays no heed to the very different conditions that would have precipitated the "former office assistant's" vulnerability as a Native American woman—including but not limited to a federal court system unresponsive to crimes on Native American reservations and centuries of Native dispossession that have left reservations with few resources for survivor defense and support. As intersectional feminists have continually insisted, narrow forms of recognition available to a privileged few do *not* transform oppressive regimes. Rather, they disguise and justify the conditions of oppression.

In fact, the future envisioned by the concluding words of "The Silence Breakers" draws directly from the vocabulary of criminalization. Zacharek et al. write, "We can and should police criminal acts," and many of #MeToo's most celebrated victories have depended on criminalization. The conviction of Bill Cosby was declared "the first big win of the #MeToo movement" (Chuck), and Harvey Weinstein's arrest marked another "pivotal turning point" in its evolution (Dockterman). When the *New York Times*'s gender editor, Jessica Bennett, surveyed the impact of #MeToo in June 2018, she focused on the development of "real, criminal consequences" for perpetrators of sexual assault ("After #MeToo"). Her examples include Weinstein's arrest, France's decision to make catcalling a "punishable offense," and the general "[erosion of] barriers to prosecuting sexual harassment" around the world. The "sheer universality" of the #MeToo movement that Bennett describes, however, does not address the erasure of women of color and working-class women that she mentioned in 2017 ("The #MeToo Moment"), let alone the plight of incarcerated women, nonbinary folks, and men who have been persecuted by the very system through which #MeToo so often pursues retribution.

The lateral inclusion modeled in "The Silence Breakers" might be seen as what Kimberlé Crenshaw terms "single axis" politics—a form of gestural recognition through which minorities are simply shuffled onto a platform structured to uphold experiences of relative privilege. As Crenshaw demonstrated in her landmark essay "Demarginalizing the Intersection of Race and Sex," the singular frameworks so often used in feminist and antiracist politics cannot account for those who experience multiple oppressions. Building on the earlier work of feminists of color, Crenshaw exposes how myopically "race based" or "gender based" approaches to justice inevitably reinforce exclusions along other axes. For Crenshaw and other intersectional feminists, liberationist movements must begin with accounts from our most precarious social intersections, creating space for those for whom it can be said, "when they enter, we all enter" (139)—a phrase attributed to Anna Julia Cooper, one of the originary voices of Black feminism.[8]

Pursuing such possibilities would actually not be a departure from #MeToo but perhaps an amplification of Tarana Burke's ongoing work. Even as Hollywood, Capitol Hill, and Silicon Valley subsumed media coverage, Burke has continually channeled attention toward the margins. She has stressed that substantive change needs to begin here—where folks' experiences archive the interlocking oppressions of our institutions. Shortly after #MeToo went viral, Burke expressed concerns that the movement would abandon the needs of marginal communities. She said:

> It defeats the purpose to not have those folks centered—I'm talking black and brown girls, queer folks. There's no conversation in this whole thing about transgender folks and sexual violence. There's no conversation in this about people with disabilities and sexual violence. We need to talk about Native Americans, who have the highest rate of sexual violence in this country. (Adetiba)

Burke and her accomplices have long been talking about these issues. Black and brown communities, people with disabilities, and trans and queer folks have been telling their stories for centuries.

Drawing together these wide-ranging knowledges, critical trans theory builds from intersectional feminism's "bottom-up" approach to social change, critical race theory's critiques of legal reform, and both disability politics' and fat politics' insights on bodily norms. What results is a directed focus on "administrative violence" that calls attention to how "systems that organize our lives in seemingly ordinary ways ... produce and distribute life chances based on violent forms of categorization" (Nichols 41). Rather than petitioning for individual rights or limited recognitions, critical trans politics works to transform the organizational structures most damaging for trans people—structures that also curtail the options and opportunities of those who experience "single-axis" harms. This focus on administrative bodies has particular efficacy in the United States where so much of our public lives are governed by agencies whose authority rests on an assumption of neutral expertise.[9]

#SurvivedAndPunished: **Transitional terms and transformative justice**

> It is important for us to document [our work] especially because our organizing work has been led by Black women, women of color, immigrants and queer/trans people, who are so often erased from history. We hope to preserve some of these histories, build solidarity, and share hope as we continue our collective struggle.
> —*#SurvivedAndPunished: Survivor Defense As Abolitionist Praxis* (2)

Whereas "The Silence Breakers" tries to extend the experiences of society's most influential to those less fortunate, *#SurvivedAndPunished* prioritizes those most frequently excluded from public life. It is the collaborative product of two organizations, "Survived and Punished" (S&P) and "Love and Protect" (L&P), both of which focus on defending criminalized survivors of gender violence. Like many contributors to #MeToo, both S&P and L&P seek to illuminate and respond to the cultural foundations of gender violence. The *#SurvivedAndPunished* toolkit culls from their organizational histories to offer a "collection of tools, tips, lessons, and resources" (Bierria et al. 2) for future defense efforts.

The core of the toolkit is a PDF, but its prolific use of hyperlinks tethers this one document to a network of other guides, essay collections, Web sites, social media, campaign archives, and other educational materials. Many of these resources were also authored by the toolkit's cocreators, which involves sixteen writers and five editors. The editors include Alisa Bierria, who researches carceral cultures and gendered violence; Marianne Kaba, who cofounded the Chicago Alliance to Free Marissa Alexander; Essence McDowell, digital activist and member of L&P; Hyejin Shim, S&P cofounder; and Stacy Suh, who now serves as the network director at Center for Media Justice. Similar to "The Silence Breakers," *#SurvivedAndPunished* also begins by detailing the experiences of a diverse range of survivors—from those of single mothers to those of immigrants, queer individuals, and transgender folks. Because all these survivors are often exploited by the criminal legal system, *#SurvivedAndPunished* necessarily envisions alternative forms of justice. Both a pragmatic and a visionary document,

#SurvivedAndPunished addresses the immediate, material needs of prison detainees while also aspiring to a world beyond prisons.

In contrast to the celebrity-driven trajectory charted by "The Silence Breakers," *#SurvivedAndPunished* foregrounds the experiences of those who are multiply marginalized, allowing their stories to direct the search for more equitable solutions. Stitching together a wide range of individual narratives, *#SurvivedAndPunished* maps these stories onto a longer history of how incarceration has been used to contain minority communities—an institution Michelle Alexander famously exposed as a "comprehensive and well-disguised system of racialized social control" (4). *#SurvivedAndPunished* thus examines the personal within a context of social responsibility, coalescing these experiences into a systemic analysis that does not abandon the significance and potency of personal accounts. In fact, the authors emphasize that the most effective defense committees consistently situate individual cases within "the broader forces and impacts of criminalization" (Bierria et al. 5). Even while working within the criminal legal system to protect and hopefully free survivors, Bierria et al. also stress the destructiveness of its machinations, and they advocate for models of justice that do not rely on caging and isolation.

Like many of the central reports on #MeToo, *#SurvivedAndPunished* targets a pervasive culture of gender violence and seeks to transform it. Through a more holistic view, however, Bierria et al. adopt a systemic approach that considers other elements of social control and their consequences. *#SurvivedAndPunished* responds to the ways anti-violence advocates have increasingly "empower[ed] the criminal legal system to intervene in gender violence by treating it as a crime" (6). As this strategy has played out over the past four decades, it has failed to reduce the epidemic rates of domestic and sexual violence. Moreover, by relying on a process that subjects marginalized survivors to further isolation and trauma, this strategy has "reinforced the systemic roots" of gender violence (6). *#SurvivedAndPunished*, by contrast, works to unearth those roots by networking the experiences of "Black, immigrant, women of color, trans, queer, disabled and poor survivors" into a vigorous critique of the criminal system and a clear set of resistive tactics (6). A focus on administrative violence and its wide-ranging consequences gives Bierria et al. the rhetorical flexibility to engage many issues entangled with gender-based violence without abandoning the centrality of gender and without compressing distinct experiences into a homogenous narrative.

Without explicitly invoking trans theory, *#SurvivedAndPunished* both thinks about and thinks *with* trans, moving into and making knowledge from "the borderlands of nonrecognition" where embodiments of gender exceed the presumed naturalness of racialized, binaristic, ableist, heterosexist, and cissexist norms (Bhanji 521). The toolkit moves liberally among individual story lines and structural analysis, deploying (trans)itional terms and concepts as connective nodes. For example, Bierria et al. consider how communities of color, immigrant communities, and queer communities are all criminalized through the legal system, but also how the specific tactics of criminalization differ depending on context. The adaptability of these transitional concepts helps articulate linkages among different topics often addressed through singular lenses: gender violence, immigration, racism, ableism, trans justice, and incarceration. Weaving among micro and macro political registers, *#SurvivedAndPunished* illustrates how so many single-issue topics are in fact embedded in mutually constitutive configurations of power.

This intricate network begins with a single story. *#SurvivedAndPunished* opens by describing the imprisonment of Marissa Alexander and the collaborative efforts that eventually secured her release. Alexander's story becomes a reference point to which the authors return periodically throughout the document, and it establishes the transitional terms through which Bierria et al. pivot to other, very different accounts of gender violence and incarceration. In the midst of an attack by her abusive, estranged husband, Alexander fired her (registered) gun into the wall. She was sentenced to a mandatory minimum of 20 years for this single warning shot. Though the bullet never touched anyone, Alexander was charged with three counts of aggravated assault with a deadly weapon. The Florida state attorney, Angela Corey, framed Alexander as an "angry Black woman" and ignored her experiences of domestic abuse. Alexander was also denied Stand Your Ground immunity the same year it was invoked in the acquittal of George Zimmerman. The ways the criminal process replicated systems of abuse—from racialized gender stereotyping to physical and emotional isolation—motivated the primary tactics for Marissa's defense. Bierria et al.'s discussion then focuses on how normative expectations of race and gender similarly constrained the options of other survivors, scripting them into the role of aggressor despite all evidence to the contrary.

By turning the focus toward cultures of discrimination, Bierria et al. refuse to render Alexander's story as an isolated event. This is not an anomalous outrage, nor yet another example to tack onto a race-blind feminist agenda. Rather, the "angry Black woman" caricature links Alexander's experience to a legacy of stereotypes weaponized specifically against Black women. Also known as the "Sapphire," the figure of a treacherous Black woman has been popularized by news and popular media (including Hollywood itself) and "projected onto any black woman who overtly expresses bitterness, anger, and rage about her lot" (hooks 86). Corey easily exploited that history when she circulated Alexander's mugshot to state legislators. Along with the images, she wrote: "Marissa Alexander to her husband: 'I've got something for your ass'" (Berry). Corey thus invoked the narratives historically used to "justify [the] de-humanization and sexual exploitation of black women" (hooks 85), adding Alexander to a long lineage of Black women criminalized for the defensive measures necessitated by their own abuse (Richie, *Compelled to Crime, Arrested Justice*; Roberts; Morris).

Bierria et al. transition back to this wider context when they incorporate a Free Marissa Now poster that reads: "Stop the legal lynching of a Black domestic violence survivor by Florida's racist mandatory minimum sentencing laws" (7). The term *lynching* not only connects the current legal system with this country's legacies of racial violence but also aligns with some of the most recognized critiques of U.S. prisons. Michelle Alexander's *The New Jim Crow*, for example, provides an extended argument for how "[t]oday's lynching is incarceration. Today's lynch mobs are professionals" (163–64). An expanding body of literature reveals how the criminalization of racial, sexual, and gender minorities pervades our everyday practices and social configurations (Richie, *Compelled to Crime, Arrested Justice*; A. Davis, *Are Prisons Obsolete?*, *Abolition Democracy*; Spade; Stanley and Smith; INCITE! Women of Color Against Violence; Morris; Rios; Ore). In concert, these formal and informal procedures create legal avenues for persecution, assault, and even murder, while policies like mandatory minimums extend the reach and power of the state.

In Marissa Alexander's experience, as in many other cases of domestic violence, the mandatory minimum meant that her husband's history of abuse and the dire circumstances of her crime were irrelevant to her sentencing. The judge asserted that the decision was "out of [his] hands"—that he could not consider domestic violence as a mitigating circumstance (Stacy). Because survivors of domestic abuse are often criminalized for the actions they take in self-defense, and because Black women and other historically disadvantaged folks are more often seen and treated as criminals, policies like mandatory minimums serve as institutional reinforcement for the ongoing disenfranchisement of particular communities. In fact, mandatory minimums have allowed prosecutors to force guilty pleas; they can "load up" cases with unlikely charges that carry extreme sentences in order to intimidate defendants into pleading guilty for lesser crimes (Alexander 88).

Situating Marissa Alexander's experience within the state infrastructure surrounding it, Bierria et al. maneuver from their opening example to a whole professionalized machinery of gendered racist oppression. They connect mandatory minimums to an arsenal of current-day policies and practices designed to disempower communities of color, including but not limited to the War on Drugs, Secure Communities, and increased police and immigration enforcement authority (Bierria et al. 7). Like mandatory minimums, these programs structure and legitimize discrimination under the guise of impartiality. As acts of administrative violence, they systematically contain and disempower racial, gender, and sexual minorities through the imposition of a new classification: criminal.

This explanation of mandatory minimums introduces criminalization as a transitional term through which Bierria et al. explore a series of personal experiences. As isolated stories, these many cases might seem like disconnected, singular issues. However, when networked together through patterns of criminalization, *#SurvivedAndPunished*'s separate examples collectively elucidate how the legal system reinforces the insecurity and persecution of marginalized peoples. These cases include the "New Jersey 4," young lesbians of color who were targeted by misogynistic, homophobic, and racist sexual violence; Marcela Rodriguez, who was forced into deportation proceedings when she reported her abusive ex-husband; Nan-Hui Jo, an immigrant mother trying to protect herself and her daughter from an abusive (U.S. citizen) partner; and Ky Peterson, a Black trans man who defended himself against a brutal physical and sexual assault. Like Angela Corey, the prosecutors in each of these cases were able to tap into racist and/or anti-immigrant and transphobic sentiments to secure their convictions.

Bierria et al. approach each story through a "wide-angle view" (Dingo, *Networking Arguments* 20) that situates each individual experience within relevant domains of state power, class relations, and gendered, racial, and ethnic discrimination. For example, like Marissa Alexander, Nan-Hui Jo was villainized through gendered racial stereotypes. A noncitizen, Jo was denied a green card when her estranged husband refused to sponsor her application. When she became trapped in an abusive relationship with a different man, Jesse Charlton, Jo had few options but to flee to South Korea. Because Jo took their daughter with her, Charlton reported Jo's departure as child abduction. Jo returned to the United States five years later, at which time she was separated from her daughter, arrested, and transferred to Immigration and Customs Enforcement (ICE) detention. A family court granted full custody rights to Charlton (Law). At every turn, U.S. administrative agencies very clearly reinforced Jo's outsider status; the police and the courts are not intended to protect her, but rather to protect "deserving" citizens from her.

As an Asian immigrant, Jo could not embody the (racialized) standards for feminine innocence that would render her a legible victim. She was portrayed as both a "manipulative illegal immigrant seeking to cheat the U.S. system" and a "'tiger mom' who was too competent to be a victim" (Bierria et al. 6). District attorney Steve Mount actually used the phrase "tiger mom" in his closing argument, concluding that Jo was so effective at protecting her own daughter that she could not possibly be a victim (Pishko). With a single phrase, Mount accessed notions of Asians as hypercompetent, emotionless, perpetual foreigners whose ambition threatened the security of "real" U.S. citizens. Jo's case, and the many others like it, demonstrates how state institutions fortify the boundaries of national belonging.

Of the five cases that *#SurvivedAndPunished* describes in detail, only one survivor remains in prison. However, the work of defense campaigns often continues well beyond the period of incarceration. Freedom as envisioned by *#SurvivedAndPunished* entails not just freedom from being behind bars. In determining an appropriate endpoint, the particularities of all survivors and their perspectives drive the campaign. Bierria et al. stress that defense committees should orient their goals toward what "'freedom' would mean for the person they are supporting" (27). Depending on the case, survivors may require funds to endure mandated home confinement. Others may require resources to secure employment. Still others might need help ensuring protection from their abusers.

For Ky Peterson, however, such considerations remain beyond his horizon of possibilities, and his defense committee has had to identify alternative freedoms to pursue. A Black trans man, Peterson occupies a racialized and gendered intersection that denies him any right to self-defense. Peterson was attacked while walking home from a grocery store in Georgia. He was knocked out from behind and regained consciousness while his attacker was raping him. That was when he shot and killed his assailant. Though the rape kit corroborated Peterson's story, the police insisted that he did not seem like a "believable victim" of rape (Bierria et al. 7; Spade and Dector 00:50–00:52). Peterson's public defender encouraged him to sign a plea deal, insisting that "self-defense" was not a viable claim because Peterson is Black and "looks stereotypically gay" (Spade and Dector 01:05–01:09). The "deal" gave Peterson twenty years in prison, which he continues to serve today.

While the committee organized on Peterson's behalf originally named themselves "The Free Ky Project," the organization has since become Freedom Overground. On their Web page, they explain:

> Ky has faced retaliation from the DOC [Department of Corrections] for the actions that he has taken to get medical care for trans inmates. Doing interviews cost him video visit privileges. Exposing negligent health care and putting the DOC under pressure has made him a target. His parole request was denied last Jan, his visitor requests have been denied, and even his [F]acebook was reported and permanently deleted. ("Ky Peterson FAQ")

Respecting Peterson's wishes to "lay low" and avoid further aggravating the DOC, Freedom Overground has shifted its tactics for now. Rather than campaigning explicitly in Peterson's name, they focus on developing programs for transgender prisoners as well as developing supportive networks and resources for transgender and gender-nonconforming people to build lives "above the underground economy." In doing so, they also hope to provide for Peterson by ensuring his employment after his release.

Because Peterson, Jo, and Alexander all occupy very different intersections of race, gender, and sexuality, their cases together demonstrate the range of experiences that fall beyond the purview of "believable victim." The politics of respectability, purity, and desirability actually deny myriad survivors any protection from gender violence and mark them as individuals whom assailants can target without fear of consequences. By emphasizing the *im*personal stereotypes that dehumanized each of these survivors before juries and the wider public, Bierria et al. not only expose the complicities of carceral politics in social violence but also tether this damaging institution to the everyday assumptions and actions that perpetuate catastrophic harms. Scripts that criminalize blackness, queerness, gender nonconformity, and other boundary crossings are magnifications of the same unexamined fears that pervade public life—that compel white suburbanites to call the police on Black children playing in their neighborhoods, that compel officers to draw their guns on unarmed suspects, and that actively endanger and end Black and Brown and trans lives all over the country with horrific regularity.

The nationwide alliances that organized for Alexander's release and for the freedom of subsequent survivors achieved their successes through a vertical analysis that links individual experience to the historical and cultural formations surrounding them. *#SurvivedAndPunished* then uses these linkages to demonstrate how state violence replicates interpersonal violence, drawing attention to the ways courts and prisons often replicate abusers' use of surveillance, isolation, and coercion to erode their victims' physical *and* emotional fortitude. Bierria et al. effectively translate their experiences defending Alexander and other incarcerated survivors into more general "tools, tips, lessons, and resources" that can systematically combat those mechanisms of control. For example, because abusive relationships *and* the criminal legal system maintain power by "making survivors believe that they caused the violence to happen," defense teams should affirm "that you believe them, that the abuse was real, and that they did not deserve it" (11). Because both abusers and the state deprive incarcerated survivors of their agency, survivor defense committees begin first by giving back as much control as possible. In fact, *#SurvivedAndPunished* advises that defense campaigns always consult with the survivor, allowing survivors to decide (as circumstances permit) the terms of their involvement and the degree and forms of communication.

The many different tactics that Bierria et al. describe cohere into a "bottom-up" approach that begins with the authority of the survivor and moves vertically to map an overarching strategy for survivor defense and combating gender violence. The three major components of this strategy are (1) enabling the self-determination of survivors; (2) seeking and creating educational opportunities about racialized criminalization, gender violence, and their interrelations; and (3) forging connections—among individuals, organizations, institutions, movements, and histories. After establishing these priorities in their account of Marissa Alexander, Bierria et al. use them as transitional concepts that open up considerations of specific survivor demographics. For transgender folks, survivor-driven advocacy might entail having the survivors determine the terms of their stories (quite literally; including names and pronouns) and mobilizing a community to shape the public messaging. For immigrants, rallying public support might require a letter-writing campaign "affirming that the person is not a threat or flight risk" (13). Defense campaigns might also consider whether they have access to an immigration attorney or trans/gender-nonconforming/queer organizations where possible. For a survivor who identifies as both immigrant and trans, defense committees may need to draw widely from all these resources. While specific actions will differ according to the particular vulnerabilities of each survivor, they still focus on allowing the survivor to set the story and deploying interpersonal and organizational networks to amplify that message.

In addition to describing how these tactics helped defend different individual survivors, Bierria et al. use these transitional terms to anchor their macropolitical discussions, modifying their tactics to address issues from sexism to racism, xenophobia, transphobia, and combinations thereof. Though all of these -isms and -phobias have distinct manifestations and impact individuals differently, they also all depend on alienation and isolation. Unsurprisingly, relationality emerges as the most crucial element for combating abuse and discrimination. At its core, #SurvivedAndPunished offers a series of options for proliferating a survivor's possible allies—from sharing lessons with other defense committees to excavating and disseminating accounts of how other marginalized peoples have been criminalized throughout history, to partnering with media outlets to boost the defense narrative. Like *TIME*'s "silence breakers," these survivors also span a tremendous range of human experience. They, too, are part of a counterhegemonic movement that has no formal name. Through #SurvivedAndPunished's abolitionist praxis, however, they speak not with one voice, but many.

The work of justice

In October 2018—almost exactly a year after Alyssa Milano's viral call for stories of #MeToo—Brett Kavanaugh was sworn in as a Justice on the Supreme Court of the United States. In the weeks leading up to his confirmation, stories emerged of Kavanaugh's violent history with women. Dr. Christine Blasey Ford, a professor of psychology and Kavanaugh's former high school classmate, testified before Congress. With the expertise of a research psychologist, she explained how a traumatic encounter from their teen years remains indelible in her memory. Nearly three decades since Anita Hill attested to Justice Clarence Thomas's sexual misconduct, Ford stood before another (predominantly white, male) Senate Judiciary Committee and recalled how Kavanaugh held her down and covered her mouth when she tried to scream. What she could not forget, Ford told senators, "is the laughter, the uproarious laughter" as Kavanaugh and his friend assailed her (Birnbaum).

Throughout Kavanaugh's confirmation, public debate replicated gender violence on a national scale. After Ford came forward with her story, accounts of sexual violence once again proliferated the news. Deborah Ramirez and Julie Swetnick also shared separate instances of assault involving Kavanaugh, and survivors across the country excavated their own pasts in support of these women. So many women and gender minorities voiced their trauma, and a male-dominated, heteropatriarchal judicial body refused to listen.

CNN cameras captured protestors Ana Maria Archila and Maria Gallagher confronting Senator Jeff Flake just before the vote on Kavanaugh's nomination (Choksi and Herndon). The camera remains on Flake's impassive expression, but Archila's voice cuts through: "On Monday, I stood in front of your office [inaudible]. I told the story of my sexual assault…. What you are doing is allowing someone who actually violated a woman to sit on the Supreme Court." Also off camera, Gallagher adds, "I was sexually assaulted and nobody believed me…. Look at me and tell me that it doesn't matter what happened to me, that you will let people like that go into the highest court of the land and tell everyone what they can do to their bodies." While Flake refused to actually look at the women, he, alongside 49 other senators who ushered Kavanaugh onto the Supreme Court, sent a clear message to the country: It does not matter what happened to you—to Maria Gallagher, Ana Maria Archila, Christine Blasey Ford, Deborah Ramirez, or any other survivors. As the accusations against Kavanaugh multiplied, these legislators could have shifted their support to one of many other conservative judges who do not carry accusations of sexual violence. Their refusal to do so cemented sexual assault as a racialized, gendered, and classed privilege—one protected by the agencies that administer "justice."

Unlike the survivors centered in *#SurvivedAndPunished*, Christine Blasey Ford meets so many of the requirements of middle-class respectability. As *New York Magazine*'s Irin Carmon notes, Blasey Ford is "[a] wealthy, white suburban woman, married, with children. Her parents are Republicans. Her father plays golf with Brett Kavanaugh's dad at Burning Tree." On paper, Blasey Ford's peers are among the 53% of white women who voted for Trump and the 45% of white women who still supported Kavanaugh's confirmation ("More U.S. Voters"). On the stand, Blasey Ford spoke with the steady confidence of a widely respected psychologist. Her calm, deferential responses contrasted starkly with Kavanaugh's outright tantrum. Despite her impossible composure, and her educational, race, and class privilege, she still had to compete with public sympathies for Kavanaugh's reputation[10]—and she lost.

Following Kavanaugh's confirmation, optimistic pundits quickly began charting a hopeful future. Within days, national attention turned toward upcoming elections and the possibility that progressives would reclaim a measure of legislative control. The symbolism of Kavanaugh's confirmation, however, remains a potent reminder of the challenge ahead. He has most likely secured a lifetime appointment on the Supreme Court. Regardless of how cultural tides shift, substantive change is difficult within governing structures engineered to protect the elite. The 2018 midterm elections might have appointed a few more progressive politicians, but such gains were made through an electoral process that is still driven by money and scaffolded by discriminatory voter ID laws, flagrant gerrymandering, and felony disenfranchisement. Analyses of administrative violence reveal the elaborate social arrangements that sustain widespread inequality by constraining courses of action. The visions of justice that emerge from such analyses demand transformative vocabularies that refuse to rely on those systems for support and instead redraw the boundaries of our intimate networks to envision more comprehensive, collaborative change.

Until this point, campaigns for prison abolition have focused largely on the experiences of men, who compose roughly 90% of incarcerated adults (Federal Bureau of Prisons).[11] Meanwhile, #MeToo and public discourse on sexual violence has centered the voices of white middle-class women. These conversations have created a racialized dichotomy in which carceral politics concern Black men and sexual violence focuses on white women. Within such limited cultural grammars, Ky Peterson becomes an unspeakable subject and Christine Blasey Ford is drowned out by Kavanaugh's "fire-and-fury performance" (Baker and Fandos). A politic that thinks *about* trans experiences and also *with* trans theory can illuminate how the categories produced by gendered racialization disempower many on behalf of the few. These categories have also naturalized artificial divisions that constrain our coalitional possibilities.

In the video where Ana Maria Archila confronts Jeff Flake, she does not stop at asking whether he believes Kavanaugh is telling the truth. Archila presses on: "Do you think [Kavanuagh] is able to hold the pain of this country and repair it? That is the work of justice. The way that justice works is you recognize hurt, you take responsibility for it and then you begin to repair it" (Choksi and Herndon). Kavanaugh's appointment demonstrates the extent to which the justice system refuses to hold powerful men accountable for the harms they inflict. This system will inevitably replicate patterns of hurt that propagate gender violence. The example provided by #SurvivedAndPunished prompts anti-violence advocates to empower marginalized survivors and to demand more imaginative, ground-up enactments of justice.

Transforming cultures of violence will require moving across, into, and beyond the divisions enacted by social taxonomies. "Trans issues" do not affect only transgender individuals. Trans lives are endangered by a multitude of housing policies, employment and health care practices, and racialized gender norms that affect most minorities in the United States. Mass incarceration has consequences beyond an individual's time behind bars. Rather, the entire institution creates forms of social, economic, and political disenfranchisement designed to restrict power to the elite few. Reforming abusive cultures surrounding gender, too, will need to be more than the purview of women and gender minorities. Those who benefit from presumed masculine authority will need to shoulder responsibility for reforming gendered behavior and values. We will have to understand power as a resource that can be shared rather than hoarded. Until such networked vocabularies and worldviews are established, Gerard Bryant is probably correct: our reactions to harm will be to isolate and contain; we will have prisons; we will have sexual abuse in prisons. That reality is ours to change.

Notes

1. Bryant was an associate warden and acting warden at the Metropolitan Detention Center in Brooklyn.
2. These statistics are drawn from the groundbreaking 2011 report on the National Transgender Discrimination Survey conducted by the National Center for Transgender Equality (NCTE) and the National Gay and Lesbian Task Force. In the 2015 follow-up study by the NCTE, statistics remained almost entirely the same. See James et al.
3. The rate of physical abuse targeting American Indian trans prisoners is 45% and sexual assault targeting Black trans prisoners is 34% (Grant et al.).

4. Statistics from 2015 are from James et al.'s 2015 U.S. Transgender Survey (USTS), which is the largest study ever conducted on the experiences of trans people in the United States. The survey had 27,715 respondents nationwide.
5. The absence of a systemic analysis also contributes to the silencing of bisexual, queer, and trans voices within LGBTQ movements.
6. According to the extensive 2015 national transgender survey from which many of these statistics are drawn, trans folks overwhelmingly prioritize anti-violence policies that protect trans people far above ones that address poverty, racism, police misconduct, and prison reform (James et al. 239).
7. For an extensive discussion of the way these structures limit the life chances of trans folks, see Dean Spade's *Normal Life*.
8. In the 1800s, when Martin Delany claimed that "where he was allowed the enter, the race entered with him," Anna Julia Cooper countered, "Only the Black Woman can say, when and where I enter . . . then and there the whole Negro race enters with me" (Crenshaw 160). The fact that Cooper first uttered those words in the 19th century, that Crenshaw echoed her point in 1989, and that today, women of color—trans and cis—are still straining to be heard suggests a pressing need for more reflexive ways to respond to different accounts of personal trauma.
9. For example, the Environmental Protection Agency, the Food and Drug Administration, the Department of Health and Human Services.
10. For example, the *Washington Post*'s Marc Thiessen equates Blasey Ford's charges with the destruction of Kavanaugh's life.
11. As the experiences of trans prisoners remind us, however, the binaristic sorting of incarcerated individuals is an entirely flawed process, so statistics are representative only of those the state labels as male.

Works cited

@Alyssa_Milano. "If You've Been Sexually Harassed or Assaulted Write 'Me Too' As a Reply to This Tweet." *Twitter*, 15 Oct. 2017, https://twitter.com/Alyssa_Milano/status/919659438700670976.

Adetiba, Elizabeth. "Tarana Burke Says #MeToo Should Center Marginalized Communities." *The Nation*, 17 Nov. 2017, https://www.thenation.com/article/tarana-burke-says-metoo-isnt-just-for-white-people/.

Alexander, Michelle. *The New Jim Crow: Mass Incarceration in the Age of Colorblindness*. The New Press, 2010.

Baker, Peter, and Nicholas Fandos. "Show How You Feel, Kavanaugh Was Told, and a Nomination Was Saved." *New York Times*, 7 Oct. 2018, https://www.nytimes.com/2018/10/06/us/politics/kavanaugh-vote-confirmation-process.html.

Bennett, Jessica. "After #MeToo, the Ripple Effect." *New York Times*, 28 June 2018, https://www.nytimes.com/2018/06/28/arts/what-is-next-metoo-movement.html?

———. "The #MeToo Moment: No Longer Complicit." *New York Times*, 7 Dec. 2017, https://www.nytimes.com/2017/12/07/us/the-metoo-moment-no-longer-complicit.html.

Berry, Elizabeth. "State Attorney Details Marissa Alexander Case for Lawmakers." *WJXT*, 19 Mar. 2014, https://www.news4jax.com/news/local/state-attorney-details-marissa-alexander-case-for-lawmakers.

Bhanji, Nael. "Trans/Scriptions: Homing Desires, (Trans)Sexual Citizenship, and Racialized Bodies." *The Transgender Studies Reader 2*, edited by Susan Stryker and Aren Z. Aizura, Routledge, 2013, pp. 512–26.

Bierria, Alisa, et al., editors. *#SurvivedAndPunished: Survivor Defense As Abolitionist Praxis*. Survived and Punished, https://survivedandpunished.org/wp-content/uploads/2018/06/survived-and-punished-toolkit.pdf.

Birnbaum, Emily. "Ford Recalls 'Uproarious Laughter' During Alleged Incident." *The Hill*, 27 Sept. 2018, https://thehill.com/homenews/senate/408738-ford-recalls-uproarious-laughter-during-alleged-incident.

Burke, Tarana. "#MeToo Founder Tarana Burke on the Rigorous Work That Still Lies Ahead." *Variety*, 25 Sept. 2018, https://variety.com/2018/biz/features/tarana-burke-metoo-one-year-later-1202954797/.

Carmon, Irin. "Christine Blasey Ford Is a Class Traitor." *Intelligencer*, 27 Sept. 2018, http://nymag.com/intelligencer/2018/09/christine-blasey-ford-is-a-class-traitor.html.

Choksi, Niraj, and Astead Herndon. "Jeff Flake Is Confronted on Video by Sexual Assault Survivors." *New York Times*, 28 Sept. 2018, https://www.nytimes.com/2018/09/28/us/politics/jeff-flake-protesters-kavanaugh.html.

Chuck, Elizabeth. "Cosby Conviction Is the First Big Win of the #MeToo Movement." *NBC News*, 26 Apr. 2018, https://www.nbcnews.com/storyline/bill-cosby-scandal/bill-cosby-conviction-first-big-win-metoo-movement-n869381.

Crenshaw, Kimberlé. "Demarginalizing the Intersection of Race and Sex: A Black Feminist Critique of Antidiscrimination Doctrine, Feminist Theory, and Antiracist Politics." *University of Chicago Legal Forum*, vol. 1989, no. 1, 1989, pp. 139–67.

Davis, Angela Y. *Abolition Democracy: Beyond Empire, Prisons, and Torture*, 1st ed. Seven Stories Press, 2005.

———. *Are Prisons Obsolete?* Seven Stories Press, 2003.

Davis, Heath Fogg. *Beyond Trans: Does Gender Matter?* New York UP, 2018.

Dingo, Rebecca. *Networking Arguments: Rhetoric, Transnational Feminism, and Public Policy Writing*. U of Pittsburgh P, 2012.

———. "Networking the Macro and Micro: Toward Transnational Literacy Practices." *JAC*, vol. 33, no. 3/4, 2013, pp. 529–52.

Dockterman, Eliana. "Harvey Weinstein's Arrest Marks a Pivotal Turning Point for the #MeToo Movement." *Time*, 25 May 2018, http://time.com/5291663/harvey-weinstein-arrest-metoo-movement/.

Enke, Anne, editor. *Transfeminist Perspectives in and Beyond Transgender and Gender Studies*. Temple UP, 2012.

Federal Bureau of Prisons. "Inmate Gender," 29 Sept. 2018, https://www.bop.gov/about/statistics/statistics_inmate_gender.jsp.

Foderaro, Lisa W. "New York State May Move to Close Rikers Ahead of City's 10-Year Timeline." *New York Times*, 15 Feb. 2018, https://www.nytimes.com/2018/02/14/nyregion/rikers-island-jail-closing-timeline.html.

Grant, Jaime M., Lisa A. Motter, Justin Tanis, Jack Harrison, Jody L. Herman, and Mara Keisling. *Injustice at Every Turn: A Report of the National Transgender Discrimination Survey*. National Center for Transgender Equality and National Gay and Lesbian Task Force, 2011, https://transequality.org/sites/default/files/docs/resources/NTDS_Report.pdf.

hooks, bell. *Ain't I a Woman: Black Women and Feminism*, 2nd ed. Routledge, 2014.

INCITE! Women of Color Against Violence, editors. *Color of Violence: The INCITE! Anthology*. Duke UP, 2016.

James, S. E., J. L. Herman, S. Rankin, M. Keisling, L. Mottet, and M. Anafi. *The Report of the 2015 U.S. Transgender Survey*. National Center for Transgender Equality, 2016, https://www.transequality.org/sites/default/files/docs/USTS-Full-Report-FINAL.PDF.

"Ky Peterson FAQ." Freedom Overground Corp, https://www.freedomoverground.org/ky-peterson-campaign. Accessed 1 Oct. 2018.

Law, Victoria. "Nan-Hui Jo's Case Shows How the System Fails Immigrant Abuse Survivors." *Rewire.News*, 4 May 2015, https://rewire.news/article/2015/05/04/nan-hui-jos-case-shows-system-fails-immigrant-abuse-survivors/.

Malinowski, Nick. "NYC Official Says Rape Is Inevitable at Rikers Island: If True, We Cannot Send Anyone There." *Huffington Post*, 26 June 2016, https://www.huffingtonpost.com/nick-malinowski/nyc-official-says-rape-is_b_10600320.html.

"More U.S. Voters Say Don't Confirm Kavanaugh." *Quinnipiac University Poll*, 1 Oct. 2018, https://poll.qu.edu/images/polling/us/us10012018_uovc95.pdf/.

Morris, Monique W. *Pushout: The Criminalization of Black Girls in Schools*. The New Press, 2016.

Nichols, Rob. "Toward a Critical Trans Politics: An Interview with Dean Spade." *Upping the Anti: A Journal of Theory and Action*, vol. 14, 2012, http://uppingtheanti.org/journal/article/14-dean-spade/.

Ore, Ersula. *Lynching: Violence, Rhetoric, and American Identity*. U of Mississippi P, 2019.

Pishko, Jessica. "After Fleeing Abuse, an Immigrant Mother Faces Losing Her Daughter Forever." *The Guardian*, 6 June 2015, https://www.theguardian.com/global/2015/jun/06/immigration-child-deportation-domestic-violence.

Richie, Beth. *Arrested Justice: Black Women, Violence, and America's Prison Nation*. New York UP, 2012.

———. *Compelled to Crime: The Gender Entrapment of Battered Black Women*. Routledge, 1996.

Rios, Victor M. *Human Targets: Schools, Police, and the Criminalization of Latino Youth*. U of Chicago P, 2017.

Roberts, Dorothy E. *Killing the Black Body: Race, Reproduction, and the Meaning of Liberty*, 1st ed. Vintage Books, 1997.

Rowley, Liz. "#MeToo Founder Says the Movement Has Lost Its Way." *The Cut*, 23 Oct. 2018, https://www.thecut.com/2018/10/tarana-burke-me-too-founder-movement-has-lost-its-way.html.

Snorton, C. Riley. *Black on Both Sides: A Racial History of Trans Identity*. U of Minnesota P, 2017.

Spade, Dean. *Normal Life: Administrative Violence, Critical Trans Politics, and the Limits of Law*, 2nd ed. Duke UP, 2015.

Spade, Dean, and Hope Dector. *Ky Peterson—Survived and Punished*. *YouTube*, uploaded by Barnard Center for Research on Women, 9 Aug. 2017, https://www.youtube.com/watch?time_continue=48&v=W7ySbCx_SwE.

Stacy, Mitch. "Woman Gets 20 Years for Firing Warning Shot." *Washington Times*, 19 May 2012, https://www.washingtontimes.com/news/2012/may/19/woman-gets-20-years-firing-warning-shot/.

Stahl, Aviva. "New York City Jails Still Can't Keep Trans Prisoners Safe." *Village Voice*, 21 Dec. 2017, https://www.villagevoice.com/2017/12/21/new-york-city-jails-still-cant-keep-trans-prisoners-safe/.

Stanley, Eric, and Nat Smith, editors. *Captive Genders: Trans Embodiment and the Prison Industrial Complex*, 2nd ed. AK Press, 2015.

Stryker, Susan. *Transgender History: The Roots of Today's Revolution*. 2nd ed., Seal Press, 2017.

Stryker, Susan, Paisley Currah, and Lisa Jean Moore. "Introduction: Trans-, Trans, or Transgender?" *Women's Studies Quarterly*, vol. 36, no. 3/4, Fall 2008, pp. 11–22. doi:10.1353/wsq.0.0112.

Thiessen, Marc A. "How Much Evidence Do We Need to Destroy Someone?" *Washington Post*, 20 Sept. 2018, https://www.washingtonpost.com/opinions/how-much-evidence-do-we-need-to-destroy-someone/2018/09/20/43343648-bcf4-11e8-be70-52bd11fe18af_story.html?noredirect=on&utm_term=.498110b6b02d.

Zacharek, Stephanie, Eliana Dockterman, and Haley Sweetland Edwards. "TIME Person of the Year 2017: The Silence Breakers." *TIME*, http://time.com/time-person-of-the-year-2017-silence-breakers/. Accessed 1 July 2018.

Expendables for Whom: Terry Crews and the Erasure of Black Male Victims of Sexual Assault and Rape

Tommy J. Curry

ABSTRACT
The sexual assault of Terry Crews by Adam Venit raises all sorts of questions about the nature of sexual violence and our reluctance to see Black men as victims of sexual assault in the United States. Despite a history of Black men and boys being raped by White men and women, there is no effort to connect the centuries-long record of sexual violence against Black males to the sexual victimization of Black men and boys currently. This article analyzes the language, history, and stereotypes deployed in our understanding of Terry Crews's victimization, even those he uses to describe himself, to better situate and describe the vulnerability of Black men and boys to sexual violence in the United States.

On October 10, 2017, Terry Crews—a Black male actor and former professional athlete in the National Football League—announced on Twitter that he was a victim of sexual assault at the hands of well-known Hollywood executive Adam Venit: "My wife n I were at a Hollywood function last year in a high level Hollywood executive came over 2 me and groped my privates. This whole thing with Harvey Weinstein is giving me PTSD. Why? Because this kind of thing happened to ME" (Crews, 2017b).

When Crews first announced himself as a survivor of sexual assault and a victim of sexual violence, many of the responses on Twitter blamed him for not defending himself from the assault and knocking the attacker out. Crews explained that Black men are not able to defend themselves from violence even when they are attacked by a weaker aggressor. If he did defend himself with violence from the groping of Venit, "'240 lbs. Black Man stomps out Hollywood Honcho' would [have] be[en] the headline the next day" (Crews, 2017a). In a June testimony before the U.S. Senate to expand the sexual assault Survivors' Bill of Rights Act, Crews explained that

> as a black man in America, you only have a few shots at success. You only have a few chances to make yourself a viable member of the community. I'm from Flint, Michigan. I have seen many, many young black men who were provoked into violence, and they were imprisoned or they were killed. And they're not here… . My wife, for years, prepared me. She said: "If you ever get goaded, if you ever get prodded, if you ever get anyone trying to push you into any situation, don't do it, don't be violent." (Kelly, 2018, paras. 4–5)

Crews, "as a Black man in America," explained to the senator that violence was not—is not—an option. No matter if he was defending himself from the sexual aggression of Venit, Crews would be framed, interpreted, seen by the public as the attacker. His physical size, skin color, and maleness made him the threat irrespective of the actual violence inflicted upon him. Black men are burdened by the threats others perceive them to be. Our belief that Black men are dangerous and in need of control and criminal sanction nullifies our ability to perceive them as victims of violence at the hands of other groups of men or even women.

Despite Crews's accusation against Venit being eerily similar to the stories and experiences of female victims of sexual harassment and assault shared under #MeToo, it is clear that #MeToo is unable to fully comprehend and incorporate Crew's vulnerability to sexual violence as a Black male. Crews has certainly been acknowledged to be a victim of Venit's toxic masculinity, but is Crews a victim because as a Black male he is vulnerable to sexual violence? Or is Mr. Crews a victim because he was victimized by a toxic male?

The increasing number of stories by male victims of sexual violence has spurred on a debate over the status of male victimization within #MeToo. I believe Crews's narrative exposes some of the discursive limitations of how #MeToo conceptualizes Black male victims of sexual assault and rape. While this article certainly builds from many of the concerns generally raised about male victims of sexual assault in #MeToo, I am particularly concerned about the ways that some of the discussions utilize feminism and patriarchy as an intuitive marker that indicates who *can be* and who *usually are* victims of rape, sexual harassment, and sexual assault in this society. The erasure of Black male victims—specifically, their disproportionate sexual victimization in the United States—persists unabated in the era of #MeToo as female victims. Women's stories and narratives continue not only to displace but also to deny the prevalence of Black male sexual victimization at the hands of other men and women. This article is critical of the discursive formulations of #MeToo asserting that men, specifically Black men, are primarily perpetrators of sexual violence and rarely victims of sexual violence.

Terry Crews's story has been accepted into #MeToo based on his victimization at the hands of another man, not his position as an actual victim of sexual assault. I want to be clear about this point as it matters to how we think about and rhetorically situate Black males in conversations about rape and sexual violence. Crews's experience of sexual assault is not being discussed as evidence of the at-large vulnerability Black men have to being sexually assaulted, raped, or made to penetrate others. Crews's narrative has been almost singularly interpreted as him being a victim of toxic masculinity. Unlike the narratives of #MeToo that emphasize women's vulnerability to sexual violence throughout U.S society, Crews is thought to simply be the victim of one man's desire; he is simply not thought of being part of a class vulnerable to sexual violence as a Black man. Crews's assault became more mainstream and part of #MeToo as he adopted more of the discursive formulations of contemporary feminism (e.g., toxic masculinity, patriarchy, male privilege) and the "male as perpetrator" paradigm of #MeToo. Even with Crews's acceptance within #MeToo, U.S. society is still reticent to acknowledge the sexual vulnerability of Black men to rape, sexual assault, and sexual coercion.

Many scholars, activists, and gender theorists consider it inconceivable that Black men (6.5%) in the United States experience contact sexual violence (which includes rape, being made to penetrate, sexual coercion, and unwanted sexual contact) as often as Black women (5.8%) in a given year, or have rates of sexual victimization higher than White women (3.6%) (Smith et al., 2017, pp. 18, 21, 28). Consequently, any data or evidence suggesting that Black men are victims of sexual violence or rape comparable to women are often rejected outright. While the National Crime Victimization Survey (NCVS) conducted by the U.S. Bureau of Justice Statistics (BJS) contains the most cited data on rape in the United States, its survey methodology has been criticized for not fully capturing women's experiences of victimization (Lynch, 1996) or the role of consent, because it emphasizes the individual's ability to identify his or her experience of rape as a crime (Groden, 2014). The Centers for Disease Control and Prevention (CDC) National Intimate Partner and Sexual Violence Survey (NISVS) is much more attuned to an individual's experience of sexual events and has consistently shown that men suffer comparable rates of sexual violence as women in the United States. According to Black et al. (2011), U.S. male victims of made-to-penetrate violence (1,267,000) are similar to the number of women rape victims (1,270,000) over a 12-month period (pp. 18–19). This statistic is largely ignored because it cuts against too many ingrained gender stereotypes concerning our popularly held assumptions about rape and the nature of patriarchy. However, wrestling with empirical data that may contradict established postulates is necessary to advance theory—especially theories about Black men and boys, who remain absent from our thinking about victims of sexual violence.

This article analyzes the assumptions directing interpretations of Mr. Crews's victimization to challenge and discredit the understanding of Black men as second-class victims of sexual violence and rape. In what follows, I argue that Crews's acceptance by #MeToo is rooted in his confirmation of the dominant feminist view that men are primarily the perpetrators of sexual violence and women are almost solely victims, a position which is actually at odds with the views of Tarana Burke, the original founder of Me Too. Then, I draw on Burke's understanding of #MeToo as a movement that urges the United States to deal with the trauma of sexual violence against both men and women. Following Burke, academics would find an analysis of sexual assault, rape, and violence that problematizes the dominant male as perpetrator view asserted by many #MeToo activists, as well as Crews himself. Specifically, I articulate a different lens through which to perceive the vulnerability of Black men generally and historicize the sexual assault against Crews. The history of Black men's rape and the data showing Black males as vulnerable to sexual violence should change how we conceptualize the risk Black men and boys have to sexual violence in the United States. In the final section, I argue that the dangerous racist and gendered stereotyping of Black men as criminals, deviants, and sexual predators is a powerful and enduring paradigm that essentializes and reifies racialized men as invulnerable to sexual violence.

Terry Crews's recognition as a victim of sexual assault in #MeToo

#MeToo rose to popularity in October 2017 when Alyssa Milano tweeted the hashtag to bring awareness to the problem of sexual harassment and assault in society. Her audience and message were specifically geared toward the sexual vulnerability of women. In her first tweet on #MeToo, Milano (2017) wrote: "If you've been sexually harassed or assaulted write 'me too' as a reply to this tweet." According to Twitter, "in less than 24 hours, 4.7 million people around the world ... engaged in the #MeToo conversation, with more than 12 million posts, comments and reactions" (Santiago and Criss, 2017, para. 32). While #MeToo certainly captured the experiences of many rich White actresses, entertainers, and celebrities, Milano actually appropriated the term "me too" from Tarana Burke, a sexual assault survivor and director of the Brooklyn-based Girls for Gender Equity, who created Me Too in 2006 to empower young women of color (Santiago and Criss, 2017, para. 4). Burke has dedicated her life to helping female victims of sexual assault and abuse. Unlike the symbolic representation of #MeToo offered by the positioning of prominent (and mostly White) women—The Silence Breakers—as *Time*'s 2017 Person of the Year, Burke has suggested that discursive innovation should take a backseat to the more real-world agenda of helping actual victims. As Burke said, "We don't need another 'thing.' If we keep on 'making statements' and not really doing the work, we are going to be in trouble" (Walden, 2018, para. 1). Burke's position demands the public help, hear, and heal victims.

For many people, #MeToo should be a feminist moment exclusively focused on female victimization and male perpetration (Haider, 2019; Mack & McCann, 2018). Over the past several months, more stories from male victims and the recent revelation of Asia Argento as the (statutory) rapist of a male teen has troubled many of the core assumptions of this moment and complicates the agreed-upon narrative that women are primarily victims to men, not perpetrators of violence toward men (Weiss, 2018). The act of sexual perpetration against men and boys has caused some debate as to the focus, theory, and political commitments of the #MeToo movement (Bowen, 2018). Various publications and critics (Bump, 2018; Chandler, 2018; Levin, 2017) have pointed out that while women are often victims of sexual harassment and assault, there are also a substantial number of male victims of sexual assault and rape that remain unheard, unseen, and silenced by the rhetoric and political ideations of #MeToo.

Remarking on the failure of the male victims of sexual assault to receive serious attention by the movement, Klee (2018) drew attention to how male victims of sexual assault like Crews and Brendan Fraser were ridiculed by having their sexual assaults lessened to jokes and playful pokes about others groping their bodies. Such ridicule toward male victims' reports is why more male victims do not come forward and share their stories. Klee (2018) wrote, "This is how we victim-blame men: not for drinking too much or wearing the wrong clothes or seeking salacious fame, but for not playing along when another guy crosses a line. The villains here invoke the same fraternity of silence that gaslights and suppresses female victims" (para. 8).

Often, male victims of sexual assault are told to ignore it, give it a pass, or interpret their assault as nothing more than a different interpretation or misguided intention of their harasser. However, appeasing this advice would simply reinforce "the toxic assumption that men are invulnerable to these attacks—that to be a victim is, essentially, to be a woman" (Klee, 2018, para. 8). Some commentators such as Norton (2017) have suggested that the recognition of male victims within #MeToo is almost impossible if not paradoxical in nature. He explained:

> Male victim rape and sexual assault are clearly neglected and under-reported, so #metoo gave some men a safe space and enough momentum to share their experiences. The

paradox is this: if women experienced #metoo as a safe space, free from the interruption and judgment, then some of them—rightfully—didn't want perceived male intrusion. Given the lack of information, shaming, and beliefs towards men vis-a-vis sexual violence (not as affected by rape, cannot be raped, must have enjoyed it, etc.), it becomes exponentially more difficult for men to speak out. (para. 20)

Crews's story of victimization thereby occupies a somewhat peculiar place in the unfolding of #MeToo as a moment and cultural narrative. While Crews's case is a specific example of the numerous male victims that have themselves been tormented by the trauma of their sexual assaults, the death of Chester Bennington or the years of therapy Tyler Perry needed to deal with his abuse have not been centered in any noticeable way in the discourse and representations of the #MeToo movement (Crary, 2018). As one male survivor said:

> Because the movement happened to get its start with women only, in a way it furthers my loneliness as a past victim…. Men are historically considered the bad guys. If some men abuse women, then we all are abusers ourselves … so therefore when it comes to our being abused, we deserve it. (Crary, 2018, paras. 4–5)

Because men are viewed primarily as perpetrators of violence and abuse, they are rarely understood to be victims and, consequently, can never be the leading subject of conversations about rape, sexual harassment, or sexual victimization.

Crews seems to rationalize his story as one of survival demonstrating the violence of toxic masculinity. Crews views #MeToo as a dialogue accommodating all victims' experiences equally. However, Crews's optimism seems to be at odds with reality—or the financial underpinnings of #MeToo. In an interview with *Deadline* in January 2018, Crews was asked about his lawsuit against Adam Venit and the Time's Up legal defense fund for victims of sexual assault and abuse. He replied:

> this is my concern, symbolic victories are no good. People tend to get satisfied by symbolic victories. I mean, when you're talking about Time's Up, hey, Time's Up is one of the greatest ideas of all time and I'm standing with these women. I am with it, I could not be more supportive, but when you let William Morris just put in $1.5 million dollars, pledged that to Time's Up, and my assailant still works there, I was hung out to dry, and now they're pledging this money in an attempt to buy your justice. To me, it's arrogance on top of arrogance. (Patten, 2018, para. 10)

In March 2018, Crews would find out that his lawsuit was rejected by the Los Angeles district attorney (Messer and Ghebremedhin, 2018). For filing a lawsuit against William Morris Endeavor (WME) Entertainment, Crews was eliminated from *The Expendables* movie franchise. Crews is now unable to take legal action against his assailant and has lost earnings from going public with his abuse.

Crews has been very clear to the public that he understood himself to be powerless when Venit sexually assaulted him. Crews's experience of sexual assault, specifically his inability to defend himself from the sexual aggression of Venit, was communicated as an effect of the fear others have of his Black male body. In June 2018, Crews explained to a Senate Judiciary Committee for the Survivors' Bill of Rights Act how anti-Black misandry, or the fear and hatred the United States has toward Black men, made him vulnerable to Venit's violence. Crews said, "Just imagine, if I had done something like that to his wife, would I get a pass? Or if he had done that and just imagine if I hit him back, would I have a career? No way. No way. That's the arrogance" (Patten, 2018, para. 12).

The inability of the United States to see a muscular Black man as a *real* victim of sexual violence hit Crews hard in the following months when it became obvious that he had no social capital or narrative of Black male sexual victimization that would mobilize others to act on his behalf. Unlike the female victims of #MeToo, his accusation alone was not powerful enough to remove his assailant from his job or force WME to sanction Venit in any serious way. As a Black man accusing a White man of sexual assault, his body and vulnerability was not sacred enough to destroy Venit's career, much less get him fired. Remember, in other cases that were not part of #MeToo but borrowed its cultural prominence, such as the anonymous letter concerning a date with Aziz Ansari (Way, 2018), the accusation (by a White woman) alone was enough to cancel his Netflix series and seriously endanger his career (Chang and O'Neill, 2018). Crews had to launch a civil suit against Venit and WME to get Venit to resign and WME to institute policies against sexual harassment (Clark, 2018).

How does Crews explain this tension (being a second-class victim, so to speak) between his sexual victimization, his racial vulnerability, and his commitment to women's issues as framed by #MeToo? At a personal level, Crews has interpreted his struggle as similar to that of Frederick Douglass, who according to Crews "fought just as hard for women's suffrage as he did for the abolishment of slavery. I mean, just as hard. Once the Emancipation Proclamation happened he switched right over into women's suffrage" (Patten, 2018, para. 27). There is, of course, a history here that needs some nuance, but this really shows how Crews sees himself and his feminist politics aligning with the goals of #MeToo, at least in theory. Materially, however, there seem to be obvious differences between his story of victimization and that of (mostly) White women. In my view, Crews knew that as a heterosexual Black male his story would never get public attention unless he could become part of #MeToo. This need to be incorporated dictated the change in the language he utilized and the rise in the popularity of his story with the public. Having realized the lack of empathy he received as a Black male victim, he became an even more adamant and outspoken feminist ally and critic of toxic masculinity.

Despite the proliferation of discursive formulations designed to convey the intrasubjective experiencing of violence and the imposition of external ideological and structural forces on gendered bodies, there is a conspicuous lack of language that conveys the sexual vulnerability and victimization of men—specifically Black men—in our society. The sexual victimization of Crews resonated with #MeToo to the extent that he was a victim of sexual assault by another male perpetrator and an ally of women. I can find no editorials or mainstream periodicals that point to the sexual assault of Crews as an example of the sexual violence Black males experience in U.S. society on the whole, as young men and children or at the hands of police. Whereas female victims of sexual assault and sexual harassment indicate a pervasive threat to women in the United States, Crews's story is individualized and particular to his person.

Increasingly, Crews has used a personalized language of victimization when he discusses his past participation in the cult of masculinity and the need for "men to hold other men accountable" for the victimization of other men and women. While he emphasizes the problem of masculinity, Crews's commentary elides a larger point about the broader cultural phenomenon of Black male sexual victimization and abuse. In recent months, his language describing sexual victimization has focused on the dangers of toxic masculinity, patriarchy, and female objectification (Santi, 2018). At the ninth annual Women in the World Summit, Crews explained:

> Masculinity can be a cult, and when I say cult, it is no different than David Koresh. It's no different than Jim Jones.... You know, the best example is slavery. It's when slaves were yelling, "Oh my god. I am being beaten and hurt." The master would look at them like I don't understand what you are saying... . It's almost like there is this disconnect, like they won't see pain. There's a lack of empathy, and this is what happens with men and women. Men who are in this cult, you can say as a woman—they talk, but that guy is not looking at you as all the way human. And this is where you have to understand there is a humanity issue here. You are like, "Why don't you hear me? Why don't you see my feelings?" And they are like "You are not all the way human. You are here for me." (Women in the World, 2018)

Crews's embrace of this particular narrative suggests that #MeToo still lacks a language to describe and center the abuse of racialized men next to women generally. Black men have higher rates of sexual victimization than White women in the United States. If masculinity is, in fact, a cult, which some White hegemonic iterations of it certainly are, then what conceptualization of male vulnerability does Crews have to explain why women are the majority of the perpetrators of sexual violence against men when we consider men reporting being made to penetrate, sexual coercion, and unwanted sexual contact (Smith et al., 2017, p. 32)? Crews makes it a point to account for the violence inflicted upon him by Venit, but in doing so he has continued to offer a narrow understanding of sexual violence and rape that focuses more on male perpetration than male victimization.

Since early 2019, Crews has become even more outspoken concerning the topic of Black masculinity and its relationship to toxicity and violence. Referencing an online article published in *The Root* titled "Straight Black Men Are the White People of the Black Race" (Young, 2017), Crews responded that the idea that Black men are the White men of the Black race is "thought provoking" (2019b) and evident given the rates of domestic abuse and his experience with his father (2019a). A far cry from his initial efforts to recognize the victimization of Black men by sexual abuse, Crews suggested that the issue requiring the most attention is Black men's violence against women as sexual predators. The article shared by Crews has warranted replies by both activists and academics (Moore, 2018; Curry & Curry, 2018). According to the article's author, Damon Young (2017), Black men "are the ones who get the biggest seat at the table and the biggest piece of chicken at the table despite making the smallest contribution to the meal" (para. 3). Following the trope that Black men do not provide for families or contribute any meaningful contribution to Black family life, Young continues that Black men are not only derelict in the duties of family but also dangerous. He writes, "And nowhere is this more evident than when considering the collective danger we pose to black women and our collective lack of willingness to accept and make amends for that truth" (para. 4).

Alongside Young's essay, Crews's rhetoric emphasizing the danger of Black men to their communities and to Black women runs contrary to fact and impedes the ability of U.S. society to empathize with Black male victims of sexual violence given their alleged sexual threats as rapists and abusers. Crews endorsed the dominant language of patriarchal (toxic) masculinity to describe the dehumanization of women that pays little attention to the differences of power, privilege, or perpetration against women based on class location or perhaps the more historically salient feature of race. A closer look at the data concerning sexual assault and rape among Blacks in the United States offers vastly different a picture of Black males than Crews describes.

Tarana Burke and other challenges to the dominant feminist paradigm of sexual victimization

The debate over the inclusion of male victims within #MeToo was the topic of many editorials at the end of 2018. In an article titled "If We Want Men to Be a Part of #MeToo, We Have to Stop Gendering the Movement," Arceneaux (2018) wrote, "If we want men to be a part of the #MeToo movement, we need to acknowledge that they too can be victims" (para. 4). Citing Burke, Arceneaux urged activists and victims alike to remember that this moment should be an analysis of power and not the inscription of gendered stereotypes that force male victims into silence (para. 11). Other articles such as Perry's (2018) "#HimToo Should Be a Conversation About Male Victims of Sexual Assault" reported that "[t]oo often, even 'woke' men talk about fighting rape culture out of a need to protect the women in their lives" (para. 5). Referencing U.S. CDC data and the work of Lara Stemple, Perry (2018) concluded "that singular focus on women victims is misguided. We're all in this together" (para. 5). Unfortunately, data do not always persuade the masses. Activists and academics have been slow to adjust gender theories to reflect this reality. Burke, however, has been extremely clear that #MeToo's core mission was to highlight sexual violence and the victims of that violence regardless of gender. As she stated in her TEDWomen talk, #MeToo is "a movement about the 1 in 4 girls and the 1 in 6 boys who are sexually abused every year and who carry those wounds into adulthood" (Burke, 2018b). Recognizing male victims of sexual violence is central to Burke's vision of #MeToo, even though she believes that such recognition runs counter to #MeToo as currently conceptualized.

Burke's activism parts with academic feminism's account of sexual violence and perpetration in many ways. The dominant feminist account of sexual violence requires an understanding of males as perpetrators of sexual violence against female victims of sexual violence (Stemple, Flores, & Meyer, 2017; Stemple & Meyer, 2014; Cohen, 2014). In feminist analysis, rape and sexual violence occur as an outgrowth of ingrained sociocultural differences between the sexes (Brownmiller, 1975). MacKinnon (1979) similarly argued, "Aggression against those with less power is experienced as sexual pleasure" for men (p. 7). Following the male as perpetrator paradigm, feminist scholar Koss (1993) maintained:

> Although consideration of male victims is within the scope of the legal statutes, it is important to restrict the term rape to instances where male victims were penetrated by offenders. It is inappropriate to consider as a rape victim a man who engages in unwanted sexual intercourse with a woman. (pp. 206–207)

Rape, as understood within the feminist analytic, applies only to or can include male victims of male perpetrators who forcibly penetrate their male bodies. A woman or other man making them penetrate their mouth or anus does not fall within the popular feminist paradigm. Cohen's (2014) book *Male Rape Is a Feminist Issue: Feminism, Governmentality, and Male Rape* similarly remarked that prevailing research by feminist academics has been driven by the idea that "rape is still the most gender specific of all crimes [where] 'only a man ... can be the actual perpetrator, only a woman the victim'" (p. 3). Much of the feminist research concerning male rape often suggests that "male rape is not prevalent overall, and that where it does occur, it only concerns homosexual communities" (Cohen, 2014, p. 17).

The inability of feminist frameworks to understand male vulnerability to rape by other men and by women to the same extent as women have to do with the construction of the woman as always vulnerable to sexual violence perpetrated by men. As Cohen (2014) explained,

> [T]he reluctance to embrace male rape within the feminist rape model, as popularly conceived, is a result of the reluctance to adapt it, not an inability to do so. But this reluctance is understandable when the model itself is presented as so enmeshed with the legitimacy of the theoretical stance. One cannot revisit the feminist rape model without supposedly impinging on the feminist paradigm as a whole. (pp. 157–158)

Stemple and Meyer (2014) also note that the dominant feminist paradigm of sexual victimization deploys various myths that erase and lessen the suffering of male victims, preferring to see males primarily as sexual aggressors; they explain, "Because dominant feminist theory relies heavily on the idea that men use sexual aggression to subordinate women, findings perceived to conflict with this theory, such as female-perpetrated violence against men, are politically unpalatable" (pp. e19–e20).

The resistance of gender scholars to seriously consider the empirical findings showing males, particularly Black males, as having similar rates of sexual victimization as women not only impedes theory but creates a discursive barrier preventing the recognition and treatment of victimized men and boys. Even when men do report rape and sexual assault, they are rarely believed and are ridiculed within our current clinical institutions. This further silences males and increases the likelihood of negative behavioral and mental outcomes (Hohendorff, Habigzang, & Koller, 2017).

This is not to say that all feminists are of the same mind about the sexual assault and rape of men in the United States. For example, feminist activist and writer Schroeder (2018) penned a powerful piece after Argento's rape of Jimmy Bennett recognizing that men were roughly half of all rape victims in the United States and are often forced into silence. However, dominant feminist frameworks and conceptualizations employed to interpret sexual violence erase male victimization generally and make Black male victimization to rape an impossibility to most academics and activists.

The case for Black men is far more complicated than merely encouraging recognition. Black males are stigmatized as violent brutes throughout multiple sectors of society. Among law enforcement, educational institutions, the at-large public, and even among many academics, Black men are theorized as terrors and popularly imagined to be pathological in nature. The dominant feminist theories coming out of the 1970s endorsed a pathological view of Black masculinity as violent and sexually aggressive. Following Wolfgang and Ferracuti (1967), Brownmiller (1975) actually argued that rape, specifically gang rape, was an attempt by Black men to project their manhood after desegregation and was a normal feature of the Negro male's subculture of violence (pp. 174–209). Brownmiller's account of Black masculinity plainly asserts that rape is a more normal, a more brutal, and a more prevalent practice among young Black males than among Whites (pp. 180–181). Many Black feminist accounts of Black masculinity actually extended Brownmiller's subculture of violence frame that interprets underclass (straight) Black males as particularly violent and beastlike—beings who take pleasure in the pain of others (Cooper, 2005; White, 2008; Garfield, 2010). In *We Real Cool: Black Men and Masculinity*, hooks (2004) argued:

> Lots of young black men are walking around assuming a gangsta persona who have never and will never commit violent acts. Yet they collude with violent patriarchal culture by assuming this persona and perpetuating the negative racist/sexist stereotype that says "all black men are carriers of the violence we dread." Then there are the large numbers of underclass black males with no hope for the future who are actively violent. Added to this group are the black males who will never act violently outside the home, who do not commit crimes in the street, but who are, inside the home, in their private lives, abusive and violent. Overall the facts reveal that black males are more violent than ever before in this nation. And they are more likely to be violent toward another black person whom they deem less powerful. Much black male violence is directed toward females. Sexism and the assumption of the male right to dominate serves as the catalyst for this violence. (p. 52)

From this perspective, hooks maintained that Black males take pleasure in cultivating the image of violence and are satisfied by the fear it creates in others, especially the larger White society. "Young black males, particularly underclass males, often derive a sense of satisfaction from being able to create fear in others, particularly in white folks," wrote hooks (2004, p. 45). This analysis mirrors Wolfgang and Ferracuti's (1967) thesis in *The Subculture of Violence*, which argues "that in many lower-class communities violence is associated with masculinity and may be not only accepted but admired behavior" (p. 305). The existing frames used to interpret Black males are narrow and make violence endemic to this group. To date, not one feminist or Black feminist text has dedicated itself to understanding the rape of Black men beyond asserting that most rapes of Black men and boys are perpetrated by other males. This is an area that has been historically and systematically neglected in the current literature (Curry and Utley, 2018; Curry, 2017).

In 2012, the Department of Justice announced a change to the definition of rape, which took effect on January 1, 2013. The old definition of rape, originating in early-20th-century case law, was "The carnal knowledge of a female forcibly and against her will" (Carbon, 2012, para. 1). This definition excluded the rape of males and various other offenses that would constitute sexual violence against a person. The new definition of rape adopted in the Uniform Crime Reporting (UCR) programs reporting system—"Penetration, no matter how slight, of the vagina or anus with any body part or object, or oral penetration by a sex organ of another person, without the consent of the victim"—attempts to capture male victims as well as other sexually coercive acts (Carbon, 2012, para 2).

For almost 100 years in the United States, rape was defined in such a way that only women could be victims of this crime. Now that society is grappling with male rape victims, there is a tendency to extend victimization to males but only insofar as they are victims to other men. We have not understood that males are susceptible to rape or that Black men are denied victimization altogether because of the historical stereotypes of them as rapists or hypersexual.

When considering the changes to the UCR, recent research has concluded that men comprise a significant number, if not half, of rape victims in the United States. According to Stemple and Meyer (2014), men and women in the United States report similar rates of nonconsensual sex in a 12-month period. Subsequent research by Stemple et al. (2017) also found surprising rates of female perpetration of sexual violence and rape against men. These findings, however, have not been widely publicized or accepted as fact because they disrupt many of the ideas we have about women in the West. In the United States, "[s]tereotypes about women, which reflect gender and heterosexist biases, include the notion that women are nurturing, submissive helpmates to men. The idea that women can be sexually manipulative, dominant, and even violent runs counter to these stereotypes" (Stemple et al., 2017, p. 303). The need to preserve the female subject as innocent and nonviolent, distinct from a male subject that is violent and driven by the will to dominate others, often accompanies the intuitive interpretations offered of sexual violence in U.S. society. To say that men perpetrate the majority of rape and sexual violence leaves undisturbed the general premise that most women do not commit sexual violence. While CDC data reports have shown that women constitute the majority of perpetrators in made-to-penetrate cases, sexual coercion, and unwanted sexual contact, our present framing of male rape victimization revolves around the visibility of the male perpetrator and toxic masculinity (Smith et al., 2017, p. 32). This is a significant obstacle in our attempts to understand Black male victims who experience higher rates of sexual violence than their White male counterparts.

Among Black Americans, we find similar sexual victimization rates between the sexes. According to the CDC's NISVS data, the incidence of rape and being made to penetrate were similar over a 12-month period. Black women reported 264,000 cases of rape, while Black men reported 272,000 cases of being made to penetrate (Smith et al., 2017, pp. 21, 28). When looking at 12-month prevalence, Black men and women both report near identical numbers of contact sexual violence. Black men report 865,000 cases and Black women report 849,000 cases of contact sexual violence (Smith et al., 2017, pp. 21, 28). Black men report higher rates of contact sexual violence (6.5%) than White men (2.8%) and White women (3.6%), Hispanic men (5.2%) and Hispanic women (4.3%), and Black women (5.8%). Despite the public availability of these data, the evidence of Black men's sexual victimization has created little societal impact or academic awareness of the sexual vulnerability of Black males in the United States. The most recent national data collected on unwanted sexual contact, rape, and being made to penetrate showed convincing evidence that sexual violence, assault, and coercion are not isolated to one sex, yet Black men remain on the periphery of conversations concerning sexual violence victimization and justice-seeking activism.

The little research published on sexual violence against Black men and boys shows that Black males are more likely than other groups of males (and some groups of females) to be victims of child sexual abuse, child physical abuse, statutory rape, and sexual coercion over the course their lives. Curry and Utley's (2018) study on Black male victims of sexual violence argued that "Black boys are often not understood to be socialized and maturing within spheres of sexual violence. Consequently, they are theorized as invulnerable to sexual coercion, sexual abuse, and statutory rape, despite their intimate proximity to these kinds of violence" (p. 234). Black children are particularly at risk for sexual abuse compared to their White counterparts, but what is often missed, given our current interpretive frames, is that Black males are more likely to be victims of completed and attempted sexual intercourse in these environments.

> Black children are at higher risk of abuse than white children, particularly black males. Children from single-parent households and of lower socioeconomic status are more common targets, as are children with physical, neurological, or emotional problems; black males are overrepresented in all those situations.... Although age of onset of abuse is similar across genders, girls are generally abused up to an older age, as boys begin to fend off abusers sooner. Actual or attempted intercourse is more common with boys, as is extrafamilial abuse. (Hernandez, Lodico, & DiClemente, 1993, p. 594)

Among racially diverse groups of men, young Black males experienced statutory rape, sexual coercion, and sexual manipulation more than other groups (French, Tilghman, & Malebranche, 2015). These experiences of sexual trauma often cause Black males to endorse negative racial and sexual stereotypes of their female abusers (French, Teti, Suh, & Serafin, 2019). Like other male victims of sexual assault, the experience of rape and child sexual abuse is linked to depression, increased sexual risk taking, and increased risk for intimate partner violence perpetration and victimization, as well as hatred toward the abuser's group (Curry and Utley, 2018; Denov, 2004; Lewis, McElroy, Harlaar, & Runyan, 2016; Turner, Taillieu, Cheung, & Afifi, 2017).

How we perceive the risk of sexual violence that Black males experience dictates how we conceptualize and interpret their realities. Our inability to recognize the data on and stories of sexual violence against Black males over the course of their lives harms this group. Our hesitancy to acknowledge that the violence and aggression we associate with Black masculinity originates in their survival of sexual violence and trauma comes from a deeply held and societally reinforced racist misandry that believes Black males are actually the cause of societal sexual violence, not its victims. As scholars, we need to focus on the vulnerability of Black males to sexual violence and how this experience of trauma influences the attitudes and behaviors of this group. We must move beyond the focus on the sex/gender of the perpetrator to an understanding of the dangers confronting the victims—why Black males are more vulnerable to sexual assault and violence than are the men and women of other racial groups.

Burke's focus on the victims of sexual violence makes her analysis more open than those coming out of the academy. Burke insisted that men and boys cannot and should not be excluded from #MeToo's recognition of victims. She explained:

> It should never have become an "us and them" thing.... #MeToo has been popular because of the moment we're in, but it's not really a women's movement: it's a movement for all survivors of sexual violence. Yes, women are the drivers because so many are victims, but we can't erase the boys who spoke up about Kevin Spacey or the millions of men who have been subjected to sexual violence, too.... Men are not the enemy and we have to be clear about that. (Walden, 2018, paras. 7–8)

Unfortunately, Burke's words often fall on deaf ears since the driving force behind #MeToo has primarily focused on high-profile celebrity cases and causes and not the disproportionate suffering and sexual violence of minority men and women or girls and boys. Burke has been adamantly critical of the framing of #MeToo as being exclusive of male victims. In August 2018, she wrote:

> I've said repeatedly that the #metooMVMT is for all of us, including these brave young men who are now coming forward. It will continue to be jarring when we hear the names of some of our faves connected to sexual violence unless we shift from talking about individuals … and begin to talk about power. Sexual violence is about power and privilege. That doesn't change if the perpetrator is your favorite actress, activist or professor of any gender. And we won't shift the culture unless we get serious about shifting these false narratives. (Burke, 2018a)

By focusing on power, Burke insisted on recognizing perpetrators of sexual violence regardless of gender. By focusing on the experiences of victims, Burke reconfigures much of the feminist paradigm determined by male perpetration and patriarchy to consider the consequences of trauma and pain carried by victims. According to Burke (2018b),

> Part of the work of the Me Too Movement is about the restoration of that humanity for survivors, because the violence doesn't end with the act. The violence is also the trauma that we hold after the act. Remember, trauma halts possibility. It serves to impede, stagnate, confuse and kill. So our work rethinks how we deal with trauma.

As such, the victims of sexual violence must be understood beyond the act of sexual violence. They must be understood as living with trauma that outlasts the event of violation. Black men and boys remain untreated and uncared for throughout their lives. They live with the pain of sexual violence and rape, and then are denied the compassion necessary for them to heal and not become burdened by their scars.

Black male vulnerability and the struggle to be a Black male victim of sexual violence

The rape of Black males in the United States has a long but unacknowledged history in contemporary theories of sexual violence. Since slavery, Black men have been used as sex toys and pornographic actors for White men who forced Black men to rape women for enjoyment (Foster, 2011; Aidoo, 2018). White men often sodomized Black males as punishment for not completing assigned tasks or for the pleasure of slaveowners who used Black male bodies to fulfill their sexual desires (Woodard, 2014). While the rapes of Black males by White men during slavery were sometimes made known to the public through legal proceedings, the rape of Black men and boys by White women were clandestine affairs. Black men were raped by White women during slavery as a form of sexual experimentation and offered a means of sexual release not possible within the puritanical norms of 19th-century America (Foster, 2011, p. 462). The rape of Black men and boys by White Americans during slavery, encoded a common occurrence, made sexual violence against Black males invisible.

Because Black males were thought to be savage hypersexual rapists, there was no way for the world to see them as victims of rape. The threat Whites claimed Black males posed as the rapists made it impossible to imagine Black males as being victims of rape.

Black men and boys were able to be sexually violated for centuries without a mention of this victimization in history books or among theorists (Curry, 2017, 2018a). During Jim Crow segregation, this stratagem became even more obvious as White women used the myth of the Black rapist to hide their rape of young Black males who worked in their homes (Curry, 2018a). Among historians and theorists alike, Black male victimization to racism and sexual violence is interpreted primarily through the act of lynching. Because Black men are imagined throughout history and within theory by their proximity to the rapist, our most general conceptualizations of Black males deny their vulnerability to rape. The fear that White society has of Black men and boys is not merely a sociohistorical stereotype but the foundation of disciplinary method and gender theory (Curry, 2017).

This history of scapegoating Black men for rape and deviance is the major obstacle to seeing Black men as victims (Curry, 2018b). In the 1950s, White sociologists documented the sexual debut of Black boys between the ages of seven and nine with much older adolescent girls (Kardiner and Ovesey, 1951). Rather than interpreting the rape of these young boys as victims of undeserved violence, Kardiner and Ovesey maintained the early sexual intercourse of Black boys was due to their innate hypersexuality and deviance. Even within their own race, Black male bodies historically were exploited as objects of others' sexual desire, yet Black boys are not thought to be able to be victimized regularly as children. Despite recent studies that suggested Black boys have sexual intercourse at earlier ages than other populations (between the ages of 12 to 14 and 9 to 12), Black males are not thought of as being reared in highly sexualized environments or endangered by early sexual experiences that fall within our current understanding of statutory rape (Biello, Ickovics, & Niccolai, 2013; Cavazos-Rehg, Krauss, & Spitznagel, 2009). As Black and male, there is an erroneous view that Black male children are men and are invulnerable to rape and sexual assault.

This historical stereotype is so strong that for many people in the United States, be they Black or White, Black men are denied being able to be victims of other people's sexually predatory acts. The association of Black males with violent threats is so strong that multiple psychologists have observed that simply seeing a Black male body or hearing a Black male's name triggers aggression, threat construction, and a fight-or-flight response among some Whites (Goff, 2008; Holbrook, Fessler, & Navarrete, 2016). This is not a problem of recognition whereby Black men are not simply seen as suffering at the hands of others. This is an ontological problem—a problem of definition and social being—wherein the very being, the kind of existence of Black men and boys, does not allow them to be harmed or affected by the actions of others. Black men have no characterological defense against the violent tropes launched against them in the United States. As dehumanized entities, Black males are thought to be capable of any and every atrocity against women, children, and society imaginable (Curry, 2017, pp. 167–168). Overshadowed by the specter of violence and deviance and death, many people do not believe Black men can be victims of rape. Black men are insatiable. They want sex; if they did not want it, they are (or should be) capable of fending off an attacker. Hypermasculinity, hypersexuality, and fear converge to make it inconceivable that these big brutes could not or would not harm whomever they believed to be capable of sexually violating them.

Crews's description of the cult of masculinity and toxic masculinity did little to offer an understanding of Black male trauma that considers the rates of victimization and violence Black males are exposed to within society. In a recent interview on Bravo's *Watch What Happens Live*, Crews was asked whose support surprised him the most after he spoke out about his sexual abuse. He said:

> I have to say this: the people that surprised me the most were Black women. Black men did not want any part of it. All my support came from Black women, straight up. And that's kind of wild. It shocked me. It shocked my family. I thought, here I am as a Black man saying some things that we've all been through, and a lot of guys [were] just like, "Man, you're weak. You're sorry. You should have hit him. You should have knocked him out. You should have did all this stuff." Black women were like, "No, no. It doesn't work like that." And I was shocked at the split within my own community. It was deep. (Boone, 2019, paras. 3–8)

Crews suggested that Black men had no interest in his victimization at the hands of Venit, despite the overwhelming number of Black male victims of sexual assault and violence in the United States. In no interview has Crews attempted to situate the silencing of Black males specifically as a potential explanation for what he perceived as a lack of support. While Crews admitted earlier in the interview that he received "no support initially" from the Black community, he failed to interrogate the responses of Black men beyond what he perceived as their toxic masculinity and aggressive response to his sexual violation. Crews has since apologized to Black men for saying they did not care about his assault and admitted if it had not happened to him he would have remained ignorant of male sexual victims (Crews, 2019c). While Crews acknowledged that he "mistakenly drew attention to the worst examples and should have remained focused on the best of who we are" (Crews, 2019d), the caricatures of Black men he perpetuated reinforced stereotypes of Black men held by popular Black feminist critics and White society more broadly.

Is anger not a legitimate response by Black men to sexual assault? Crews suggested in his testimony to Congress that he too felt anger but did not defend himself against Venit because of what the media and the White world would say about a Black man beating up a White man. Was his initial impulse to attack Venit his toxicity? No. It is a natural and justifiable response. Whereas our society often accepts a woman's right to defend herself against sexual violence, Crews and many of his supporters place an additional burden on Black male victims. Because our society believes that Black men are violent, it is now the responsibility of Black men not to fulfill this stereotype by finding other ways to address sexual assault against their bodies. What Crews shows us in his hesitancy to defend himself through violence, as well as the lack of empathy for his victimization as a Black man, is that he in fact recognizes that his masculinity is not like the dominant White masculinity. He recognizes that his ability to be recognized as a victim of sexual violence is intimately tied to how the White public sees him, not whether he actually suffered a sexual assault. Crews knows he has to be respectable and peaceful enough for the U.S. public not to be afraid of him. In doing so, he distances himself from the experience and marginalization that other Black men who do not have the opportunity to be recognized as victims of sexual violence, or anything else, endure.

For more than a century, racist caricatures of hypersexuality, deviance, and danger have obscured Black men's sexual victimization and rape. Black males are the only group throughout the history of the United States who have endured "Negrophilic and Negrophobic relations simultaneously—as both the victim of rape and the supposed perpetrator of rape" (Curry, 2018a, p. 149). The Black male has been raped throughout history but has been denied being seen as a victim of rape because he is feared to be the rapist. The fear of being seen as a Black beast, the insatiable sexual savage, a violent animal, was so powerful that it stopped Crews from defending himself from sexual assault. Crews understood at a visceral level that if he defended himself from sexual violence, he would become the epitome of violence—the dangerous Nigger. As a Black man, Crews had to decide which act of violence he could endure: to be sexually assaulted and groped by a White man in public in front of his wife or judged by White America as the savage Nigger who attacked a White man. For many Black men, this is a far too common and impossible choice.

Crews's victimization at the hands of a White man unsettles our habitual thinking about sexual violence. To say that racism and desire work simultaneously toward Black male bodies in the form of an aggressive homoeroticism by White men and dangerous sexual aggression by White women disrupts the illusion of danger Black male bodies pose. When we consider the mutilation and violence inflicted on Black men, we now have to consider that what we are reflecting on is libidinal outrage, the frustration one has in not being able to completely possess the body of the despised Nigger, and how that frustration manifests itself throughout history as lynching, the castration of Black men, and the sodomization of Black male bodies. By extricating sexual vulnerability from the history under which Black men and boys suffer, we contribute to the thinking that holds the only thing that can hurt Black men are bullets—that their primary suffering is rooted in death (Curry, 2014, 2016, 2017).

Crews's victimization poses a problem and a complication in the traditional feminist narrative of patriarchy. Whereas female victims of sexual assault and harassment are viewed as vulnerable because all women are vulnerable to and thought to be victimized by the patriarchal power of men (who are thought to be a class of perpetrators and violent), male victims are thought to be situational. Male victims may exist, but they are victims of particular individuals, not victimized historically by a class of perpetrators or offenders who make their position as subordinate men in the society vulnerable to sexual violence. Black Male studies scholars hold that racialized men are the primary targets of White patriarchal rage (Curry, 2017, 2018b; Miller, 1991, 1994) and cannot benefit from hegemonic male power. Within these racialized patriarchies, racialized men are subject to extreme forms of violence, such as lynching, murder, and rape. Crews's victimization is an opportunity to rethink how Black men exist as a racialized class of men who have always been particularly vulnerable to sexual violence within patriarchy. The issue is not that Crews was sexually assaulted by a White man. The issue is that Terry could be assaulted by a White man and no one in the United States would believe that he was actually a victim of sexual assault or rape because he is a Black man.

Conclusion

Terry Crews's story provides an opportunity to rethink how we formulate cultural narratives of sexual violence and rape that exclude the experiences of Black men. While it is of the utmost importance to respect the story of Crews and his experience of marginalization in society as a Black man and as a Black male victim within #MeToo, it is equally important for scholars, activists, and survivors to interrogate how we come to understand and interpret the vulnerability of Black men and boys to sexual violence in this society through his victimization. The question posed to #MeToo by Crews is not whether this moment can recognize the stories of Black male victims without apology. The question the victimization of Crews poses is whether the history of sexual vulnerability presented to the world as the terror of patriarchy actually captures the reality of rape and sexual violence against Black men in this society. #MeToo has not begun to address the history of rape against Black men in the United States and how stereotypes of Black men as hypermasculine misogynists and rapists ensure the erasure of Black men's sexual vulnerability and victimization. #MeToo ignores the role that homoeroticism and sexual fetishization have played in the rape and sexual victimization of Black men and boys throughout history while asserting that the presumed hypermasculinity of Black men makes them more likely to be rapists and threats to women.

To accept that a Black man is just as likely as any woman—and more likely than a White woman—to be sexually victimized destroys the long-standing belief that rape is particular to the female body. This is a particularly controversial position, because it is the uniqueness of rape as gendered violence toward women that imparts a particular moral force. Black males continue to endure sexual violence at rates similar to women but are refused recognition as victims of this violence. If we confront this neglect of Black male pain, we quickly realize that it is our fear of Black men that prevents us from seeing their reality. Black men's caricatures as rapists and brutes have limited the ways through which we theorize their existence and the violence to which they are subject in the real world. Theory needs them to be boogeymen, so academics and activists imagine them as such (Curry, 2018b).

To accept that Black men are victims of rape because of racism and that some of these rapists are women or other men would mean not only the collapse of the gender analytic that makes patriarchy the sole cause of all rape and sexual violence against women but a reorientation of feminist theory such that the moral force of the claim that condemns all men for their capacity to harm women is lessened. While it is perhaps not debilitating to say some men are victims of rape by other men, it is threatening to the presumed operation of gender within Western patriarchal societies to say that all Black men suffer under the threat of rape because of their inferior status in the United States as racialized men. The violence and sexual victimization of Black men and boys concretized by Crews stands opposite to the valorization of the White woman victim and demands for us to think about the structural and cultural arrangements of patriarchy that continue to make the rape of Black men and boys a deliberately neglected chapter in the history of rape and sexual assault in the United States.

References

Aidoo, L. (2018). *Slavery unseen: Sex, power, and violence in Brazilian history*. Durham, NC: Duke University Press.

Arceneaux, M. (2018, August 28). If we want men to be a part of #MeToo, we have to stop gendering the movement. *Glamour*. Retrieved from https://www.glamour.com/story/me-too-movement-men-sexual-assault-survivors?verso=true

Biello, K., Ickovics, J., & Niccolai, L. (2013). Racial differences in age at first sexual intercourse: Residential racial segregation and the Black–White disparity among U.S. adolescents. *Public Health Reports, 128*(1), 23–32. doi:10.1177/00333549131282S103

Black, M. C., Basile, K. C., Breiding, M. J., Smith, S. G., Walters, M. L., Merrick, M. T., Chen, J., & Stevens, M. R. (2011). *The National Intimate Partner and Sexual Violence Survey (NISVS): 2010 summary report.* Atlanta, GA: National Center for Injury Prevention and Control, Centers for Disease Control and Prevention.

Boone, K. (2019, January 15). We're not surprised! Terry Crews say Black women supported him the most after his sexual assault. *Essence.* Retrieved from https://www.essence.com/celebrity/terry-crews-black-women-supported-him-after-sexual-assault/

Bowen, A. (2018, August 21). Amid Asia Argento accusation, what a #MeToo moment can be like for male victims. *Chicago Tribune.* Retrieved from http://www.chicagotribune.com/lifestyles/sc-fam-asia-argento-men-me-too-0828-story.html#

Brownmiller, S. (1975). *Against our will: Men, women, and rape.* New York, NY: Fawcett.

Bump, B. (2018, April 17). Male victims deserve their own #MeToo movement, state officials say. *Times Union.* Retrieved from https://www.timesunion.com/news/article/Male-victims-deserve-their-own-MeToo-movement-12842188.php

Burke, T. (2018b, November). MeToo is a movement, not a moment [Video file]. Retrieved from https://www.ted.com/talks/tarana_burke_me_too_is_a_movement_not_a_moment

Burke, T. [TaranaBurke]. (2018a, August 20). I've said repeatedly that the #MeTooMVMT is for all of us, including these brave young men who are now coming forward. It will continue to be jarring when we hear the names of some of our faves connected to sexual … [Tweet]. Retrieved from https://twitter.com/taranaburke/status/1031498206260150272

Carbon, S. B. (2012, January 6). *An updated definition of rape.* Washington, DC: U.S. Department of Justice. Retrieved from https://www.justice.gov/archives/opa/blog/updated-definition-rape

Cavazos-Rehg, P., Krauss, M. J., & Spitznagel, E. L. (2009). Age of sexual debut among U.S. adolescents. *Contraception, 80*(2), 158–162. doi:10.1016/j.contraception.2009.02.014

Chandler, M. A. (2018, April 8). Men account for nearly 1 in 5 complaints of workplace sexual harassment with the EEOC. *Washington Post.* Retrieved from https://www.washingtonpost.com/local/social-issues/men-account-for-nearly-1-in-5-complaints-of-workplace-sexual-harassment-with-the-eeoc/2018/04/08/4f7a2572-3372-11e8-94fa-32d48460b955_story.html

Chang, M., & O'Neill, G. (2018, January 15). Should Aziz Ansari's career be ruined by these sexual misconduct allegations? *Elle Australia.* Retrieved from https://www.elle.com.au/culture/should-aziz-ansari-lose-his-career-15572

Clark, T. (2018, September 6). The Hollywood agent Terry Crews accused of sexual assault is stepping down. *Business Insider.* Retrieved from https://www.businessinsider.com/wme-agent-terry-crews-accused-of-sexual-assault-will-step-down-from-wme-2018-9

Cohen, C. (2014). *Male rape is a feminist issue: Feminism, governmentality, and male rape.* New York, NY: Palgrave MacMillan.

Cooper, F. R. (2005). Against bipolar Black masculinity: Intersectionality, assimilation, identity performance, and hierarchy. *University of California Davis Law Review, 39*(3), 853–904.

Crary, D. (2018, April 19). #MeToo movement "furthers my loneliness," male sexual assault victims say. *Global News.* Retrieved from https://globalnews.ca/news/4154420/male-sexual-assault-victims-metoo-left-behind/

Crews, T. [TerryCrews]. (2017a, October 10). "240 lbs. Black Man stomps out Hollywood Honcho" would be the headline the next day. (5/cont.) [Tweet]. Retrieved from https://twitter.com/terrycrews/status/917838656500506625

Crews, T. [TerryCrews]. (2017b, October 10). My wife n I were at a Hollywood function last year n a high level Hollywood executive came over 2 me and groped my privates [Tweet]. Retrieved from https://twitter.com/terrycrews/status/917838500061253632.

Crews, T. [TerryCrews]. (2019a, January 25). My father. And toxicity was when he was punching my mother in the face. Next question? [Tweet]. Retrieved from https://twitter.com/terrycrews/status/1088958538066448384

Crews, T. [TerryCrews]. (2019b, January 25). This article is THOUGHT-PROVOKING Straight Black Men Are the White People of Black People https://verysmartbrothas.theroot.com/straight-black ... via @verysmartbros [Tweet]. Retrieved from https://twitter.com/terrycrews/status/1088802324535902209

Crews, T. [TerryCrews]. (2019d, March 12). I mistakenly drew attention to the worst examples and should have remained focused on the best of who we are [Tweet]. Retrieved from https://twitter.com/terrycrews/status/1105491277573840897

Crews. T. [TerryCrews]. (2019c, March 12). I'd like to also apologize to the Black men that were hurt by my comments regarding a lack of support regarding my sexual assault [Tweet]. Retrieved from https://twitter.com/terrycrews/status/1105491274419777536

Curry, T. J. (2014). Michael Brown and the need for a genre study of Black male death and dying. *Theory and Event*, *17*(Suppl. 3). Retrieved from https://muse.jhu.edu/article/559369

Curry, T. J. (2016). Eschatological dilemmas: The problem of studying the Black male only as the deaths that result from anti-Black racism. In J. Lee & F. L. Hord (Eds.), *I am because we are* (pp. 479–499). Amherst: University of Massachusetts Press.

Curry, T. J. (2017). *The man-not: Race, class, genre, and the dilemmas of Black manhood*. Philadelphia, PA: Temple University Press.

Curry, T. J. (2018a). He's a rapist, even when he's not: Richard Wright's account of the Black male vulnerability in the raping of Willie McGee. In J. Gordon & C. E. Zirakzadeh (Eds.), *The politics of Richard Wright: Perspectives on resistance* (pp. 132–154). Lexington: University of Kentucky Press.

Curry, T. J. (2018b). Killing boogeymen: Phallicism and the misandric mischaracterizations of Black males in theory. *Res Philosophica*, *95*(2), 235–272. doi:10.11612/resphil.1612

Curry, T. J., & Curry, G. (2018). Taking it to the people: Translating empirical findings about Black men and Black families through a Black public philosophy. *Dewey Studies*, *2*(1), 42–71.

Curry, T. J., & Utley, E. (2018). She touched me: Five snapshots of adult sexual violations of African American boys. *Kennedy Institute of Ethics Journal*, *28*(2), 205–241. doi:10.1353/ken.2018.0014

Denov, M. S. (2004). The long-term effects of child sexual abuse by female perpetrators: A qualitative study of male and female victims. *Journal of Interpersonal Violence*, *19*(10), 1137–1156. doi:10.1177/0886260504269093

Foster, T. (2011). The sexual abuse of Black men under American slavery. *Journal of the History of Sexuality*, *20*(3), 445–464. doi:10.1353/sex.2011.0059

French, B. H., Teti, M., Suh, H. A., & Serafin, M. R. (2019). A path analysis of racially diverse men's sexual victimization, risk-taking, and attitudes. *Psychology of Men and Masculinities*, *20*(1), 1–11. doi:10.1037/men0000159

French, B. H., Tilghman, J., & Malebranche, D. (2015). Sexual coercion context and psychosocial correlates among diverse males. *Psychology of Men and Masculinity*, *16*(1), 42–53. doi:10.1037/a0035915

Garfield, G. (2010). *Through our eyes: African American men's experiences of race, gender, and violence*. Piscataway, NJ: Rutgers University Press.

Goff, P. A. (2008). Not yet human: Implicit knowledge, historical dehumanization, and contemporary consequences. *Journal of Personality and Social Psychology*, *94*(2), 292–306. doi:10.1037/0022-3514.94.2.292

Groden, C. (2014, September 8). Why is it so hard to determine exactly how many women are raped each year? *New Republic*. Retrieved from https://newrepublic.com/article/119364/cdcs-report-one-five-women-raped-other-statistics-disagree

Haider, M. (2019, January 23). The next step in #MeToo is for men to reckon with their male fragility. *Slate*. Retrieved from https://slate.com/news-and-politics/2019/01/men-male-fragility-metoo-progress.html

Hernandez, J. T., Lodico, M., & DiClemente, R. J. (1993). The effects of child abuse and race on risk taking in male adolescence. *Journal of the National Medical Association*, *85*(5), 593–597.

Hohendorff, J. V., Habigzang, L. F., & Koller, S. H. (2017). "A boy, being a victim, nobody really buys that, you know?": Dynamics of sexual violence against boys. *Child Abuse and Neglect, 70*, 53–64. doi:10.1016/j.chiabu.2017.05.008

Holbrook, C., Fessler, D., & Navarrete, C. D. (2016). Looming large: Racial stereotypes illuminate dual adaptation for representing threat versus prestige as physical size. *Evolution and Human Behavior, 37*(1), 67–78. doi:10.1016/j.evolhumbehav.2015.08.004

hooks, b. (2004). *We real cool: Black men and masculinity*. New York, NY: Routledge.

Kardiner, A., and Ovesey, L. (1951). *The mark of oppression: A psychosocial study of the American Negro*. New York, NY: W. W. Norton.

Kelly, E. (2018, June 27). Terry Crews explains why he didn't fight back during alleged sexual assault in emotional speech to U.S. Senate. *Metro*. Retrieved from https://metro.co.uk/2018/06/27/terry-crews-explains-didnt-fight-back-alleged-sexual-assault-emotional-speech-us-senate-7663513/

Klee, M. (2018, June 7). Brendan Fraser's #MeToo story is why more male victims don't speak out. *MEL Magazine*. Retrieved from https://melmagazine.com/en-us/story/brendan-frasers-metoo-story-is-why-more-male-victims-dont-speak-out

Koss, M. P. (1993). Rape: Scope, impact, interventions, and public policy responses. *American Psychologist, 48*(10), 1062–1069. doi:10.1037/0003-066X.48.10.1062

Levin, S. (2017, October 31). Hollywood actors speak of "rampant" problem of male abusers targeting men. *The Guardian*. Retrieved from https://www.theguardian.com/world/2017/oct/31/hollywood-male-abusers-boys-gay-men-kevin-spacey

Lewis, T., McElroy, E., Harlaar, N., & Runyan, D. (2016). Does the impact of child sexual abuse differ from maltreatment but non-sexually abused children? A prospective examination of the impact of child sexual abuse on internalizing and externalizing behavior problems. *Child Abuse and Neglect, 51*, 31–40. doi:10.1016/j.chiabu.2015.11.016

Lynch, J. P. (1996). Review: Clarifying divergent estimates of rape from two national surveys. *Public Opinion Quarterly, 60*(3), 410–430.

Mack, A. N., & McCann, B. J. (2018). Critiquing state and gendered violence in the age of #MeToo. *Quarterly Journal of Speech, 104*(3), 329–344. doi:10.1080/00335630.2018.1479144

MacKinnon, C. A. (1979). *Sexual harassment of working women: A case of sexual discrimination*. New Haven, CT: Yale University Press.

Messer, L., & Ghebremedhin, S. (2018, March 8). Authorities reject Terry Crews' sexual assault case. *ABC News*. Retrieved from https://abcnews.go.com/GMA/Culture/authorities-reject-terry-crews-sexual-assault-case/story?id=53595423

Milano, A. [Alyssa_Milano]. (2017, October 15). If you've been sexually harassed or assaulted write "me too" as a reply to this tweet [Tweet]. Retrieved from https://twitter.com/alyssa_milano/status/919659438700670976

Miller, E. (1991). *Men at risk*. Kingston: Jamaica Publishing House.

Miller, E. (1994). *Marginalization of the Black male: Insights from the teaching profession*. Kingston, Jamaica: Canoe Press.

Moore, A. [tonetalks]. (2018, March 9). How #MeToo forgot Terry Crews—Why this is about power not gender—Dash Radio [Video file]. Retrieved from https://www.youtube.com/watch?v=aaH01ahXZwg

Norton, P. (2017, October 24). The problem with men saying #MeToo. *The Good Men Project*. Retrieved from https://goodmenproject.com/featured-content/problem-men-saying-metoo-lbkr/

Patten, D. (2018, January 20). Terry Crews talks Sundance relevance, today's respect rally, and changing America. *Deadline*. Retrieved from https://deadline.com/2018/01/womens-march-sundance-terry-crews-frederick-douglass-sorry-to-bother-you-1202263753/

Perry, D. M. (2018, October 19). #HimToo should be a conversation about male victims of sexual assault. *Pacific Standard*. Retrieved from https://psmag.com/social-justice/himtoo-and-male-victims-of-sexual-assault

Santi, C. (2018, June 27). Terry Crews condemns "toxic masculinity" during sexual assault testimony. *Ebony*. Retrieved from https://www.ebony.com/entertainment-culture/terry-crews-toxic-masculinity-sexual-assault-testimony

Santiago, C., & Criss, D. (2017, October 17). An activist, a little girl, and the heartbreaking origin of "Me Too." *CNN*. Retrieved from https://www.cnn.com/2017/10/17/us/me-too-tarana-burke-origin-trnd/index.html

Schroeder, J. (2018, August 23). Yes, men can be sexually assaulted. Gender stereotypes make it hard to talk about. *Vox*. Retrieved from https://www.vox.com/first-person/2018/8/23/17772712/asia-argento-news-jimmy-bennett

Smith, S. G., Chen, J., Basile, K. C., Gilbert, L. K., Merrick, M. T., Patel, N., … Jang, A. (2017). *The National Intimate Partner and Sexual Violence Survey (NISVS): 2010–2012 State Report*. Atlanta, GA: National Center for Injury Prevention and Control, Centers for Disease Control and Prevention. Retrieved from https://www.cdc.gov/violenceprevention/pdf/NISVS-State ReportBook.pdf

Stemple, L., Flores, A., & Meyer, I. (2017). Sexual victimization perpetrated by women: Federal data reveal surprising prevalence. *Aggression and Violent Behavior, 34*, 302–311. doi:10.1016/j.avb.2016.09.007

Stemple, L., & Meyer, I. (2014). The sexual victimization of men in America: New data challenge old assumptions. *American Journal of Public Health, 104*(6), e19–e26. doi:10.2105/AJPH.2014.301946

Turner, S., Taillieu, T., Cheung, K., & Afifi, T. O. (2017). The relationship between childhood sexual abuse and mental health outcomes among males from a nationally representative United States sample. *Child Abuse and Neglect, 66*, 64–72. doi:10.1016/j.chiabu.2017.01.018

Walden, C. (2018, March 9). #MeToo founder has mixed feelings about how it unfolded. *The Age*. Retrieved from https://www.theage.com.au/lifestyle/life-and-relationships/metoo-founder-has-mixed-feelings-about-how-it-unfolded-20180309-p4z3l6.html

Way, K. (2018, January 13). I went on a date with Aziz Ansari. It turned into the worst night of my life. *Babe*. Retrieved from https://babe.net/2018/01/13/aziz-ansari-28355

Weiss, B. (2018, August 21). Asia Argento proves, once again, that women are human beings. *New York Times*. Retrieved from https://www.nytimes.com/2018/08/21/opinion/asia-argento-avital-ronell-weinstein.html

White, A. (2008). *Ain't I a feminist? African American men speak out on fatherhood, friendship, forgiveness, and freedom*. Albany: State University of New York Press.

Wolfgang, M., & Ferracuti, F. (1967). *The subculture of violence: Towards an integrated theory in criminology*. Abingdon, United Kingdom: Tavistock.

Women in the World. (2018, April 14). Terry Crews: Men don't see women as "all the way human" [Video file]. Retrieved from https://www.youtube.com/watch?v=GibE058a4P0

Woodard, V. (2014). *The delectable Negro: Human consumption and homoeroticism with U.S. slave culture*. New York: New York University Press.

Young, D. (2017, September 9). Straight Black men are the White people of Black people. *The Root*. Retrieved from https://verysmartbrothas.theroot.com/straight-black-men-are-the-white-people-of-black-people-1814157214

#AzizAnsariToo?: Desi Masculinity in America and Performing Funny Cute

Ali Na

ABSTRACT
By attending to racialized tropes of masculinity and sexuality in U.S. media, this article explores how the #MeToo response to comedian Aziz Ansari is supported by a history of Asian American masculine media representation in the United States. The article forwards two theoretical concepts—Desi masculinity and performing funny cute— to explain the cultural response to Ansari as simultaneously desexualized as sexually undesirable *and* sexually deviant in his noncompliance with white normative masculinity. Through a critical cultural approach, these concepts thus offer a theoretical feminist approach to #MeToo that is positioned within histories of accumulated and perpetually reiterated tropes of racialized gender and sexuality.

On January 13, 2018, Babe.net shifted the conversation around the #MeToo movement. The then little-known web site published an article titled "I Went on a Date With Aziz Ansari. It Turned Into the Worst Night of My Life." The piece recounted, from the perspective of the pseudonymous author, Grace, the events of her date with Ansari, which involved unwanted sexual contact. Ansari, perhaps best known for his supporting role as Tom Haverford on the television satire *Parks and Recreation* and his leading role as Dev on the Netflix comedy-drama *Master of None*, is also a writer, director, producer, stand-up comedian, and coauthor of the *New York Times* best-selling book *Modern Romance: An Investigation*, which, for some, marks Ansari as something of an expert on dating.[1]

In the Babe.net piece, Grace recounts that Ansari asked her to put her phone number into his phone after she approached him at a 2017 Emmys after-party. They texted for about a week, went on a dinner date, and then went to Ansari's apartment at his urging. At his apartment, Grace was uncomfortable with how quickly things escalated. He told her he was going to get a condom; she responded, "Whoa, let's relax for a sec" (Way). He performed oral sex on her and requested the same. Throughout the piece, Grace's recounting is sexually detailed, and she notes that she felt as though he "wouldn't let *her* move away from him," even though she engaged in "verbal and non-verbal cues to indicate how uncomfortable and distressed she was" (Way). For example, in response to Ansari repeatedly asking "Where do you want me to fuck you?" Grace bluntly responded, "Next time." Following more undressed kissing and oral sex, Ansari repeated the query with overt sexual posturing, to which Grace responded "no" (Way). They got dressed and watched television, which is when Grace indicates how it really "hit [her] that [she] was violated," and the evening closed with more kissing, which she describes as gross and forceful (Way). Grace reveals that she cried and reached out to friends for support on her way home.

The next day, Grace received a text from Ansari: "It was fun meeting you last night. I just dropped my roll of film today. Fingers crossed for some solid shots!" She replied, "Hey Aziz nice meeting you too. I hope you have some good shots on the roll. Last night might've been fun for you, but it wasn't for me. When we got back to your place, you ignored clear non-verbal cues; you kept going with advances. You had to have noticed I was uncomfortable" (Way). She goes into detail about the encounter and how it negatively affected her. He responded, "I'm so sad to hear this … . Clearly, I misread things in the moment and I'm truly sorry" (Way). In a statement release, Ansari writes,

> [W]e ended up engaging in sexual activity, which by all indications was completely consensual. The next day I got a text from her saying that although "it may have seemed okay," upon further reflection, she felt uncomfortable. It was true that everything did seem okay to me, so when I heard that it was not the case for her, I was surprised and concerned. I took her words to heart and responded privately after taking the time to process what she had said. I continue to support the movement that is happening in our culture. It is necessary and long overdue. (Way)

As with prior instances of #MeToo, many quickly and forcefully condemned Ansari's behavior as misogynistic. At the same time, Grace's story elicited—more so than similar allegations leveled against other male celebrities—more polarized and polarizing reactions from feminist viewpoints.

I address this seemingly unparalleled variance from a critical cultural feminist of color approach. The feminist responses to Grace's story compel me to ask: How do U.S. cultural formations of race, gender, and sexuality affect and sustain our conversations around the allegations of sexual conduct leveled against Aziz Ansari? Situating Ansari's cultural reception in a history of representation and American cultural interpretation, I want to take seriously sexual power and racial power in context. This article works from the assumption that one cannot disarticulate race, gender, and sexuality from conversations of sexual violence and practices enabled by sexual dominance. As such, I am interested in *how* identity constructions play a part in feminist responses to Ansari. I approach identity as a diffuse category that accumulates and divests meaning in context. It, in general, projects constructed histories and representations through perceived physical and social attributes shared by a group. In addition to this broad sense of identity, I am also interested in how it is "verified" through the particular. With Ansari, this connects his public image as a celebrity to his personal life. My investment in identity should not be taken to say it is the only or overriding factor in approaching #MeToo. But I take it as a given that identity is a necessary prerequisite to untangling cultural responses to sexual assault and patriarchal power.

Throughout this piece, I maintain that the frisson of the #MeToo response to Ansari is inflected by a history of media representation. I contend that the diametrically opposed feminist responses to Ansari require an inquiry into the history of racialized masculinity and sexuality as manifest in American cultural understanding. In this effort, I propose two concepts: *Desi masculinity* and *performing funny cute*. *Desi* is a term broadly used to refer to people from the Indian subcontinent. However, as Shalini Shankar maintains in attending to how the term is predominantly used, "*Desi* marks the inception of a particular type of diasporic, racially marked, generationally influenced consciousness at the beginning of the millennium" (1). In line with this sense of the term, I mobilize *Desi* in its diasporic manifestation to attend to racialized masculinity in America. I use Desi masculinity to refer to how Indian American masculinity has been culturally produced in media and cultural discourse, rather than how Desis have practiced their own masculinity.

In the context of this article, Desi masculinity is about how identity has been affixed to certain bodies through dominant social conceptions. It is a starting point for thinking about how Ansari's perceived identity, as secured through his public image, follows and diverges from histories of pan–Asian American masculinity. Hence, I focus on the characters that Ansari plays as a way to track how representations become attached to particular formations of identity. Specifically, the concept of performing funny cute establishes how Ansari's career has consolidated tropes of Desi masculinity. Ansari combines humor with cuteness in his characters in a manner that sutures these representations to his public reception *as* sexed and racialized identity. My aim is to illustrate that an understanding of Desi masculinity, as characterized by prevailing representational practices in conjunction with Ansari's roles, is necessary to interpret the #MeToo disagreements. I argue that by doing the work of contextualizing Ansari through Desi masculinity in relation to performing funny cute, an overriding cultural framing emerges. This framing, in turn, produces Ansari as simultaneously desexualized as sexually undesirable *and* sexually deviant in his noncompliance with white normative masculinity. This ambivalence is a (sometimes invisible) cultural bias solidified through Ansari's career of performing funny cute. Ansari's roles thus give license to digital discussions that actualize tropes of Desi masculinity.

#Race: Feminist responses' common thread

Feminist responses in digital publications quickly followed the Babe.net story and ranged from adamant defense to dismayed condemnation. Through myriad responses, race continually emerges as something to consider in reckoning with Ansari and Grace. This common thread does not uniformly map onto a racialized tone but rather is a recurrent touchstone. Contrary to what I am advocating, an abstracted reading of #MeToo articles would seize on this lack of racial continuity as a reason to relegate race to a nonissue. In other words, it does not appear that racism is at work in the feminist responses to Ansari, so there is a temptation to think race does not inflect the varied rejoinders. My argument is meant to address the clear impulse to racialization present in the digital debates. Race operates in a complex cultural framing, not just as overt racism.

A vocal group of #MeToo advocates (and some anti-feminist reactionaries) rushed to Ansari's defense. An oft-cited and critically received article in *The Atlantic* by Caitlin Flanagan gives the starkest position in defense of Ansari:

> Was Grace frozen, terrified, stuck? No. She tells us that she wanted something from Ansari and that she was trying to figure out how to get it … . He wasn't interested … . And what she and the writer who told her story created was 3,000 words of revenge porn. The clinical detail in which the story is told is intended not to validate her account as much as

it is to hurt and humiliate Ansari. Together, the two women may have destroyed Ansari's career, which is now the punishment for every kind of male sexual misconduct, from the grotesque to the disappointing.

Sidestepping normative assessment of Flanagan's position, I nonetheless cite hers as a feminist response because Flanagan enacts her judgment from the position of a self-identifying feminist who came of age in the late 1970s. For Flanagan, the Babe.net piece feels like a rift in feminism, and Grace's perspective is unfathomable from her own point of view. To close her piece, Flanagan attributes the condemnation of Ansari by others to his race, writing, "I thought it would take a little longer for the hit squad of privileged young white women to open fire on brown-skinned men." Grace's race is not revealed in the Babe.net piece but has been widely speculated on and assumed in multiple directions. Flanagan's response is meant to use Ansari's race as a tool of silencing further discussion about sexual power dynamics. Dissimilarly, I want to center race as it is historically and contemporarily relevant. Unlike Flanagan, I do not mark Ansari's race in passing or as a condemnation of those who would denounce his actions. One's race does not predetermine innocence or guilt but rather operates to infiltrate social conceptions of guilt and innocence.

On the other side of the argument, Adrija Bose and others write more critically of Ansari. Seemingly unlike Flanagan, Bose condemns his actions as hypocritical—the discrepancies of what she calls a "woke misogynist":

> On social media, a lot of people have gone on to defend Ansari saying this wasn't a sexual assault. Many are questioning the woman on why she didn't leave. And, that is the problem with us. Yes legally, Ansari has done nothing wrong. But in 2018, the conversation has to go beyond that. The whole Ansari incident doesn't feel like assault because it's so deeply rooted in our dating culture that it is considered just another "normal" sexual encounter. Many men and in fact, a lot of women say that the women could have left, no one had stopped her. No, of course not. But at that moment, you are not sure what you are supposed to do. "Will he hurt me if I yell? Will he force himself? Maybe I should just let him do what he wants to do."

Bose proposes that due to gendered acculturation Grace could not have easily left the situation, rooting the problem instead in the disjuncture between Ansari's public image as "woke"—attuned to issues of social justice—and his private actions as a misogynist. Bose brings to the fore an important distinction between the representational quality of Ansari's public persona and his private actions. While Flanagan closes with Ansari's race, Bose frames her response to Ansari with her own personal story, not unlike Grace's, which occurred in Calcutta. Race again plays into the feminist response to Ansari, this time as an initial entrance into the story, aligning two instances of brown men pressuring women into unwanted sexual contact. To be clear, I do not think Bose has done something individually problematic in this racial association; rather, she has shared a resonant experience that is deeply personal. When this personal description is read more broadly in light of impersonal cultural conceptions, it makes race a structuring element of the digital conversation.

Much has been made about the details of Grace's allegations and the manner of their reporting as explanations for the divisiveness of the Ansari case. Certainly, the account treads in a cloudier area (around questions of consent, power, violence, and journalistic transparency) than some of the more prominent #MeToo moments.[2] But acknowledging this need not keep us from exploring the role of Ansari's comedic persona and racialized identity in prompting polarized responses. Many responses to the exposé indicated that Ansari was a celebrity whom some feminists did not want to lose as an ally and whom others were determined to restore to a pre-#MeToo image. Writers frequently bandied the term "imperfect ally" in the wake of the allegations against Ansari to signal what they perceived as a self-defeating zealotry in #MeToo: "If we reflexively guillotine every imperfect ally like Aziz Ansari without finding out his side of the story, we will have no allies left. There is a whole spectrum between a bumbling, clueless lover and alleged predators like Weinstein and Trump" (Brawley). As I argue, the characterization of Ansari as "bumbling" and "clueless" is tied at least in part to his racialized comedic persona and not purely to the account of his private actions.

Race also functions as something that some writers look to disentangle from Ansari and project onto other men of color. Notably, for mothers of color, Ansari's race has provided an opportunity to discuss their sons. For Sonora Jha, it offers an occasion to talk to her own Indian American son. Even as she and her son disagree about the intersectional identities at play, she urges other mothers who want to raise feminist sons to do the same. Aliya S. King takes the opportunity to explore "what we need to tell our black and brown sons about consent," because, unlike Ansari, they will not have the affordances of celebrity but will still deal with the pressures of having to represent not only themselves but all men of their race. King's assertion that Ansari is shielded by his celebrity and position of power should be considered. Indeed, social and material capital inure Ansari from structural repercussions of the state and everyday acts of vigilante retaliation. However, in terms of cultural scrutiny, Ansari's celebrity and wealth amplify the #MeToo moment, elevating it to a national debate. Moreover, such attention performs an accumulative effect of representation, as Ansari is made to perform the exemplative function of Desi masculinity, illustrated by how many responses felt dismayed by what Ansari's actions mean for Indian American role models. As such, I would argue that it is damaging to the broader social conversation to mark Ansari as unraced by his celebrity.

Despite the apparent incongruity of feminist responses to the sexual allegations against Ansari, I contend that they are actually two sides of a Janus-faced understanding of Desi masculinity that is configured through performing funny cute. The negative backlash to Ansari may seem to be rooted in surprise and unexpected disgust: "How could someone so woke betray us?" But by tracing the cultural backdrop of Ansari's public image, I argue that repugnance always lurks in the multifaceted surface of the impulse to regard Ansari as cute and harmless. Histories of Asian American masculinity in representation are necessary to understand the cultural response to Ansari as concurrently desexualized in his primary public image *and* sexually aberrant in his secondary alter egos.

Desi masculinity

Desi masculinity is entwined in a history of Asian American masculinity as culturally produced. In particular, popular media representations repeatedly work to construct Asian American men as simultaneously feminine and sexually aberrant (Ono and Pham

71–72). I suggest that Desi masculinity repeats this trope but diverges in contemporary society through its relation to brownness as terrorist threat. Ansari is culturally attached to Desi masculinity as a representational practice and Desi masculinity as a socially constructed truth of himself. It is important, again, to distinguish the representational and cultural repetition of Desi masculinity that I am tracking from alternative forms of masculinity as practiced by Desi men. For instance, in Stanley I. Thangaraj's work on Desi pickup basketball in America, his sociological method demonstrates both queer expression in sports (176–88) and pressures to "man up" (11). Thangaraj's study illustrates that these practices are often pushbacks to dominant narratives of effeminacy. Distinctively, Desi masculinity, as normatively conceptualized in representation, functions to imbricate tropes as truth in the bodies of Desi men. This is particularly the case with Ansari, given how his representations have assisted the themes of Desi masculinity.

Ansari is often described as Desi. His parents are Muslim and immigrated from India to the United States. He was born and raised in South Carolina. Ansari's characters have sometimes shared his racial, regional, and religious heritage, as did his character Tom Haverford on *Parks and Recreation*:

> Leslie: You're not from here, right?
>
> Tom: No. I'm from South Carolina.
>
> Leslie: But you moved to South Carolina from where?
>
> Tom: My mother's uterus.
>
> Leslie: But you were conceived in Libya, right?
>
> Tom: Wow. No. I was conceived in America. My parents are Indian.
>
> Leslie: Where did the name "Haverford" come from?
>
> Tom: My birth name is Darwish Sabir Ismael Gani, and I changed it to Tom Haverford because, you know, brown guys with funny-sounding Muslim names don't make it really far in politics.
>
> Leslie: What about Barack Obama?
>
> Tom: Okay, yeah, fine, Barack Obama. If I knew a dude named Barack Obama was going to be elected president, yeah, maybe I wouldn't have changed it. ("The Stakeout")

The joke of assuming racial difference as national otherness echoes what Lisa Lowe describes as a long history of Asian Americans as perpetual foreigners. In the context of Ansari's mediated public image, his characters are often closely tied to his own identity categories. As such, it is imperative to see his representation as integral to interpreting the #MeToo response to Ansari. Racialized gender and sexuality underlie Ansari's sexual assault framings and responses. Within a predominantly American context, they racially and culturally shape how his masculinity is understood differently from that of others. In a response to the Babe.net piece, Harnidh Kaur wrote that "Aziz Ansari is not the woke Desi feminist we thought he was." This is a problem of identity because, as Kaur continues, Ansari has been made into "a poster boy for representation" by being "someone [who] contextualised the Desi south Asian identity instead of merely exploiting it" and as such "the allegations of sexual misconduct against Ansari hit a very raw, uncomfortable nerve for many of his Indian audience." The Indian diasporic or international audience that Kaur references is acutely aware of how Ansari's perceived identity matters because it is a shared identity exported onto others.

Ansari is also racialized in the broader context of media representations of Asian American masculinity. David Eng argues that American film, drama, and literature have produced Asian American masculinity as materially and psychically feminized, conflating "Asian" with "anus," and that such strategies have the effect of racial castration (2–3). Eng's arguments about racial castration suggests that there is an assumption of phallic power that can be excised by racial perception. This serves to underscore white patriarchy and Asian male subordination. As Celine Parreñas Shimizu explains, "'Unnormal' gender and sexuality dominate the discourses of Asian American masculinity" (15). This is to say that they are made abnormal. One lesson that Eng's work brings to the case of Ansari is that whiteness and masculine heterosexuality have been coconstitutive components of American society, which are supported by materializing representational tropes of Asian American men's sexuality as nonnormative and incoherent to racial normativity (Eng 130). Ansari's gender and sexuality are preconfigured by a history of subjugating practices that make him deviant from the desired norm. This is an often-ignored facet of Asian American masculinity imperative to understanding the cultural response to Ansari's #MeToo moment. Ansari is represented as without sexual capacity. The foreign distinction casts him as nonnormative; and nonnormative sexuality is by definition deviant. Culture has taught Americans to fear Asian American masculinity; for in feminization prowls a peril.

As I approach Ansari's #MeToo response as racialized, it is simultaneously imperative to note that cultural contextualization is distinct from Ansari's actions as they may perpetuate toxic heteronormative masculinity. In fact, practices of toxic masculinity or normative masculinity are sometimes initiated by Asian American men in order to work against the tropes of Asian American masculinity as effeminate or desexualized. Several scholars have demonstrated this in their analysis of Frank Chin. For instance, Kent Ono and Vincent Pham explain that Chin works to reclaim a masculinity that does not challenge normative conceptions (72). Eng, likewise, critiques Chin as aligned with homophobia (93). Because of the representational continuity of emasculation, scholars have noted that some Asian American men in turn develop patriarchal prejudices in their everyday practices (Ling). As Parreñas Shimizu cautions, "We need to beware that the representation and criticism of Asian American men in the movies can also be straitjacketed into a narrowly circumscribed vision of masculinity, informed by a reactionary claim to male power and privilege" (2). In addition, some scholars, including Tan Hoang Nguyen, have sought to rearticulate the accretion of representation as effeminacy in order to allow for what Nguyen calls "bottomhood," redirecting the logics of homophobic rejection and typified masculinity (2). My argument is in no way incompatible with Ansari's exercise of toxic masculinity. Rather, I look to contextualize how displays of masculinity by Desi men are situated in relation to dominant depictions of sexual aberrance as innate. Thus, prevailing racialized assumptions about Desi men in the United States precede and inflect the #MeToo response to Ansari's actions, whether or not his actions in a vacuum constitute sexual violence. The degree of Ansari's culpability should not preclude scholars from considering the role of racialized identity in the collective response to the event.

Effeminacy as a characteristic of Indian men's sexuality and gender presentation has been continually constructed through amassing Western practices of power. As Revathi Krishnaswamy explains, effeminization was projected onto Indian males by empire to align them with womanliness and passivity, thus justifying colonial domination. This mode of disempowerment continues in contemporary American representations. Building on scholars such as Eng and Richard Fung, Shilpa Davé argues that effeminate materializations apply in the case of Indian American representation, primarily manifesting in a form of otherized brownface practiced through thick and stereotyped Indian accents. For example, Davé explores the animated characters of Apu on *The Simpsons* and Gandhi on MTV's *Clone High*. With both, Davé investigates the ways in which Eng's work is productive in describing shared tropes of Asian American masculinity. For instance, one episode of *Clone High* portrays the problematic character of Gandhi as unable to "get a girl," so he seeks help from the show's resident white masculine heartthrob, JFK, who teaches Gandhi how to be like him: desirable to women (Davé 65, 77, 82).

Davé demonstrates that the accented other persists through the "characteristics of an assimilated brownface performance [that] are present in the roles of the model-minority immigrant[s] and the second-generation Indian American[s]" (61–62). To distinguish the effect of consistent cultural feedback and formation, I propose that Desi masculinity provides a useful peculiarity from other adult immigrant experiences in the United States. In Davé's survey of second-generation brownface performance, she examines actor Kal Penn's roles in the *Harold and Kumar* and *Van Wilder* movies (62). These characters portray Indian American men as desexualized or lacking sexual appeal and ability, needing the aid and guidance of white American virility in archetypal male leads. As with the *Clone High* example, the character Taj in the *Van Wilder* movies seeks the aid of normative masculinity found in whiteness through the title character, Van (Davé 71). Likewise, Ansari's character of Tom exerts much energy in learning how to "pick up" women, echoing the trope exhibited by Penn's character in the *Van Wilder* movies. Like Taj, Ansari's Tom is formed around having a strong sex drive that is unable to be sated because of his ineptitude in attracting women.

Ansari's roles have in part attempted to undo problematic stereotypes but have failed to disarticulate racialized sexuality from dominant narratives. In the *Master of None* episode "Indians on TV," Ansari's character Dev confronts how only limited, accented, stereotypical roles exist for Indians in television and film. In addition to pointing out the American history of brownface (in which white actors play stereotyped Indian roles), the episode indicates that the form of racism experienced in these stereotypes should not be conflated with other forms of racism, such as anti-black racism. The episode falls short of addressing the question of masculinity and second-generation representation. (In the *Master of None* Emmy Award–winning episode "Parents," writers Ansari and Alan Yang do explore the concept of second-generation Asian American identity but not in relation to media representation or masculinity.)

Desi masculinity in the case of Ansari relies on performance to solidify his person as simultaneously lacking sexual appeal *and* being threateningly sexual. This form of threat is characterized by an oscillation present in the model minority/yellow peril ambivalence (Ono and Pham 89). The South Asian model minority is simultaneously brought into the nation through diaspora while being excluded through strategies of national security surveillance (Puar and Rai 76–77). In the United States, "[r]acial definitions are further complicated by the aftermath of 9/11, which has left some Desis even more invested in separating themselves from others who may be mistaken for enemies of the state" (Shankar 15). This anxiety might be responsible for the shift in Ansari's characters from *Parks and Recreation* to *Master of None*. As outlined, Tom Haverford is aware of the threat sparked by his birth name, Darwish Sabir Ismael Gani, because it is "Muslim-sounding." The character's choice to separate himself from the name makes evident the desire to maintain an identity detached from Islamophobia. However, in *Master of None*, Ansari's character has a Hindu name, no longer sharing Ansari's Muslim heritage, following Shankar's observation that Desis sometimes look to align themselves with more nonthreatening images. In light of mainstream U.S. culture, Ansari forgoes markers of Muslim identity.

Such opacity of identity is marked by brownness, which I suggest works to distinguish the way in which threat is perceived in Desi masculinity. In the context of Desi men, Thangaraj notes that the "racial category 'brown' is a reference to certain racial ambiguity that comes with flexible racial subjectivity and its subsequent shifting racial classifications" (17). These shifts are not limited to how individuals seek to produce their own identities but also apply to how individual identity formations are culturally produced by others. As Kumarini Silva explains, in a post-9/11 United States, brown is a category now extended to include South Asians and works through a process of identification—that is to say, how one is culturally understood and produced, often in popular culture (10). In this way, perception and interpretation become the overriding factors of intelligibility. These are not alleviated by ethnic difference or religious practice. Identification functions as the deciding factor of who someone is. These productions create a sense of "real identity" and append brownness to other "deviancies," such as nonnormative sexuality (15). As Thangaraj further suggests, these associations create "a racial illegibility that produces gendered valences about what type of 'brown' men they are" (17). Jasbir Puar warns that these stakes are deeply tied to understandings of sexuality, which is ignored in public discourse, and yet the image that inhabits the U.S. consciousness persists through "the invocation of the terrorist as a queer, perversely racialized other" as a "part of the normative script of the U.S. war on terror" (37). Desi masculinity is thus central to how brownness is experienced and understood in dominant cultural discussion. However, because sexuality is the unnamed facet of the brown threat, the overriding narrative of brown men as sexually aberrant through desexualization is a *latent* threat rather than a readily acknowledged one. In this way, Desis are conceived of as a brown threat along with others. However, Desi masculinity is unique due to its historical manifestation within Asian American masculinity, functioning as an especially resonant container for expected deviance in projected disempowerment.

This imbalanced multiplicity is actualized in Ansari's representational narrative. The danger of deviant sexuality coupled with Islamophobia in a figure such as Ansari is often present but shielded by the ambivalent nature of Desi masculinity, as in, for example, the lesser-known character Raaaaaaaandy. The character created by Ansari first appears in the 2009 film *Funny People* and then in Ansari's stand-up act, a Web series, and radio guest spots. Randy, spelled with eight *A*s, is excessive. He is posed as painfully unfunny. He is obnoxious. Part of the joke about the character is that he is divorced from social expectation of Ansari himself. Seth Rogen, fellow comic and one the stars of the film, noted in an interview alongside director Judd Apatow that Raaaaaaaandy is a real person but that he and "Aziz" are not the same person. Rogan echoes the general emphasis of why we laugh at Raaaaaaaandy. Social laughter arises from the disjuncture between Ansari and the fact that we do not like Randy with eight As. He is a crass and unfunny annoyance to the comedy world. In a post-Babe.net world, Raaaaaaaandy's attributes creepily emerge in Grace's narrative. Raaaaaaaandy likes to "eat pussy," "get his dick sucked," and "get his fuck on." He "fucks" the audience from behind, thrusting his penis over and over again. Grace indicates that Ansari, too, continually jammed his penis against her in such a fashion while he asked where she wanted to "get fucked." Raaaaaaaandy wants to fuck women in his kitchen, the setting of Grace's first sexual encounter with Ansari. The joke of Raaaaaaaandy is that the setting is ridiculous and ultimately incongruous with Ansari himself. Grace's recounting of the worst night of her life recasts the joke into abhorrence. Some might see Babe.net's article as a moment where the lie of Tom and Dev are replaced with the truth of Raaaaaaaandy. However, when read through Desi masculinity, Ansari's characters instead demonstrate that Raaaaaaaandy is always the minor threat of Tom and Dev. Even as his characters shift, Ansari's brownness remains the same.

Performing funny cute

Desi masculinity constructs Ansari's sexuality broadly as racialized in an oscillation of desexuality and threat. These characteristics are amplified through the repetition of Ansari's public self, seemingly confirming of stereotype. This repetition occurs through what I call performing funny cute, which further entrenches the tropes of Desi masculinity while also creating a possessive sense of relationship between viewers and Ansari.

Ansari performs as funny and cute. These two elements work together to enmesh his characters to Ansari himself. Ansari's career frequently operates by creating a slippage between performance (of characters) and performativity (of personhood). This slippage sutures Ansari's characters to himself, marking the repetition of his identity as reality. I offer performing funny cute as a concept that attends to the ways in which Ansari's performances are naturalized to his person. By making his characters seem organic and expected, these representations activate a possessive and aggressive form of relation. By performing funny cute, Ansari conjures two types of response: endearment and suspicion. Cuteness is the driving force of this combination, working to evince feelings of adoration as a thin veil to practices of superiority. In this section, I argue that the incapacity displayed by Ansari's roles inscribes his body as funny cute, which reifies the tropes of Desi masculinity as true.

Ansari perpetually performs what I would describe as defunct sexuality. By defunct sexuality, I mean that Ansari's sexuality is seen as intrinsically lacking the expectation encompassed by normative White masculine male sexuality. Ansari's sexuality is there, perhaps overly so, but not in working order because ultimately the White norm defines functionality. Ansari's portrayal of Tom on *Parks and Recreation* played an important role in establishing Ansari as a feminist ally. In a feminist response to the Babe.net piece that explores the "problem with 'male feminists,'" Karishma Upadhyay writes,

"Since Ansari catapulted to fame as Tom Haverford, the universally loved serial entrepreneur on *Parks and Recreation*, he has been an ardent campaigner for feminism" (para. 3). Several responses to Ansari's #MeToo moment lament the loss of Tom. Upadhyay positions the universal love for Tom as the source of her feelings of betrayal in response to the allegations against Ansari. Tropes of Desi masculinity enable the dual action of loving funny cute and yet always already experiencing it as potentially threatening in its deviation from normative desirable masculinity.

The expressed loss of Tom Haverford for fans after Grace's narrative should attune social interpretation to the racialized elements present in what made Tom "lovable"— laughing at his lack of sex appeal. The joke of Tom is that he is not sexy, even as he is adorable. In the first season of the show, Tom exerts much energy in learning how to "pick up" women. And the show plays on the viewer's expectation that these endeavors will be futile by introducing Tom's wife, Wendy, who is inexplicably beautiful, successful, and cool. Ultimately confirming a pitying interpretation of Tom's illusory desirability, the second season explains his "mismatch" with Wendy as, in fact, a sham—the product of a green-card marriage. This marriage is ended without sentiment by Wendy and much to Tom's chagrin, after which Wendy dates Tom's (white) boss, who is configured as truly sexually desirable and normatively masculine. What these moments exhibit is an inelasticity of essence. At his core, Tom is incapable of adapting to a white privileged form of masculinity. Humor is filtered through tropes of Desi masculinity, creating a uniquely racialized version of funniness.

Tom is funny according to the simple logic of slapstick. He tries too hard and fails too easily, always tripping over the same obstacles. But Tom's obstacles are sexual rather than physical; they are little more than the encoded norms of white masculinity, which Tom can only approach clumsily. This recurs throughout Ansari's roles. The comic appeal of Ansari's characters lies in the rigidity of essentialized tropes of Desi masculinity. He is sexually clumsy, which is to say he is unable to perform a normatively desirable white masculinity. The impotence configures him comically charming. Try as he might, he cannot amend his embodiment of racialized gender and sexuality, so Ansari is funny.

I suggest that Ansari's humor is imperative to understand how his performances slip into performativity. In *The Mating Mind*, Geoffrey F. Miller argues that humor serves an evolutionary purpose and that being funny evolved by sexual selection as a marker of intelligence. In other words, saying "You're funny" is, in a heterosexual and ultimately procreative context, likened to saying "I want to mate with you." This is funny sexy. Miller's argument is about evolutionary practices but is also perpetuated throughout cultural representation in the United States, solidifying funniness as a feature of sex appeal. Popular depictions repeatedly condition audiences to see otherwise undesirable white masculine men as a catch due to their humor. Unlike normative white masculine enactments, humor is generated from Ansari's character in a uniquely racialized manner. The inelasticity of Ansari's Desi masculinity confirms racial expectation. It is perpetuated as a truth of racial difference and persists as part of the social practice of keeping funny sexy *white*. "You're funny" in relation to Ansari is a way of deauthorizing his sexual desirability but not his sexual drive. Ansari continually materializes these tropes through his performances, legitimizing the dominant cultural view of Desi masculinity.

Dissimilar to funny sexy, Ansari is funny cute. The specificity of Ansari's cuteness as Desi masculine is illuminated by Sianne Ngai's aesthetic theorization of cuteness. She describes "cute objects" as having "no edge to speak of, usually being soft, round, and deeply associated with the infantile and the feminine" (813–14). Ansari, as the cute object, can be tossed around. He is soft, posing no danger; one would not throw around a knife with the same attitude, even though it might be small. His size is figured by cuteness, and he is easily handled, but not having an edge does the work of removing the threat of masculinity, making it into a form of femininity. By imbuing Ansari's character with childlike qualities, his adultness is dislocated, highlighting immaturity through clumsiness and self-doubt. Ansari's characters cannot talk to women and do all the wrong things. These wrong things are sometimes endearing, but they nonetheless solidify his romantic and sexual incompetence.

In a *Parks and Recreation* scene, Tom's girlfriend Lucy breaks up with him but reaffirms his funny cute appeal:

> Lucy: I believe you when you say that you're not in love with Wendy anymore, but you're definitely not cool with her dating Ron. You talk about it constantly.
>
> Tom: Well, I can't help it, okay? I mean, he's so manly, and he's my boss. Imagine if your boss was Angelina Jolie, and then one day, she just started dating your ex-boyfriend. Wouldn't that freak you out a little bit?
>
> Lucy: Well, not if I had a great new boyfriend, dumbass. Look, Tom, I like you. You're really cute and you're funny, and you're small enough for me to throw you around. ("Time Capsule")

In this scene, Tom is insecure in his masculinity when compared to Ron, played by Nick Offerman, who exudes normative white masculinity. To infuse Tom with a sense of desirability, Lucy, played by Natalie Morales, lets him know he is funny and cute; he is funny cute. His cuteness is exemplified by paralleling him to an object or child that could be easily tossed around. Throughout the series, Ansari's performance of funny cute configures his character's insecurities as well as his relationship to threat.

In the episode "Gin It Up!," Tom is described as oscillating between cute and threatening. April, played by Aubrey Plaza, is charged with getting Tom a date, and the premise of the interaction is that Tom is incapable, weird, and bordering on frightening. Nadia, played by Tatiana Maslany, is inherently out of Tom's league.

> April: Tom wants me to tell you that all the screw-ups were my fault, but really, he kept messing up so that you would stay in Pawnee as long as possible because he is super into you.
>
> Nadia: Okay. Several questions. Is any part of him British?
>
> April: No.
>
> Nadia: So, that was just weird, panicky dude behavior?
>
> April: Yeah.
>
> Nadia: Okay. I'm just trying to figure out if acting that insane is, like, romantic or totally scary. I'll go with romantic. He is kind of cute. What's his deal?
>
> April: He's sweet, he's cool, and you're, like, way out of his league, so there's literally no risk for you at all here.

This scene establishes Ansari's character as incompetent in the realm of sexual expression, which is humorous. But cute, here, also serves an inoculative function. Tom's sexual eagerness evokes a suspicion that is defrayed by pathetic cuteness, which casts the suspicion within the realm of a risk-free encounter. In addition to being explicitly named, cuteness functions as an overriding characteristic of Tom through dismissal and disempowerment.

By filtering Ansari's masculinity through feminine qualities, cuteness also creates a form of otherization. As Ngai elaborates, cuteness is found not only in a description of physical appearance (Ansari's smallness) but also "becomes identified with a 'twittering' use or style of language, marked as feminine or culturally and nationally other" (814). Ansari's performance of linguistic confusion or uncertainty outlined in these scenes mark him as outside the cultural norm of U.S. masculinity. I offer these examples as connective entanglements between the inherent and compounded relationship between Desi masculinity and funny cute. These qualities of feminine otherization are compounded and anxiously repeated through his roles, confirming a particular normative cultural perception. As Ngai notes, feelings are derived from "the formal properties associated with [cute]" and "call forth specific affects: helplessness, pitifulness, and even despondency" (816). And this helplessness in turn characterizes how society is compelled to feel about Ansari himself.

Ansari's cuteness is furthered developed in his show *Master of None*, which has, much more than *Parks and Recreation*, taken on issues of gender, sexuality, and race and expanded notions of Asian American masculinity as desirable. Since Ansari is one of the creators, writers, and stars of *Master of None*, it, more so than *Parks and Recreation*, is interpreted as an extension of himself. This enlargement of Asian American masculinity nevertheless functions within the matrix of cute. In an early episode of the show, "Hot Ticket," two of the primary characters, Dev, played by Ansari, and Brian, played by Kelvin Yu, both Asian American, are described in terms of their dating appeal. Denise, played by Lena Waithe, gives Dev advice on how he is socially perceived.

> Dev: It's been two days. I haven't heard anything back.
>
> Denise: So, she doesn't like you. What's the debate? I'm confused.
>
> Dev: Hey! Why you got to be so pessimistic?
>
> Denise: Dude, she ain't text you in two days, it means she don't want to go. This is a very clear and unambiguous situation.
>
> Dev: Or maybe she really likes me and she's nervous. And she's sitting around with three of her buds trying to figure out what to text this guy. What about that scenario?
>
> Denise: No. She doesn't like you, man.
>
> Dev: Why you got to crush my dreams? Think I'm just gonna send a little question mark.
>
> Denise: Question mark? Did Brian tell you to do that?
>
> Dev: Yeah.
>
> Denise: I told you, stop taking advice from him, dude. Look, it don't matter what he texts these girls. All girls like his ass.

Brian: It's true.

Dev: It's just a light check-in. It's just like, "Oh?"

Denise: No. When he does it, it's cute. If you do it, it's needy; it's sad. ("Hot Ticket")

Ansari's characters are incapable of expressing the appropriate response to women, as evidenced by his needing help constructing flirtatious text messages. What is transgressive about the representation at play in the episode is that Brian, an Asian American man with parents from Taiwan, is seen as desirable. He is opposed to Dev, an Asian American man with parents from India, who is seen as pathetic and trying too hard. However, even in the character of Brian, cuteness is descriptive of desirability. The script for the episode was written by Ansari and Yang and demonstrates a cognizant understanding of trope but not of the implications of Asian American masculinity in relation to cuteness. Importantly, this resistant move highlights the difference between Ansari's funny cute and Yu's sexy cute. Sexy cute secures a nonthreatening version of sexuality that is simultaneously desirable, as, for example, is the case of Japanese and Korean pop stars. Instead, funny cute dislocates sexiness through the attribution of femininity as nonnormative in masculinity.

Ngai's theorization of cute offers a productive complication of my characterization of Ansari's humor. If Ansari's sexual slapstick owes to a rigid inability to conform to white normative masculinity, Ngai suggests by way of contrast that cuteness is about malleability. As an aesthetic concept, Ngai explains that cuteness is "fundamentally about minorness," and "it is crucial to cuteness that its diminutive object has some sort of imposed-upon aspect or mien; that is, that it bears the look of an object not only formed but all too easily deformed under the pressure of the subject's feeling or attitude towards it" (816). Ansari's characters exhibit such minorness in their deference to white masculinity and incapacity to rise above the infantile qualities of cuteness. What comes out of this diminished capacity for normative masculine expectation is the sense that one who is cute can be bent to the will of the subject. In this way, by seeing Ansari as cute, the cultural anticipation becomes that he will bear our expectations by conforming to them. I have argued that Ansari is funny in large part because of rigidity— because his humor confirms the tropes of Desi masculinity as immutable. But Ansari is simultaneously cute because all other components of his personhood are seen as malleable to social demand. Cuteness introduces a power dynamic into the social relationships by projecting malleability. Therefore, cuteness functions as a minoritarian position to be dominated, shaped, and protected.

Put simply, cuteness is fundamentally about power. According to Ngai, there is "an unusual degree of synonymy between objectification and cutification"; in seeing this, it becomes easier "to see how cuteness might provoke ugly or aggressive feelings, as well as the expected tender or maternal ones" (816). This cutification exaggerates passivity and vulnerability "to excite a consumer's sadistic desires for mastery and control as much as his or her desire to cuddle" (816). The cuteness generated by Ansari's career thus enables objectification to ensure both aggressive feelings (illustrated by those who contend he is a "woke misogynist") as well as maternal or protective responses to Ansari (as the victim of "revenge porn"). Both responses are generated out of what Ngai describes as an exaggerated passivity that follows from cutification. What follows is that, in each narrative and position, there is a social power to condemn or to cuddle Ansari. By continually reaffirming the person as cute, as thing, these underlying assumptions of helplessness and incapacity are transformed into antagonistic and even violent dimensions of cuteness (Ngai 855). Power and powerlessness converge and create an "oscillation between domination and passivity, or cruelty and tenderness, uniquely brought forward by the aesthetic of cuteness" (846).

Power functions not only to affect the seemingly disparate responses to Ansari but also to secure his figure to a form of powerlessness. Ngai indicates that the "aesthetic of cuteness calls attention … to the 'latent threat' attending all strategies of rhetorical personification" because "if things can be personified, persons can be made things" (833). By claiming control over that which is cute, the cute person becomes objectified and mutable not only to the subject's desire but also to an accretion of objecthood. The aesthetic of cuteness "always involves a hyperintensification of the thingishness of things," which for Ngai dovetails with a fetishistic understanding of that which is cute (844). Through the intensification of powerlessness, agency is removed from cuteness. In applying this sense to Ansari's representational image, the powerlessness of his characters is transfused into his body through the performance of funny cute. Unlike white comics, such as Jack Black, who play up cuteness as a capacity of their identity formations, Ansari's cuteness becomes more than an act and is instead appended to his racialized sexual identity. The removal of agency that comes with cuteness combined with the racialized rigidity that comes with the humor of failing to adapt to white normative masculinity informs a cultural response that pulls Ansari's persona apart under the multiple and multiplying pressures of desexualization and sexual deviance.

#MeToo assemblages

So what is the relationship between funny cute and Desi masculinity? Can they be understood as separate issues? And to what extent do these concepts demand relation to Ansari and #MeToo? Returning to Puar, it is productive to think of the processes of Desi masculinity, performing funny cute, the #MeToo feminist response, and Ansari as assemblage. Puar writes that

> turban wearers, usually male, bear the burden of safeguarding and transmitting culture and of symbolizing the purity of nation typically ascribed to women. But this does not automatically or only feminize turbaned men. And here we are pressed to rethink race, sexuality, and gender as concatenations, unstable assemblages of revolving and devolving energies. (195)

I suggest assemblage is also apt for thinking through the ways in which Desi masculinity functions as a convergence of cultural ideas that accumulates detachable elements (performing funny cute). Together, these concepts pathologize brown bodies and enact a form of desubjectification through regimes of representation. They do not have to belong to one another and indeed function differently in their discrete occurrences. As such, performing funny cute is not unique to Desi masculinity but does uniquely function in relation to Desi masculinity as a mode of merging raced and sexed bodies. In this particular assemblage, Ansari's body and actions fuse these functions together and inform the varying speeds of affective receptions found in the feminist #MeToo divergences.

On the axis of brown bodies and feminist passions, the assemblage of Desi masculinity and performing funny cute form myriad lines of expression. The power of cuteness in its malleability and the rigidity of humor in its subordination of minoritarian bodies emerge alongside the blurring of identity and identification. The fusion of deviant threat and disempowered feminization work by merging and dismantling expectation—all while functioning in the collective assemblage at play in Ansari's #MeToo event. These interminglings of race, sexuality, and gender as experienced in Ansari's roles undergo transformation in a post-Babe.net world. They speed up and take on new structures of affective response. Each of these experiences is coconstitutive of the cultural assemblage at work in Desi masculinity and Ansari's performing funny cute.

Performing funny cute is a uniquely raced, gendered, and sexualized interaction among cultural representation, bodily materialization, and social expectation. To understand this, we must also attend to how destabilizations of expectation—Ansari's betrayal—emerge in the depth of the surface. For with betrayal also comes the desire to cuddle Ansari as hapless. These form the multiplying and seemingly incongruous interpretations of racialized sexuality. I suggest that these factors distinguish the response to Ansari from simultaneous #MeToo moments for other celebrities and comics. It is precisely the fervor of response to Ansari that is informed, forecast, and culturally authorized by performing funny cute. Because of the ways in which Desi masculinity entangles performing funny cute onto Ansari's personhood, the anticipation of lurking sexual deviance was instrumentalized to make him worse than others—worse in deserving more scrutiny and worse off in needing more protection. While many of the social and news media respondents attribute hypocrisy (e.g., he is not the woke Desi feminist that people thought he was) as the reason for why Ansari's #MeToo rejoinder should be more pronounced, I contend that it was not surprise but confirmation that drove the cultural response. Ansari's primary public image reaffirms the trope of his racialized body as lacking normative sexual capacity. This inelasticity of his character attached to his expected cultural position in masculinity makes him endearing as the comic; and his dovetailing cuteness, in turn, rewrites the allocation of power and subjecthood to the observer, making him into the object of tenderness or control. This performance of funny cute then rekindles the implicit threat of nonnormative non-white sexuality as aberrant. In his divergence from the white masculine norm, fear and disgust at his sexuality is ever ready to emerge.

The assemblage described herein is meant to identify power and control in the #MeToo response to Ansari, not as a casual indictment but as a complex accretion of representational public memory. My terms describe positive, negative, and mixed commentary, rather than condemn one point of view or legitimize another. Acknowledging the historical power behind divergent views is necessary to address how racial subordination, sometimes painfully, is reified in difficult discussions about sexual dominance and assault. Bracketing cultural inheritances only further entrenches tropes as generally true. Understanding social historical antecedents of racialized gender and sexuality is not equivalent to being incapable of condemning sexual assault. Feminists have long disagreed with one another, and their continued disagreements are vital to having important conversations. I advocate for feminist practice to be better informed and culturally located. By culturally contextualizing how particular bodies in our society are produced socially, feminists can better attend to the visceral messiness of what #MeToo brings.

Notes

1. At the time this article was written, Ansari had only two public appearances: once at a Knicks basketball game with other celebrities, including fellow comedian Chris Rock; and a five-night stand-up comedy appearance, always as a surprise guest, at Manhattan's Comedy Cellar. The Babe.net piece was published during awards season, and Ansari notably did not attend the 2018 Screen Actors Guild Awards, at which he was nominated for outstanding performance by a male actor in a comedy series for *Master of None*. Prior to the Babe.net piece's publication, Ansari was seen walking the red carpets in solidarity with feminist movements in Hollywood, notably Time's Up, established in response to #MeToo's reach in the entertainment industry. The movement works against sexual assault, harassment, and inequality in the workplace and provides legal defense funds for sexual assault and harassment cases. Since acceptance of this article, Ansari has released a new Netflix special, *Right Now*. In it, he addresses his #MeToo controversy, among other cultural issues of racism and sexism. Two moments are particularly relevant for this article. First, Ansari begins the set with a joke about how he is mistaken on the street for the comic Hasan Minhaj. Minhaj is also from a Muslim Indian family and was born and raised in the United States. This is meant to highlight the dominant perception of interchangeability among minoritarian people. Ansari rebuffs this racial conflation and the person on the street realizes the mistake, instead listing Ansari's major television roles. Ansari repeatedly says, yes, *that* is me, until the person mentions sexual misconduct, at which point Ansari delivers the punchline, "*that* was Hasan." Ansari then proceeds to speak seriously about how he has felt "embarrassed" and "terrible" about the "whole thing." Later in the set, Ansari also reflects about how his 2019 self sees the problematic nature of his prior roles, highlighting how he would not now accept a script that he did in the past, in which Tom Haverford spies on his girlfriend Ann Perkins, played by Rashida Jones, with a hidden nanny cam. The special arguably does some of the work that many critics requested of him in earlier responses to Grace's story.
2. Some news media responses were critical of Babe.net's reporting rather than of either party. See Filipovic and Escobedo Shepherd. Many take the angle that Ansari's actions represent ordinary and deeply problematic sexual practices that need to be addressed to reconfigure cultural norms. See also Gray and North.

Works cited

Bose, Adrija. "Let's Talk About Aziz Ansari and the Woke Misogynist of Our Times." *News 18*, 15 Jan. 2018, https://www.news18.com/news/opinion/lets-talk-about-aziz-ansari-and-the-woke-misogynist-of-our-times-1632331.html. Accessed 28 Jan. 2018.

Brawley, Lucia. "Let's Be Honest About Aziz Ansari." *CNN*, 18 Jan. 2018, https://www.cnn.com/2018/01/17/opinions/lets-be-honest-about-aziz-ansari-brawley/index.html. Accessed 15 Oct. 2018.

Davé, Shilpa. *Indian Accents: Brown Voice and Racial Performance in American Television and Film*. U of Illinois P, 2013.

Eng, David. *Racial Castration: Managing Masculinity in Asian America*. Duke UP, 2001.

Escobedo Shepherd, Julianne. "Babe, What Are You Doing?" *Jezebel*, 16 Jan. 2018, https://jezebel.com/babe-what-are-you-doing-1822114753. Accessed 4 March 2018.

Filipovic, Jill. "The Poorly Reported Aziz Ansari Exposé Was a Missed Opportunity." *The Guardian*, 16 Jan. 2018, https://www.theguardian.com/commentisfree/2018/jan/16/aziz-ansari-story-missed-opportunity. Accessed 4 March 2018.

Flanagan, Caitlin. "The Humiliation of Aziz Ansari." *The Atlantic*, 14 Jan. 2018, https://www.theatlantic.com/entertainment/archive/2018/01/the-humiliation-of-aziz-ansari/550541/. Accessed 28 Jan. 2018.

"Gin It Up!" *Parks and Recreation*, written by Matt Murray, directed by Jorma Taccone, created by Greg Daniels and Michael Schur, season 6, episode 5, NBC, 2013.

Gray, Emma. "On Aziz Ansari and Sex That Feels Violating Even When It's Not Criminal." *Huffington Post*, 18 Jan. 2018, https://www.huffingtonpost.com/entry/aziz-ansari-sex-violating-but-not-criminal_us_5a5e445de4b0106b7f65b346. Accessed 4 March 2018.

"Hot Ticket." *Master of None*, written by Aziz Ansari and Alan Yang, directed by James Ponsoldt, created by Aziz Ansari and Alan Yang, season 1, episode 3, Netflix, 2015.

"Indians on TV." *Master of None*, written by Aziz Ansari and Alan Yang, directed by Eric Wareheim, created by Aziz Ansari and Alan Yang, season 1, episode 4, Netflix, 2015.

Jha, Sonora. "To Raise a Feminist Son, Talk to Him About Aziz Ansari." *The Establishment*, 17 Jan. 2018, https://theestablishment.co/to-raise-a-feminist-son-talk-to-him-about-aziz-ansari-1ae7fd41b074/. Accessed 4 March 2018.

Kaur, Harnidh. "Aziz Ansari Is Not the Woke Desi Feminist We Thought He Was." *Quartz Media*, 19 Jan. 2018, https://qz.com/1183677/aziz-ansari-is-not-the-woke-Desi-feminist-we-thought-he-was/. Accessed 28 Jan. 2018.

King, Aliya S. "What We Need to Tell Our Black and Brown Sons About Consent After Aziz Ansari." *BET*, 20 Jan. 2018, https://www.bet.com/celebrities/news/2018/01/20/sons-consent-aziz-ansari.html. Accessed 4 March 2018.

Krishnaswamy, Revathi. *Effeminism: The Economy of Colonial Desire*. U of Michigan P, 1999.

Ling, Jinqi. "Identity Crisis and Gender Politics: Reappropriating Asian American Masculinity." *An Interethnic Companion to Asian American Literature*, edited by King-Kok Cheung, Cambridge UP, 1997, pp. 312–37.

Lowe, Lisa. *Immigrant Acts: On Asian American Cultural Politics*. Duke UP, 1996.

Miller, Geoffrey F. *The Mating Mind: How Sexual Choice Shaped the Evolution of Human Nature*. Anchor Books, 2000.

Ngai, Sianne. "The Cuteness of the Avant-Garde." *Critical Inquiry*, vol. 31, no. 4, 2005, pp. 811–847. doi:10.1086/444516.

Nguyen, Tan Hoang. *A View from the Bottom: Asian American Masculinity and Sexual Representation*. Duke UP, 2014.

North, Anna. "The Aziz Ansari Story Is Ordinary. That's Why We Have to Talk About It." *Vox*, 16 Jan. 2018, https://www.vox.com/identities/2018/1/16/16894722/aziz-ansari-grace-babe-metoo. Accessed 4 March 2018.

Ono, Kent A., and Vincent N. Pham. *Asian Americans and the Media*. Polity Press, 2009.

"Parents." *Master of None*, written by Aziz Ansari and Alan Yang, directed by Aziz Ansari, created by Aziz Ansari and Alan Yang, season 1, episode 2, Netflix, 2015.

Puar, Jasbir. *Terrorist Assemblages: Homonationalism in Queer Times*. Duke UP, 2007.

Puar, Jasbir, and Amit S. Rai. "The Remaking of a Model Minority: Perverse Projectiles Under the Specter of (Counter)Terrorism." *Social Text*, vol. 22, no. 3, 2004, pp. 75–104. doi:10.1215/01642472-22-3_80-75.

Right Now. Written by Aziz Ansari, directed by Spike Jonze, produced by Jason Baum and Spike Jonze, Netflix, 2019.

Shankar, Shalini. *Desi Land: Teen Culture, Class, and Success in Silicon Valley*. Duke UP, 2008.

Shimizu, Celine Parreñas. *Straitjacket Sexualities: Unbinding Asian American Manhoods in the Movies*. Stanford UP, 2012.

Silva, Kumarini. *Brown Threat: Identification in the Security State*. U of Minnesota P, 2016.

Thangaraj, Stanley I. *Desi Hoop Dreams: Pickup Basketball and the Making of Asian American Masculinity*. New York UP, 2015.

"The Stakeout." *Parks and Recreation*, written by Rachel Axler, directed by Seth Gordon, created by Greg Daniels and Michael Schur, season 2, episode 2, NBC, 2009.

"Time Capsule." *Parks and Recreation*, written and directed by Michael Schur, created by Greg Daniels and Michael Schur, season 3, episode 3, NBC, 2011.

Upadhyay, Karishma. "Aziz Ansari and the Problem With 'Male Feminists': It's Time to Look Beyond Labels and Pins on Tuxedos." *Firstpost*, 17 Jan. 2018, https://www.firstpost.com/entertainment/aziz-ansari-and-the-problem-with-male-feminists-its-time-to-look-beyond-labels-and-pins-on-tuxedos-4307035.html. Accessed 4 March 2018.

Way, Katie. "I Went on a date With Aziz Ansari. It Turned Into the Worst Night of My Life." *Babe*, 13 Jan. 2018, https://babe.net/2018/01/13/aziz-ansari-28355. Accessed 28 Jan. 2018.

Anger's Volumes: Rhetorics of Amplification and Aggregation in #MeToo

Emily Winderman

ABSTRACT
Building an archive of avowed public engagements with anger in the #MeToo movement, this article lends conceptual specificity to understanding anger regulation through the rhetorical vocabulary of volume. Volume illuminates how anger is rhetorically rendered available for some to mobilize around while simultaneously limiting the emotional expression—and thus the political potential—of others. Specifically, volume illuminates how anger waxes and wanes through public life along raced, gendered, and classed lines that too often elevate the righteous expression of privileged anger while ignoring or silencing the anger of those most marginalized. Two forms of volume regulate public anger: the *amplification* and *diminishment* of affective intensity or sound and the *aggregation* and *dispersion* of bodies, interests, and collective energies. Volume invites critics to assess how different angers circulate under the heading of a social movement to determine how they can suture collective norms of emotional expression.

On September 27, 2018, Dr. Christine Blasey Ford testified before the Senate Judiciary Committee about her experiences with Supreme Court nominee Brett Kavanaugh. Framed as "an abrupt, unexpected litmus test of the #MeToo movement," Blasey Ford was one of three women, including Deborah Ramirez and Julie Swetnick, who reported having been victims of Kavanaugh's sexual misconduct (Smith). Following Blasey Ford's compelling testimony, Kavanaugh faced the committee. In a testimony that has been overwhelmingly summarized as angry, Kavanaugh radiated contempt. With his furrowed brow, narrowed gaze, and pinched lips, Kavanaugh delivered his entire testimony in a curt cadence with short declarative sentences, lamenting the irreversible loss to his reputation. Two days later, *Saturday Night Live* (*SNL*) mocked Kavanaugh's angry intensity using the metaphor of a volume dial. As actor Matt Damon as Kavanaugh entered *SNL*'s courtroom set, sniffling, he declared, "Let me tell you this: I'm gonna [sic] start at an eleven and take it to a fifteen *real quick*." Damon's performance centered Kavanaugh's anger as having an inappropriate volume. Although activists, politicians, journalists, and attorneys alike rebuked Kavanaugh's anger, he was eventually confirmed as an associate justice of the Supreme Court.

Kavanaugh's anger refused to silence Latinx activists Ana Maria Archila and Maria Gallagher, however. Before the confirmation vote, the women confronted Arizona senator Jeff Flake, bellowing him into the corner of a small elevator. Their angry intensity and ability to take up volume within the elevator space compelled Flake's attention. As his eyes sheepishly darted away from Gallagher, she demanded: "Look at me when I'm talking to you. You are telling me that my assault doesn't matter … and that you're going to let people who do these things into power…. Don't look away from me" (Chokshi and Herndon). Archila framed her anger similarly, as serving a collective national interest:

> Do you think that [Kavanaugh is] able to hold the pain of this country and repair it? That is the work of justice. The way that justice works is you recognize hurt, you take responsibility for it and then you begin to repair it. You are allowing someone who is unwilling to take responsibility for his own actions and unwilling to hold the harm he has done to one woman, actually three women, and not repair it. (Chokshi and Herndon)

Archila made her intention clear: "I wanted him to feel my rage" (Chokshi and Herndon). Motivated by #MeToo and the act of bravery she witnessed during Blasey Ford's testimony, Archila reflected, "When the #MeToo movement broke out, I thought about saying it—but I wrote things and deleted it and eventually decided I can't say 'Me too,' … but when Dr. Blasey did it, I forced myself to think about it again." Archila and Gallagher's angry elevator confrontation is directly at odds with Kavanaugh's angry testimony. Kavanaugh's anger took the form of a reputational status slight that Paul Krugman described as a "high-end resentment, the anger of highly privileged people who nonetheless feel that they aren't privileged enough." As survivors of sexual violence, Archila and Gallagher circulated a different form of outrage that Alison Bailey named "knowing resistant anger." Inspired by Audre Lorde, knowing resistant anger "pushes back against the normalizing abuse of silencing practices" in service of the well-being and restoration of a larger collective dignity (Bailey 103).

Early in the emergence of the hashtag, one article celebrated #MeToo's anger as a force that could energize a feminist project: "Women's anger must be harnessed now and pulled out of the Twittersphere and into gatherings and meetings" (Sanders). A *New York Times* article argued that with #MeToo "the public outrage is deeper and more sustained, and the dominoes continue to fall" (Bennett). The jacket of Rebecca Traister's *Good and Mad: The Revolutionary Power of Women's Anger* contextualizes the acute anger of the #MeToo moment: "In 2018, it may feel as if anger has suddenly erupted into the political conversation. But long before the Women's March and #MeToo, women's anger had been a nation-shaping force." While anger may be pervasive and productive, there are hazards in uncritically homogenizing the anger associated with #MeToo. Maiysha Kai laments,

> I, like many other black women, am angry and tired of continuing to feel marginalized and unrecognized within a movement created with us in mind; of the colonizer constantly reminding us that she, too, has been oppressed. And that her rage is the one that should be heard the loudest.

For Kai and others who have felt left behind by #MeToo, public representations that feature a unified form of anger translate into an erasure of the specificities of their experiences.

Considering this double bind—that public anger is a laudable part of #MeToo but also that it has been a restricted emotional resource for those whom the original movement was designed to serve—this article advances a critical understanding of anger in the #MeToo movement. By building an archive of avowed public engagements with anger in the #MeToo movement, I lend conceptual specificity to understanding the regulation of anger through the rhetorical vocabulary of volume. Volume is a pathos of anger that illuminates how the emotion is rhetorically rendered available for some to mobilize while simultaneously limiting the emotional expression—and thus the political potential—of others. Specifically, volume illuminates how anger waxes and wanes through public life along raced, gendered, and classed lines that too often elevate the righteous expression of privileged anger while ignoring or silencing the anger of those most marginalized. There are two forms of volume that work to regulate public anger: the *amplification* and *diminishment* of affective intensity or sound and the *aggregation* and *dispersion* of bodies, interests, and collective energies. Volume invites critics to assess how different angers circulate under the heading of a social movement to determine how they can work to suture collective norms of emotional expression.

This article proceeds in four parts. I begin by reviewing literature about the cultural politics of anger expression in order to theorize anger and volume. Next, I explicate volume as amplification and diminishment, demonstrating how these rhetorics authorize and discipline different angry intensities. The following section illuminates aggregation and dispersion to describe how volume rhetorics encourage bodies to collectivize. The article concludes by expanding the possibilities of volume and tethering the concept to attending to one's own volume in the critical process.

Anger, silence, and volume

Anger is a claim of injustice that can orient bodies around shared concerns. "Loaded with information and energy," as Audre Lorde asserts, anger contains within it contextually situated assertions of harm. In an Elle.com interview titled "Patrisse Cullors and Tarana Burke: Anger, Activism, and Action: The Founders of Black Lives Matter and the #MeToo Movement on Making Change," Burke, originator of the Me Too movement, and Cullors, a cofounder of #BlackLivesMatter, discussed their respective motivations for activism. Burke affirmed Cullors's assertion that "[m]ost of us start this work because we are angry. We're angry about what's been done to us, we're angry about what we've witnessed, we're angry about what we continue to witness." Anger invites shared adjudication of the severity and impact of a shared moral norm violation (Condit, *Angry Public Rhetorics*). The perceived legitimacy of anger is based on whether the judgment rendered by the anger is shared *and heard* by a critical mass, rendering the emotion inherently rhetorical and contingent upon relations of power. Within Burke's Me Too and the subsequent emergence of #MeToo, anger is neither solely a feeling possessed by an individual whose experience of sexual violence has gone unheard, nor solely a social discourse formation impressed upon collectives that have experienced sexual violence. Rather, anger's circulation throughout the movement delineates and fortifies the boundaries between bodies, collectives, and shared objects of concern (Ahmed, *Cultural Politics*).

Anger is a public pivot that can be mobilized to both perpetuate and ameliorate what Miranda Fricker terms "epistemic injustice." As a form of harm inflicted on marginalized persons as knowers, epistemic injustice is tethered both to the credibility of one's testimony *and* one's expression of emotion. José Medina lists examples of epistemic injustice, including "unequal access to and participation in knowledge practices, vitiated testimonial dynamics, [and] phenomena of hermeneutical marginalization" (3). In other words, epistemic injustice occurs through multiple rhetorical forms that intersect with voices deemed as non-ethos-bearing. Anger is a notable way of both perpetuating and contesting epistemic injustices. Bailey argues that "[s]ilencing anger exacerbates the harms of epistemic injustices because silencing neutralizes or renders invisible the knowledge speakers have of the injury their anger communicates" (3). Importantly, these designations mark a collectively held claim rooted in prolonged subordination and are complicated by the intersectional identities of those speaking.

When claims of injustice are shared, anger can collectivize and fuel emergent movements like Me Too or #MeToo. Collective anger requires the continual production of shared identities or demands that can establish "the range of feelings that can be experienced" (Condit, *Angry Public Rhetorics* 65). In the nascent days of the birth control movement, for example, Margaret Sanger authored and circulated *The Woman Rebel*, a publication designed for a readership of working-class white women and men. The publication circulated an angry rhetorical form that also appealed to the capacity of its readership to *get* angry based on the shared experience of unjust reproductive and factory labor conditions (Winderman). A separate example is The Furies, a 1970s lesbian separatist group that "used its own name to both acknowledge the importance of political anger and to play on classical stereotypes demeaning angry women" (Jasper 210). Anger also was a pivotal social glue within ACT UP (Gould). Anger not only forms an in-group/out-group relationship; the emotion can also modulate an already existing collective identity, especially when one's comfortable subject position has contributed to organizational racism. Audre Lorde's angry rhetoric engaged a strategy of shifting subjectivities to hold white "allies" accountable for their role as "oppressors and oppressed" while perpetuating racism within the National Women's Studies Association (Olson). Anger can constitute and redraw affiliative boundaries, making the emotion both central to marginalized groups claiming power and a lever upon which such groups can claim the dignity of justice.

Contextualizing anger draws out a matrix of power relationships that often determines whose anger is heard as responding to injustice and whose is heard as illegitimate (Lyman). The boundaries of legitimate anger expression occur on the basis of at least gender, race, class, and ability, and people are disproportionately silenced, muted, and dismissed at the intersections of identity (Sparks). If, as Fricker notes, epistemic injustice occurs "when a gap in collective interpretive resources puts someone at an unfair disadvantage when it comes to making sense of their social experiences," it matters whose speech can be interpreted as justifiably angry. The term *emotionology* indexes the differing judgments accorded to the anger of different persons based on hegemonic cultural norms. Aristotle's *Rhetoric*, for instance, explains anger as a typical response to a reputational status slight, but that anger was only intelligible to and available for landowning men within the polis (Glenn). By defining socially (un)acceptable anger, emotionology forms a society's standards for proper emotion display that shapes "expectations [and] influence[s] actual emotional experience" (Stearns and Stearns 15). Dominant emotionological standards have historically been defined by white and middle-class Protestants, whose anger has more easily been appraised as justified (Stearns and Stearns 16). White women's anger, by contrast, has a long history of being labeled as irrational, medicalized as hysteria, and pejoratively dismissed (Smith-Rosenberg; Micale).

Anger can also perpetuate white fragility and epistemic injustice, particularly when Black identity is figured as the justified object of white rage. Structurally, "[W]hites have not had to build the cognitive or affective skills" to sit with racial discomfort. Performing one's outrage or dismissing the anger of others are two of the many "defensive moves" to offload noxious feelings associated with white fragility (DiAngelo 57). Antoine J. Banks similarly asserts that "anger is the dominant public emotional underpinning of contemporary racism" (3). Whereas disgust had once been a central lever to perpetuate white supremacy through purity appeals that justified segregation, subsequent post–civil rights attempts to produce racial equality ultimately transitioned racism toward anger through appraisals of so-called unfair policies like affirmative action and social safety nets (Banks 14–15). Not only has anger functioned as a central political emotion to perpetuate contemporary racism; attempts to meet racial injustice with anger are often dismissed and disciplined. Ahmed reflects on the paradox of women of color's anger:

> So you might be angry *about* how racism and sexism diminish life choices for women of color. Your anger is a judgment that something is wrong. But then in being heard as angry, your speech is read as motivated by anger. Your anger is read as unattributed, as if you are against x because you are angry rather than being angry because you are against x. ("Embodying Diversity" 50)

The exhausting entanglement of this circular emotional logic erodes the capacity of non-white persons to be heard for what their anger communicates. Brittney Cooper elaborates that "Angry Black Women are looked upon as entities to be contained, as inconvenient citizens who keep on talking about their rights while refusing to do their duty and smile at everyone" (3).

Reducing complex people and movements to their anger further harms those who experience epistemic injustice because it limits the perceived range of their emotional expressions. As the previously cited video "Patrisse Cullors and Tarana Burke: Anger, Activism, and Action" clarifies, anger must be one part of a larger set of shared emotions. Audre Lorde's 1981 address to the National Women's Studies Association proclaimed, "Every woman has a well-stocked arsenal of anger potentially useful against those oppressions, personal and institutional which brought that anger into being" (127). Tarana Burke affirms but nuances the role of anger in this arsenal, asserting that any meaningful social movement of "radical collective healing" must have a robust repertoire of collective emotion:

> Anger is probably a small part of the arsenal. It's sort of a jump off or a place where you can get a spark but the rest is driven by love and compassion and humanity and humility. Anger can't drive you.... And also in both Me Too and [Black Lives Matter] people don't understand it, there's also an undergirding of *joy*. We're not angrily saying Black Lives Matter, we're declaring it.... We want to be seen as robust human beings to have anger *and have joy*. And we want to be able to freely have that joy. ("Patrisse Cullors and Tarana Burke: Anger, Activism, and Action")

Burke's statement reflects Cooper's closing pages of *Eloquent Rage:* "When we lack joy, we have a diminished capacity for self-love and self-valuing and for empathy" (275). Without these other emotions, such as joy, love, compassion, and shame, movements defined solely by their anger risk reinscribing a reductive view of community. When a group is denied the attribution of a full range of human characteristics—including full emotional capacity—the ground becomes fertile for dehumanization to take root (Haslam). This, of course, places women like Burke in the double bind that Ahmed describes, simultaneously limiting their ability to express anger about epistemic injustice while also reducing their identity to an emotional expression such as "Sapphires" or "Angry Black Women" (Collins).

By reclaiming historically marginalized anger, scholars and activists have sought to amplify anger as a justified and strategic response to injustice. Celebrating the "Angry Black Woman," Cooper describes her "eloquent rage" as a superpower, and Rachel Alicia Griffin's repeated claim that "I AM an angry Black woman" bolsters her justification to perform Black feminist autoethnography. Bailey names this emotional orientation as "knowing resistant anger," which "not only restores the collective epistemic confidence of angry selves, it is also an essential ingredient in the creation and sustenance of resistant epistemic communities" (113). Combined, the historical silencing of anger and the simultaneous efforts of scholars and activists to amplify angry and epistemically oppressed voices demonstrates the need to carefully trace how various forms of anger emerge, function, and disperse within the fragmented texture of social movements like #MeToo.

Because a wide range of collectives can use, modify, and co-opt anger, the remainder of this article introduces volume as a critical framework that describes the modulation of collective anger as a rhetorical practice of pathos. As "the deliberate art for the construction of shared public emotion," analyses of pathos trace how shared anger is cultivated, mobilized, and disciplined—how anger is rhetorically made to wax and wane throughout different dimensions of public life (Condit, "Pathos" 3). I argue that volume constitutes a pathos appeal that strategically amplifies, diminishes, and modulates anger. The *Oxford English Dictionary* describes volume in three ways that inform this framework: "a particular bulk, mass, or quantity as an attribute," "to be highly expressive or significant," and the "quantity, strength or power, combined mass of sound." Volume rhetorically regulates public emotion, tracing how the anger of those most marginalized is "turned down," while the anger of those who are the most egregious perpetrators of epistemic injustice is elevated. Volume offers critics a rhetorical vocabulary to describe how the multiple angers associated with social movements like #MeToo move between, among, and against different advocates. This framework invites critical attention to how anger is nourished and legitimated or diminished and silenced based on the intersectional features of anger's sociality. Reading an archive of public discourse for anger's volumes accounts also for the gendered, raced, and classed gradients of how some anger is rendered righteous while other anger is muted. Volume explains how anger intensifies and wanes as an effect of overlapping emotionological norms and visceral engagement through two distinct forms of modulation: amplification/diminishment and aggregation/dispersion. The next section explicates volume's capacity to amplify and diminish angry intensity and sound before tracing how the presence of these volumes throughout

#MeToo discourse works to suture the white emotional centeredness of the movement. The penultimate section of this article follows a similar format to explicate volume's capacity to aggregate and disperse bodies, energies, and interests associated with the movement.

Amplifying and diminishing the volume of #MeToo's angers

WARNING: This section contains vivid descriptions of anti-LGBTQ sexual violence and may be triggering, especially for those who have experienced related violence.

Although Tarana Burke's nuanced approach to anger within Me Too predates the emergence of #MeToo, the hashtag-based form of the movement has been dominated by highly visible white voices whose anger (or repudiation thereof) has been repeatedly centered as movement defining (Garcia). *TIME* magazine's 2017 Person of the Year, for instance, featured the "Silence Breakers" of #MeToo, opening with actress Alyssa Milano as the originator of the Twitter movement, while relegating Burke's origination of "Me Too" to the article's halfway point (Zacharek, Dockterman, and Edwards). #MeToo public discourse has yielded several norms for emotional regulation that silence precarious voices' anger expression. Anger's volumes have been rhetorically amplified and diminished since the emergence of #MeToo, especially among white, cisgender celebrities and at the expense of those like Burke who are central to the movement's founding.

Volume as the amplification or diminishment of affective intensity or sound allows critics to trace the ebbs and flows of angry intensities as the emotion circulates throughout #MeToo discourses and among the bodies of those impacted by sexual violence. Volume amplification distinguishes between high-decibel expressions of anger as righteous or appropriate and the muting of anger from historically marginalized publics. Beginning with volume diminishment, "it is important to think about the expulsion of anger and rage from democratic deliberations as a political act that normalizes and naturalized prevailing sets of racial formations" (Thompson 464). Whether these democratic deliberations occur in an institutional setting or more squarely within popular culture, a number of strategies can dissolve the credibility of anger. Several tone management strategies function as epistemically unjust anger diminishment mechanisms: "tone vigilance prompts an audience either to listen for a speaker's angry testimony, or to fold a perceived or imagined anger into the testimony … trigger[ing] an insidious anger-silencing spiral, where reasonable judgments and observations are reduced to the angry nature of a particular group" (Bailey 110). Regardless of political affiliation, any interpersonal or public rhetorical action that implicitly or explicitly delegitimates anger's volume constructs the available range of emotion for that subject position. On the other hand, amplifying and listening to the testimonial intensities of sexual assault survivors can legitimate the visceral (and often righteously angry) fallout from their experiences and even "challenge legal discourses' efforts to sanitize and constrain" emotion in the process of seeking justice (Larson 125).

Volume amplification and diminishment do not only regulate the intensity of emotional expression; volume also articulates anger to sound practices aimed at effecting social change. Amplifying the decibel volume of protest chants, cheers, and song authorizes advocates to take up space together in the service of pursuing justice. Connecting the aural volume of sonic expression to the spatial volume of corporeal occupation reminds us that anger is often a shared, embodied practice of social orientation. Greg Goodale identifies the "protective cocoon" as a vocalized sound strategy that can both amplify in-group support and sonically sideline deliberative action. As Goodale writes, "[B]y enveloping ourselves in a comforting sound, we reassure and support ourselves, often in a time when we feel threatened" (220). If protest can be likened to an endurance activity, then sound's amplitude energizes, sustains, and channels enthusiasm through its participants. As I demonstrate in the following analysis, volume as the amplification and diminishment of emotional intensity and sound strategically legitimates some anger while delegitimating others'.

When #MeToo-related anger is celebrated, it is often for the agents' ability to control and restrain their emotions, demonstrating a subtle volume diminishment of anger. After an *Access Hollywood* reporter asked actress Uma Thurman about the #MeToo speak-outs, Thurman expressed not feeling able to comment "in a tidy soundbite" because of her ballooning anger: "I'm not a child, and I've learned that when I've spoken in anger I usually regret the way I express myself. So I've been waiting to feel less angry. And when I'm ready, I'll say what I have to say" (Thurman). While her narrowed gaze, flared nostrils, clenched jaw, and tempered speech visibly marked her as angry, she refused to elaborate. Her response certainly reflects the gendered cultural proscription that anger is a childish interference to reasoned argument. Bailey, however, identifies Thurman's response and four months of silence as mindful introspection and self-protection in the wake of her abuser, Harvey Weinstein, being identified as such: "[W]hen we sit with anger's rhythms we are made aware of the epistemically damaging effects practices of silencing have on us" (Bailey 110; Dowd). For Bailey, Thurman's decision to diminish the volume intensity of her anger in that moment is a recognition of her rhetorical constraints: Unrestrained anger would not likely be intelligible in this interview. Thurman's volume diminishment is framed as the first step of carving new spaces to express anger that are free from pejorative interpretations that further entrench epistemic injustice.

While Thurman's decision to diminish her own anger's volume may well have been a self-protective gesture as a survivor of sexual violence, the uptake of Thurman's suppressed anger celebrated her diminished emotional intensity and modeled it as an appropriate and "relatable" response to #MeToo (Saccone). The U.K. *Independent* called hers a "powerful response" (Loughrey). Shannon Carlin of *Refinery29* was "in awe" of Thurman's "poised and controlled response," and cited Huffington Post editor Lydia Polgreen's tweet that "[t]he controlled rage here is incredible." It is unsurprising that her lack of amplification was celebrated considering "silence is one form, perhaps the only form, of socially acceptable anger" (Glenn 104) and falls within the range of emotionological norms equating suppressed white feminine anger with proper social conduct (Stearns and Stearns). Celebrating Thurman's diminished anger encourages a disproportionately muted response to moments of epistemic injustice, preventing the knowing resistant angers of marginalized voices from coming to the foreground of public representation.

Volume diminishment also occurs when individuals place proximal distance between someone else's anger and their own self-concept. This form of epistemic injustice can occur when a more privileged individual neglects the injustice that another's anger is communicating. Drew Barrymore, a white actress who hails from an extended family of Hollywood performers, diminished public anger of #MeToo during an interview on *The Late Show with Stephen Colbert*. Lamenting anger she deemed nonsensical, Barrymore decried:

> I think [#MeToo is] phenomenal and overdue and wonderful.... I don't want anything to have a tone of anger.... I've never been an angry person. So I want—I hope for people they won't do it with anger and expectation, because what you really have to do is prove you're capable, and what this important time is about is those doors opening.

Conflating #MeToo's anger with the "expectation" of earning acting roles, Barrymore perpetuates epistemic injustice by diminishing the volume of angry testimony about sexual violence and reducing knowing resistant anger into a reputational status slight of someone who is ostensibly bitter for not yet attaining career fulfillment. Donnelly framed Barrymore as having inappropriately turned down anger, admonishing her for "tone-policing the new generation of women creators—which just happens to include more women of color." Centering the ability to earn roles in Hollywood, rather than the industry's systemic neglect of sexism and racism, both Barrymore and #MeToo "silence breakers" celebrated on magazine covers ultimately silence the unique needs of non-white survivors of sexual violence. The epistemic injustice produced through the volume diminishment of #MeToo's anger occurs both in the celebration of muted white rage and the diminishment of anger based on privileged individuals' inability to understand anger's motivation from marginalized speakers.

#MeToo is not simply marked by volume diminishment; amplifying the volume of anger occurs with both productive and problematic epistemic implications. Hannah Gadsby's comedy special *Nanette* demonstrates how the volume amplification of sonically resonant, visceral anger modulates the emotional range of #MeToo. Gadsby, a white lesbian comedian described as "angry, articulate, and unapologetic," employs volume amplification in the context of disclosing her rape and physical assault (Zainab). *Nanette* simultaneously features an extensive meditation upon the propriety of amplifying anger in the public sphere and a visceral display of Gadsby's own outrage toward a cultural tolerance of sexual violence. The performance employs dry humor to capture her experience growing up in Tasmania's anti-queer culture, discovering her lesbian identity, and facing the shame she carries from her youth. As one example, Gadsby discusses her close call with anti-LGBTQ violence when a man confronted her for speaking with his girlfriend. After realizing Gadsby was a woman, the man stated, "Sorry, I got confused, I thought you were a fucking faggot ... trying to crack on to my girlfriend." Gadsby lightens the room's tension by joking about the heteronormativity of the statement but also declares she must quit comedy because it "froze an incredibly formative experience at its trauma point and sealed it off into jokes." For Gadsby to control the tension in the room and make the audience comfortable in the comedic setting, she admits silencing aspects of her story for the sake of its public performance. She then declares it is time for her to tell her story, marking the beginning of *Nanette*'s most viscerally resonant anger.

Engaging her available sonic resources, Gadsby's volume amplification of angry intensity crafts a visceral resonance of shareable angry experience. Oscillating between the poles of booming force and self-effacing restraint, Gadsby refigures sexual violators as appropriate objects of collective anger. Gadsby's transition from a quick-witted dry humor into a sound-resonant anger emerges during a pointed critique of the comedy industry. Lamenting how many comedians pursue the "easy punchlines" of "priests being pedophiles," Donald "Trump grabbing the pussy," and "Monica Lewinsky," Gadsby amplifies her anger in a slow crescendo with the following declaration:

> Maybe, if comedians had done their job properly, and made fun of a man who abused his power, then perhaps we might have had a middle-aged woman with an appropriate amount of experience in the White House, instead of, as we do, a man who openly admitted to sexually assaulting vulnerable young women *because he could.*

With the pointed staccato *"because he could"* completing her crescendo of outrage, the audience erupts in a protective cocoon of applause, sonically affirming her anger's volume amplification. Like Archila and Gallagher, Gadsby models angry amplification as an appropriate response to sexual violators ascending to the United States' highest realms of power despite ample evidence of abuse. Gadsby then lists Trump, Pablo Picasso, Weinstein, and Roman Polanski as examples of abusers who have escaped accountability because of a misplaced public "obsession with reputation … and we don't seem to mind so long as they get to hold onto *their precious reputation.*" While *Nanette* aired well before Brett Kavanaugh's angry testimony that asserted he was victim of a "character assassination," Gadsby's anger illustrates how protecting perpetrators' reputations places the burden of epistemic injustice on survivors of sexual assault, especially LGBTQ youth whom she observes have been "soaked in shame."

Gadsby then stops—and the silence resonates throughout the cavernous space of the Sydney Opera House, which is designed for classically trained singers to fill without additional sound-amplification technology. Diminishing the sonic intensity of her anger to a full stop, Gadsby provides her audience a moment of quiet introspection to align their own feeling-states with the anger she is sharing. Following this long moment, Gadsby returns to the emotionological norms of the stand-up comedic context: "I'm not very experienced in controlling anger. It's not my place to be angry on a comedy stage." Diminishing the volume of her angry intensity sets the stage for a rejoinder to her earlier story: that she modified her close call with assault for her audience's comfort:

> I couldn't tell the story as it actually happened. Because I couldn't tell the part of the story where that man realized his mistake. And he came back and he said, "Oh, no, I get it. You're a *lady* faggot. I'm *allowed* to beat the shit out of you," *And he did! He beat the shit out of me and nobody stopped him*!

The italicized portions reflect Gadsby's amplification of sound volume and index her anger's ability to claim sonic space within the opera house. Gadsby's voice becomes quiet again, lamenting she did not go to a hospital or report the crime "because that's all I thought I was worth." Gadsby's viscerally angry performance both expresses her own feeling and simultaneously works to create an empathic orientation with audience members as they follow her through the emotional ebbs and flows of the performance.

Yet Gadsby accompanies the sonic amplification of her own anger with a paradoxical gesture that diminishes the volume of a potentially collectivizing anger. Despite feeling justified in her own anger, Gadsby maintains she must cap her angry display enough to prevent its public circulation:

> But this is why I must quit comedy. Because the only way I can tell my truth and put tension in the room is with anger. And I am angry, and I believe I've got every right to be angry! But what I don't have a right to do is spread that anger. I don't. Because anger, much like laughter, can connect a room full of strangers like nothing else.

As a comedian who recognizes her capacity to conduct the flow of public emotion in her performances, Gadsby appears cautious to volumize her audience's anger. While Gadsby's assertion reflects an awareness of anger's socially motivating capacities, she does so through a contagion model of anger and presumes sharing anger is solely destructive. Akin to Gustave Le Bon's late-nineteenth-century theory of crowd psychology that feared collective anger and thus drew a diametric opposition between reason and the emotions, Gadsby appears similarly eager to prevent what she sees as destructive crowd mobilization.

Gadsby's move to diminish the volume of audience anger ultimately downplays an extensive history of politically potent anger that has fueled social change. By "transforming justified queer rage … into a fault within herself," Gadsby deftly individuates her anger (Moskowitz). In diminishing the value of sharing her own anger (and by extension those who are engaged in meaningful queer coalition), Gadsby also elides the nuances of transformative queer anger within social movements like ACT UP and found in the polemics of Larry Kramer (Gould; Rand). Moskowitz puts it well: "By telling us we need to challenge our anger, sublimate it into love and understanding … [Gadsby is] challenging her fellow queers to be more respectful, more civil, to display our pain in a way that cis, straight people can appreciate." Through the ebbs and flows of Gadsby's sonically resonant performance, volume amplification and diminishment serve as a collective tuning fork while simultaneously limiting the political mobilization of a legitimate shared anger at the systemic protections offered to perpetrators of sexual violence.

This section has argued that throughout #MeToo anger discourse, volume rhetorics of amplification and diminishment orient the movement and its accompanying reservoir of public emotion toward hearing the anger of highly visible, predominantly white voices. By admiring muted anger and admonishing anger that lacks intelligibility for privileged audiences, #MeToo anger discourses both obfuscate and silence voices that exceed the rather narrow range of acceptable anger expression. Amplifying the sonic intensity of anger in shared spaces built for resonances can co-orient large groups so long as the productive political potential of the emotion is not diminished and siloed into an individuated feeling-state.

The next section examines how volume rhetorics aggregate angry activists while suturing institutional emotional norms.

The aggregation and dispersion of #MeToo's angers

While volume rhetorics distinctly work to amplify or diminish the intensity of angry expression, anger's volumes also *aggregate* or *disperse* bodies, interests, and energies toward or away from physical or online spaces. Volume aggregation is the process by which seemingly individuated angers accumulate within a shared social repository until they form a collective demand for social change. For instance, Ahmed calls for a "deposit system to show the scale of sexism," envisioning a strategy that can collect a volume aggregation of wrongs that evidence the severity of injustice disproportionately impacting non-white persons (*Living a Feminist Life* 30). While these "deposit systems" may have once been confined to whisper networks that hold the collective memories of repeat sexual offenders, anti–sexual violence hashtag campaigns work to render these deposited narratives public (Lokot; Stenberg). In publicly externalizing this deposit system, a cultural logic of aggregation "is shaped by our interactions with social media and generates particular patterns of social and political interaction that involve the viral flow of information and subsequent aggregations of large numbers of individuals in concrete physical spaces" (Juris 266). A viral moment like #MeToo's aggregation is documentable in a volume of tweets, messages, images, and corporeal bodies. In other words, volume aggregation argues for the sheer enormity of an issue. An abundance of angry bodies in close digital or physical proximity represents taking up space.

Aggregated angry bodies that are physically or symbolically co-oriented together provide a visceral power in numbers, potentially nurturing collectivization. For instance, when Anita Hill disclosed the sexual harassment she experienced while working for Clarence Thomas, 1,600 Black women took out a full-page advertisement, titled "African American Women in Defense of Ourselves," in the *New York Times*. Reprinted in eight other major newspapers, the advertisement listed each woman's name and declared their collective efforts should be interpreted as an aggregated anger: "We are particularly outraged by the racist and sexist treatment of Professor Anita Hill, an African American woman who was maligned and castigated for daring to speak publicly of her own experience of sexual abuse." Their stand articulates the aggregation of Black women's names with their anger's volume when they declare: "We will not be silenced."

Anger modulates through rhetorics of aggregation and dispersion, accounting for how anger gathers or spreads bodies, energies, and interests. Alyssa Milano's initial tweet that mainstreamed #MeToo expressed outrage by calling for volume as an aggregation of responses: "If all the women who have been sexually harassed or assaulted wrote 'Me Too' as a status, we might give people a *sense of the magnitude of the problem*." One reason anger has been an abundant resource for #MeToo is the aggregative connectivity offered by social media infrastructure and the hashtag itself. As "a coordinating signal of commonality," hashtags like #MeToo compress the time and space that divides participants and thereby help to "constitute publics in digital space through the organized yet open-ended circulation of texts" (McVey and Woods 2). The hashtag is a "storytelling device" with profound "connective potential" that materializes "distinct personal frames" (Papacharissi 70). #MeToo experiences extensive viral circulation in part because of the structuring sociality of the hashtag. Typical to techniques of improvisation wherein participants are encouraged to affirm other participants' contributions with a "yes-and," #MeToo carries a similar narrative structure. To disclose #MeToo is really to say "Yes, and ... me too." Together, "Yes, and ... me too" creates a network in which the implied affirmative response increases the aggregate volume of the collective it constitutes. Of central concern is whether the connective action of #MeToo, coupled with the sheer aggregation of those impacted by sexual violence, can be the "deposit system" Ahmed desires. In an interview with *Ebony*, Tarana Burke declared that "[Me Too] wasn't built to be a viral campaign or a hashtag that is here today and forgotten tomorrow. It was a catchphrase to be used from survivor to survivor to let folks know that they were not alone." More a whisper network than a bullhorn, Burke envisioned Me Too as acts of disclosure and listening to encourage radical healing, not as the momentary incantation of a capricious public. The volume aggregation of anger certainly offers affordances that render the magnitude of sexual violence visible.

The aggregated volume of the #MeToo disclosures aligns with anger's dispersion in the form of emotional exhaustion at the number of testimonies. In some cases, the abundance of stories has fueled anger to the point of affective burnout. As Amanda Petrusich cogently writes in *The New Yorker*, "[T]he volume of accusations had the unexpected side effect of making me so hot with anger that there were days when I simply couldn't catch my breath." As the *Washington Post* explains, "Lucia Lorenzi saw #MeToo and she immediately felt tired: 'Anyone else feeling like they're drowning in stories, their own or others?'" (Ohlheiser, "#MeToo Made the Scale"). This "drowning" is the energetic snag in Milano's call for volume aggregation. Anger, after all, requires profound energy and sustained emotional labor over a long timeline of chronic abuses. Visibility without actionable redress diffuses that energy; Wagatwe Wanjuki's tweet, shared 17,000 times, explains that she refuses to say "me too" "because I know, deep down, it won't do anything. Men who need a certain threshold of survivors coming forward to 'get it' will never get it" (Ohlheiser, "#MeToo Made the Scale"). Wanjuki frames the aggregation of disclosures as a way to activate in-group solidarity rather than to persuade reluctant audiences. Nevertheless, the feeling of #MeToo's success that is predicated upon appeals to aggregative volume relies upon the connective potential and the emotional labor facilitated by those willing to share their trauma.

Volume aggregation also occurs through a homogenization of anger, which disseminates a flattened and white-oriented emotional reservoir, obfuscating a more diverse set of experiences from the margins. When Megan Garber of *The Atlantic* hailed Uma Thurman's muted response as a #MeToo referendum, it was to reflect on a changing emotionology in a piece titled, "All the Angry Ladies." Garber argues #MeToo has been transformative to women's anger: "There is anger in the ether.... And women ... have been embracing the emotion for which, in earlier eras, they were so efficiently punished." Garber celebrates that women have been successfully amplifying their anger's volume: "The stories have taken the emotion that women have been traditionally asked to squelch and smother and ignore and brought it to the surface." Despite the larger emotional range ostensibly available for "All the Angry Ladies," the article only briefly accounts for anger's racial inequities. The first references Shirley Chisholm's departure from Congress and cites a 1982 *New York Times* epideictic piece that reduced the complexities of her career to the headline "Rep. Chisholm's Angry Farewell." The second cites Roxane Gay's pre-#MeToo *New York Times* article titled "Who Gets to Be Angry?" in order to meditate upon the inevitability that "rage will, inevitably, rise." While the article works to aggregate "*All* the Angry Ladies," it constitutes their anger as unified, even as it gestures toward the unequal distribution of angry expression among non-white advocates.

Although the article briefly offers these examples of how anti-blackness shapes anger expression and uptake, it does not proceed beyond these momentary acknowledgments. Doing so removes the focus from those whose anger expression is historically saturated with silence, placing the anger conversation in the terms of whiteness. Garber does not cite "Who Gets to Be Angry" in order to problematize the racialized distribution of anger; Garber simply cites Gay's declaration that she anticipates a fallout from all the anger she has swallowed down. This homogenization disperses the political potentialities of combating epistemic injustice with the knowing resistant anger of those at the most precarious intersections of identity. The visual rhetoric of the article also homogenizes women as both white and cisgendered, dispersing the potential for introspection among women's rights advocates. For instance, the image of a pink pussy hat from the 2017 Women's March anchors the piece as the visual masthead, which has drawn critique for both reifying a sex-based approach to womanhood and normalizing white women's pink genitalia (Stoltzfus-Brown). This gesture implies *all* women equally share the burden of oppressive emotionological constraints to anger expression and state-sponsored gender violence that inflict epistemic injustice and silencing. Homogenizing anger within #MeToo may initially appear to build a larger in-group to combat sexual violence, but without attention to the racial axes that present a disproportionately higher cost of anger expression, *The Atlantic* article prevents readers from critically engaging with racial discomfort within the movement. As Tynesha McCullers cogently remarks, "White women get to be loud and angry; Black women do not." The volume aggregation of "*All* the Angry Ladies" ultimately disperses the potential for meaningful and reflexive coalition within the movement.

Volume aggregation can also diminish the volume of collective support for anger that falls outside of a proper emotionological range. Following Brett Kavanaugh's testimony, critiques of his anger turned toward his judicial temperament and the reputational harm the nominee might do to the Supreme Court institution. Legal scholars and law professors sought to diminish what they saw as Kavanaugh's inappropriate volume amplification with their own volume aggregation: the copious rhetorical listing of their dissent (Conley). Indeed, Kavanaugh's angry performance was disqualifying to an aggregate of more than 2,400 law professors who signed a letter delivered to the US Senate on October 4, 2018. The letter argues that Kavanaugh "did not display the impartiality and judicial temperament requisite to sit on the highest court of our land" ("Senate Should Not Confirm"). The list affirms that despite "differing views about the other qualifications of Judge Kavanaugh," the legal profession had come to this consensus regarding his disqualifying anger. Similarly, The American Bar Association took the "new information of a material nature regarding temperament" to open a reevaluation of Kavanaugh's judicial rating (Folley).

Aggregating their voices, these professional organizations diminished the volume of Kavanaugh's anger to reassert the emotionological norms of occupying the subject position of a US judge. Within scholarship about judicial temperament, Maroney cites Aristotle's *Nicomachean Ethics* to argue it is unrealistic to expect judges *not* to experience anger. Instead, "righteous judicial anger is, first, based on an accurate perception of reality … reflects beliefs and values that are worthy of a judge in a democratic society" and is "enabled by strong emotion-regulation skills" (1283–84). Maroney's perspective is helpful but worthy of further elaboration based on the framework of this article. If anger is a response to a perceived harm or injustice, a judge's ability to recognize and process (rather than repress) those feelings is a crucial step toward self-reflexivity.

Moreover, having an accurate grasp of reality must also imply a keen understanding of how the very justice system they serve is rooted in institutionalized racism and sexism, such that sexual violence does not often rise to the level it should (Mack and McCann). Finally, the ability to hold strong emotional regulation skills demonstrates a judge must have a working understanding of volume. Sometimes elevated anger is appropriate; sometimes it is not. Ultimately, aggregation may amplify righteous anger, as with the 1,600 Black women who signed in solidarity with Anita Hill. As the list of 2,400 professors illustrates, however, volume aggregation can also sometimes condemn anger deemed to fall outside an appropriate contextual range.

Despite the similar aggregations of the pro-Hill and anti-Kavanaugh lists, the silencing of Hill's legacy and the muting of support for Blasey Ford fell along distinct racial axes. It is important to remember precisely why the aggregated letter supporting Hill existed in the first place. As Lisa A. Flores reminds us, "[E]very local racial moment is linked, across space and time, to a host of racial moments and racial bodies that have come before and will come after" (16). The day Blasey Ford and Kavanaugh testified, Kimberlé Crenshaw, who had assisted with Hill's legal team, recalled how Hill was "trapped between an antiracist movement that foregrounded black men and a feminism that could not fully address how race shaped society's perception of black victims." Crenshaw explains how Hill's story was diminished because she was labeled as angry: "Inside the hearing room, committee members painted her as an angry and sexually deranged woman," and "we despaired as it became clear that our organizing on Anita Hill's behalf was ineffective in the face of outrage over a black woman who had dared to turn on a fellow African-American at the cusp of enormous judicial power." The aggregation of Hill's supporters was the rhetorical outcome of "a gaping hole" produced in between white feminist and antiracist interests and the perception that both movements would be unwilling to legitimate Hill's testimony (Crenshaw). The intuitive parallel between the copious listings of support for Hill and against Kavanaugh is anything but; whereas Hill's *New York Times* advertisement reflected a collective response to Hill's experience of epistemic injustice, the law professors deriding Kavanaugh's anger aggregated their signatures in service of the judicial system that too often leaves marginalized Black, Latinx, indigenous, and queer voices silenced (DeGagné 142). These comparative aggregations demonstrate the orienting function of anger, which is neither solely an individuated expression nor a social discourse but a pivot around which sociality, status, race, gender, and justice are oriented, diminished, and silenced.

Following Kavanaugh's confirmation to the Supreme Court, the aggregated anger of the #MeToo movement did not dissipate and has remained a dominant public emotion. Much as Archila and Gallagher took up space by outnumbering Flake two to one, corporeal aggregation is a form that can modulate public anger. Following the vote, and at the precipice of his swearing in, a contingent of protesters descended on the Supreme Court. Bodies poured onto the stairs with chants such as "Whose Court? Our Court" and "Arrest Sexual Predators, Not Protesters." As Kavanaugh was sworn in, protesters banged on the doors and chanted so the bodies within would hear them. The volume was striking for CNN journalist Ariane de Vogue: "You're usually not allowed on those stairs, you're not allowed up there" ("Protesters Pound"). Occupying the prohibited stairways and chanting through the swearing-in, protesters engaged the dual senses of volume, both as amplification and as aggregation. This protest display was capped by the iconic image of a white woman who climbed the statue of Lady Justice, sat in her lap, and held up a fist and a small handwritten sign reading "#MeToo."

Conclusions: Volume, sharing anger

Within Me Too and #MeToo, anger circulates in different ranges and intensities, marking the boundaries of collectives and their standards of justice. Anger's volumes help critically interrogate the raced, gendered, and classed dynamics that amplify and aggregate collective anger in the service of whiteness while diminishing and diffusing nonwhite perspectives. Volumes trace the public movement of the emotion and determine how voices are elevated and marginalized within anger discourse. Anger writ large does not belong to any particular ideological affiliation and must be understood as such if we are to fully grasp the range of its political power (Condit, *Angry Public Rhetorics*). The shared ability to experience and deploy anger necessarily requires a critical orientation to whose anger is being publicly privileged in order to avoid homogenizing the emotion within a social movement. A heterogeneous orientation to anger modulation, which the concept of volume allows, assists in understanding the historical specificities behind an emergent anger without dismissing the inventional, embodied, and collectivizing resources of the emotion. For the privileged like Kavanaugh, amplifying anger in response to a status slight helps to fortify white supremacy's durable shielding of sexual violence by indexing wrongs done to individual reputations. For others, like Burke, Archila, and Gallagher, anger's force is collectivizing because it names *shared* harms, injustices, and improprieties, eyeing a future that might nurture collective healing. Identifying anger's volumes within a social movement dissects anger at important social positional intersections to allow these important nuances to come into relief.

Anger's volumes also allow critics to hear claims of injustice. Author Ijeoma Oluo responded to those who were "scratching their heads in concern and confusion" about some of #MeToo's anger: "The rage you see right now, the rage bringing down previously invulnerable men today, barely scratches the surface. You think we might be angry? You have no idea how angry we are." Her final line, that so many "have no idea" the vicissitudes of rage speaks to the implications of considering volume in discussions of public anger within #MeToo. Confusion is only possible for those whose social position has refused to hear those who have been most impacted by sexual violence. Bailey reminds us that "[knowing resistant anger] has particular textures and features which will only be intelligible in particular resistant worlds" (104). #MeToo reflects a cultural-technological juncture where so many individuals' "knowing resistant anger" (Bailey) or "eloquent rage" (Cooper) can no longer be fully enclaved, requiring critical tools to discern the makers and markers of public anger. This analysis demonstrates that the diminishment of anger is not always an explicit silencing. Rather, by failing to cede space to knowing resistant anger, support for white anger creeps into the crevices of public attention.

This article also holds implications for the necessity for critical introspection by those seeking to attend to public emotions. Reflecting on the practice of doing rhetorical criticism, several scholars have recently called for increased reflexivity in critical practice.

Condit has invited authors to account for the "attention to one's own pathos, especially the affiliations one is crafting" while doing rhetorical criticism ("Pathos in Criticism" 20). Similarly, Lisa M. Corrigan calls for rhetorical critics to consider "white fragility as an impediment to provocative criticism" and specifically attend to the ways "scholars at the margins" navigate the emotional labor of doing rhetorical criticism in a field inhospitable to their positionality (87–88). While ignoring the emotions of the critic disavows the embodied process of writing, becoming mired in one's own emotion without the ability to enact self-distance to feel *with* others outside of one's positionality can reinscribe the same problems of white-centered anger that this article critiques. To productively analyze anger's volumes, critics must similarly be willing to sit with the visceral discomfort of angry emotionality but not dwell there at the expense of survivors whose oppression is far more exigent.

To ultimately align #MeToo with Tarana Burke's goal of cultivating a movement marked by empathy and a full repertoire of emotions, future work might productively expand on volume to think about strategically cultivating other public emotions that can fight against the silencing of survivors. Volume is potentially applicable to emotions beyond anger, such as empathy, fear, and, perhaps most importantly, joy. Expanding the emotional reach of the volume framework attunes critics and discourse creators to imagine public emotions as fungible and contingent, granting a sense of agency to amplify some emotions while diminishing others. Any inventional capacity available with this critical framework must be willing to center the emotions of those most harmed by sexual violence. As we listen to the anger that is symptomatic of regimes of epistemic injustice, we must be willing to amplify that anger, especially when it is uncomfortable to do so.

Acknowledgments

The author would like to thank Lisa Corrigan, Kristen Hoerl, and the two anonymous reviewers for their meaningful engagement with this piece throughout the revision process. The author is grateful to Atilla Hallsby, Heather Woods, Caitlin Bruce, Michael Lechuga, Zornitsa Keremidchieva, Wendy K. Z. Anderson, and Nicole Hurt for generative discussions and feedback on this project throughout its stages.

Works cited

Ahmed, Sara. *The Cultural Politics of Emotion*. Routledge, 2004.
———. "Embodying Diversity: Problems and Paradoxes for Black Feminists." *Race Ethnicity and Education*, vol. 12, no. 1, 2009, pp. 41–52. doi:10.1080/13613320802650931.
———. *Living a Feminist Life*. Duke UP, 2017.
Aristotle. *The Rhetoric*, translated John Henry Freese, Harvard UP, 2000.
Bailey, Alison. "On Anger, Silence, and Epistemic Injustice." *Royal Institute of Philosophy Supplement*, vol. 84, 2018, 93–115. doi:10.1017/S1358246118000565
Banks, Antoine J. *Anger and Racial Politics: The Emotional Foundation of Racial Politics in America*. Cambridge University Press, 2014. doi:10.1017/CBO9781107279247.
Bennett, Jessica. "The 'Click' Moment: How the Weinstein Scandal Unleashed a Tsunami." *New York Times*, 5 Nov. 2017, https://www.nytimes.com/2017/11/05/us/sexual-harrasment-weinstein-trump.html. Accessed 30 July 2018.

Carlin, Shannon. "Uma Thurman Is Seriously Angry About Sexual Misconduct in Hollywood." *Refinery29*, 4 Nov. 2017, https://www.refinery29.com/en-us/2017/11/179684/uma-thurman-sexual-misconduct-hollywood-emotional-response. Accessed 30 July 2018.

Chokshi, Niraj, and Astead W. Herndon. "Jeff Flake Is Confronted on Video by Sexual Assault Survivors." *New York Times*, 28 Sept. 2018, https://www.nytimes.com/2018/09/28/us/politics/jeff-flake-protesters-kavanaugh.html.

Collins, Patricia Hill. *Black Feminist Thought: Knowledge, Consciousness, and the Politics of Empowerment*. Routledge, 2002.

Condit, Celeste. *Angry Public Rhetorics: Global Relations and Emotion in the Wake of 9/11*. U of Michigan P, 2018.

———. "Pathos in Criticism: Edwin Black's Communism-As-Cancer Metaphor." *Quarterly Journal of Speech*, vol. 99, no. 1, 2013, 1–26. doi:10.1080/00335630.2012.749417

Conley, Thomas M. "The Beauty of Lists: Copia and Argument." *Journal of the American Forensic Association*, vol. 12, no. 2, 1985, pp. 96–103. doi:10.1080/00028533.1985.11951307.

Cooper, Brittney. *Eloquent Rage: A Black Feminist Discovers Her Superpower*. St. Martin's Press, 2018.

Corrigan, Lisa M. "On Rhetorical Criticism, Performativity, and White Fragility." *Review of Communication*, vol. 16, no. 1, 2016, pp. 86–88. doi:10.1080/15358593.2016.1183886.

Crenshaw, Kimberlé. "We Still Haven't Learned from Anita Hill's Testimony." *New York Times*, 27 Sept. 2018, https://www.nytimes.com/2018/09/27/opinion/anita-hill-clarence-thomas-brett-kavanaugh-christine-ford.html.

DeGagne, Alexa. "On Anger and its Uses for Activism." *Contemporary Inequalities and Social Justice in Canada*, edited by Janine Brody, University of Toronto Press, 2018.

DiAngelo, Robin. "White Fragility." *International Journal of Critical Pedagogy*, vol. 3, no. 3, 2011, pp. 54–70. http://libjournal.uncg.edu/ijcp/article/view/249/116

Donnelly, Erin. "Drew Barrymore Blasted for 'Tone-Deaf' Comments About #MeToo After Urging Women Not to be Angry." *Yahoo*, 20 Mar. 2018, https://www.yahoo.com/lifestyle/drew-barrymore-blasted-tone-deaf-comments-metoo-urging-women-not-angry-161220971.html. Accessed 15 July 2018.

Dowd, Maureen. "This Is Why Uma Thurman Is Angry." *New York Times*, 3 Feb. 2018, https://www.nytimes.com/2018/02/03/opinion/sunday/this-is-why-uma-thurman-is-angry.html. Accessed 30 July 2018.

"Drew Barrymore Recalls Flashing David Letterman." *YouTube*, uploaded by *The Late Show with Stephen Colbert*, 20 Mar. 2018. https://www.youtube.com/watch?v=4AcHXdIDsig. Accessed 30 July 2018.

Flores, Lisa A. "Between Abundance and Marginalization: The Imperative of Racial Rhetorical Criticism." *Review of Communication,* vol. 16, no. 1, 2016, pp. 4–24. doi:10.1080/15358593.2016.1183871.

Folley, Aris. "American Bar Association Reopening Kavanaugh Investigation Due to 'Temperament,'" *The Hill.com*. 5 Oct. 2018. Accessed 28 June 2019.

Fricker, Miranda. *Epistemic Injustice: Power and the Ethics of Knowing*. Oxford UP, 2007.

Gadsby, Hannah. *Nanette*. Directed by Jon Olb and Madeleine Parry, performance by Hannah Gadsby, *Netflix*, 19 June 2018. https://www.netflix.com/watch/80233611

Garber, Megan. "All the Angry Ladies." *The Atlantic*, 6 Nov. 2017, https://www.theatlantic.com/entertainment/archive/2017/11/all-the-angry-ladies/545042/. Accessed 30 July 2018.

Garcia, Sandra. "The Woman Who Created #MeToo Long Before Hashtags." *New York Times*, 20 Oct. 2017, https://www.nytimes.com/2017/10/20/us/me-too-movement-tarana-burke.html. Accessed 30 July 2018.

Gay, Roxane. "Who Gets to Be Angry?" *New York Times*, 10 June 2016, https://www.nytimes.com/2016/06/12/opinion/sunday/who-gets-to-be-angry.html. Accessed 30 July 2018.

Glenn, Cheryl. *Unspoken: A Rhetoric of Silence*. Southern Illinois UP, 2004.

Goodale, Greg. "The Sonorous Envelope and Political Deliberation." *Quarterly Journal of Speech*, vol. 99, no. 2, 2013, pp. 218–24. doi:10.1080/00335630.2013.775702.

Gould, Deborah B. *Moving Politics: Emotion and ACT UP's Fight Against AIDS*. U of Chicago P, 2009.

Griffin, Rachel Alicia. "I AM an Angry Black Woman: Black Feminist Autoethnography, Voice, and Resistance." Women's *Studies in Communication*, vol. 35, no. 2, 2012, pp. 138–57. doi: 10.1080/07491409.2012.724524.

Haslam, Nick. "Dehumanization: An Integrative Review." *Personality and Social Psychology Review*, vol. 10, no. 3, 2006, pp. 252–64. doi:10.1207/s15327957pspr1003_4.

Jasper, James M. "Constructing Indignation: Anger Dynamics in Protest Movements." *Emotion Review*, vol. 6, no. 3, 2014, pp. 208–13. doi:10.1177/1754073914522863.

Juris, Jeffrey S. "Reflections on #Occupy Everywhere: Social Media, Public Space, and Emerging Logics of Aggregation." *American Ethnologist*, vol. 39, no. 2, 2012, pp. 259–79. doi:10.1111/j.1548-1425.2012.01362.x.

Kai, Maiysha. "White Woman #101: Believe It or Not, Rose McGowan Is a Member of #MeToo, Not Its Messiah." *The Root*, 9 Oct. 2018, https://theglowup.theroot.com/white-woman-101-believe-it-or-not-rose-mcgowan-is-a-1829610299. Accessed 25 Jan. 2019.

Krugman, Paul. "The Angry White Male Caucus." *New York Times*, 1 Oct. 2018, https://www.nytimes.com/2018/10/01/opinion/kavanaugh-white-male-privilege.html.

Larson, Stephanie R. "'Everything Inside Me Was Silenced': (Re)defining Rape Through Visceral Counterpublicity." *Quarterly Journal of Speech*, vol. 104, no. 2, 2018, pp. 123–44. doi:10.1080/00335630.2018.1447141.

Lokot, Tetyana. "#IAmNotAfraidToSayIt: Stories of Sexual Violence As Everyday Political Speech on Facebook." *Information, Communication, and Society*, vol. 21, no. 6, 2018, pp. 802–17. doi:10.1080/1369118X.2018.1430161.

Lorde, Audre. *Sister Outsider: Essays and Speeches*. Rev. ed., Crossing Press, 2012.

Loughrey, Clarisse. "Uma Thurman's Powerful Response to Sexual Misconduct in Hollywood: 'I've Been Waiting to Feel Less Angry.'" *The Independent*, 5 Nov. 2017, https://www.independent.co.uk/arts-entertainment/films/news/uma-thurman-response-sexual-harassment-assault-hollywood-weinstein-spacey-ratner-a8038331.html. Accessed 30 July 2018.

Lyman, Peter. "The Domestication of Anger: The Use and Abuse of Anger in Politics." *European Journal of Social Theory*, vol. 7, no. 2, 2004, 133–47. doi:10.1177/1368431004041748.

Mack, Ashley N., and Bryan J. McCann. "Critiquing State and Gendered Violence in the Age of #MeToo." *Quarterly Journal of Speech*, vol. 104, no. 3, 2018, pp. 329–44. doi:10.1080/00335630.2018.1479144.

Maroney, Terry A. "Angry Judges." *Vanderbilt Law Review*, vol. 65, no. 5, 2012, pp. 1207–86. https://www.vanderbiltlawreview.org/wp-content/uploads/sites/89/2012/10/Maroney_65_Vand_L_Rev_1207.pdf

Medina, José. *The Epistemology of Resistance: Gender and Racial Oppression, Epistemic Injustice, and Resistant Imaginations*. Oxford UP, 2013.

McCullers, Tynesha. "As a Black Woman, I Won't Say #MeToo in Rose McGowan's Movement." *Black Youth Project*, 9 Jan. 2018, http://blackyouthproject.com/as-a-black-woman-i-wont-say-metoo-in-rose-mcgowans-movement/. Accessed 30 July 2018.

McVey, James Alexander, and Heather Suzanne Woods. "Anti-Racist Activism and the Transformational Principles of Hashtag Publics: From #HandsUpDontShoot to #PantsUpDontLoot." *Present Tense*, vol. 5, no. 3, 2016, pp. 1–9. http://www.presenttensejournal.org/wp-content/uploads/2016/05/McVeyWoods.pdf

Micale, Mark S. *Approaching Hysteria: Disease and Its Interpretations*. Princeton UP, 1995.

Moskowitz, Peter, "The Nanette Problem." *The Outline*, 20 Aug. 2018, https://theoutline.com/post/5962/the-nanette-problem-hannah-gadsby-netflix-review?zd=2&zi=6qmmmhgg.

Ohlheiser, Abby. "#MeToo Made the Scale of Sexual Abuse Go Viral. But Is It Asking Too Much of Survivors?" *Washington Post*, 16 Oct. 2017, https://www.washingtonpost.com/news/the-intersect/wp/2017/10/16/metoo-made-the-scale-of-sexual-abuse-go-viral-but-is-it-asking-too-much-of-survivors/?noredirect=on&utm_term=.49596ddf6b55. Accessed 30 July 2018.

Olson, Lester C. "Anger Among Allies: Audre Lorde's 1981 Keynote Admonishing the National Women's Studies Association." *Quarterly Journal of Speech*, vol. 97, no. 3, 2011, pp. 283–308. doi:10.1080/00335630.2011.585169.

Oluo, Ijeoma. "Does This Year Make Me Look Angry?" *Elle*, 11 Jan. 2018, https://www.elle.com/culture/career-politics/a15063942/ijeoma-oluo-women-and-rage-2018/. Accessed 30 Sep. 2018.

"Patrisse Cullors and Tarana Burke: Anger, Activism, and Action: The Founders of Black Lives Matter and the #MeToo Movement on Making Change." *Elle.com*, 13 Mar. 2018, https://www.elle.com/culture/career-politics/a19180106/patrisse-cullors-tarana-burke-black-lives-matter-metoo-activism/. Accessed 30 July 2018.

Papacharissi, Zizi. *Affective Publics: Sentiment, Technology, and Politics*. Oxford UP, 2015.

"Protesters Pound on the Doors of the Supreme Court," *CNN*, 6 Oct. 2018, https://www.msn.com/en-us/video/l/protesters-pound-on-doors-of-supreme-court/vp-BBO1TRD.

Rand, Erin J. "An Inflammatory Fag and a Queer Form: Larry Kramer, Polemics, and Rhetorical Agency." *Quarterly Journal of Speech*, vol. 94, no. 3, 2008, pp. 297–319. doi:10.1080/00335630802210377.

Saccone, Lauren. "Uma Thurman Filled With Rage at All the Sexual Misconduct in Hollywood Is the Most Relatable Thing You'll See All Weekend." *Hellogiggles*, 5 Nov. 2017, https://hellogiggles.com/celebrity/uma-thurman-rage-sexual-misconduct/. Accessed 30 July 2018.

Sanders, Mia. "#MeToo: The Personal Is Still Political." *Green Left Weekly*, 27 Jan. 2018, https://www.greenleft.org.au/content/metoo-personal-still-political. Accessed 30 July 2018.

"The Senate Should Not Confirm Kavanaugh: Signed, 2400+ Law Professors," *New York Times*, 3 Oct. 2018, https://www.nytimes.com/interactive/2018/10/03/opinion/kavanaugh-law-professors-letter.html.

Smith, David. "Anita Hill and the Senate 'Sham Trial' That Echoes Down to Kavanaugh." *The Guardian*, 23 Sept. 2018, https://www.theguardian.com/law/2018/sep/22/brett-kavanaugh-christine-blasey-ford-anita-hill-clarence-thomas-senate-judiciary-committee.

Smith-Rosenberg, Carroll. "The Hysterical Woman: Sex Roles and Role Conflict in 19th-Century America." *Social Research*, vol. 39, no. 4, 1972, pp. 652–78.

Sparks, Holloway. "Mama Grizzlies and Guardians of the Republic: The Democratic and Intersectional Politics of Anger in the Tea Party Movement," *New Political Science*, vol. 37, no. 1, 2015, 25–47. doi:10.1080/07393148.2014.945252.

Stearns, Carol Zisowitz, and Peter N. Stearns. *Anger: The Struggle for Emotional Control in America's History*. U of Chicago P, 1986.

Stenberg, Shari J. "'Tweet Me Your First Assaults': Writing Shame and the Rhetorical Work of #NotOkay." *Rhetoric Society Quarterly*, vol. 48, no. 2, 2018, pp. 119–38. doi:10.1080/02773945.2017.1402126.

Stoltzfus-Brown, Lars. "Trans-Exclusionary Discourse, White Feminist Failures, and the Women's March on Washington, D.C." *Transgressing Feminist Theory and Discourse*, edited by J. C. Dunn and J. Manning, Routledge, 2018, pp. 105–17.

Thompson, Debra. "An Exoneration of Black Rage." *South Atlantic Quarterly*, vol. 116, no. 3, 2017, pp. 457–81. doi:10.1215/00382876-3961439.

Traister, Rebecca. *Good and Mad: The Revolutionary Power of Women's Anger*. Simon & Schuster, 2018.

"Uma Thurman Gets Emotional About Women Speaking Out on Sexual Harassment in Hollywood." *YouTube*, uploaded by Access 18 Oct. 2017, https://www.youtube.com/watch?v=Rs4gK8DuuWY. Accessed 30 July 2018.

Winderman, Emily. "S(anger) Goes Postal in The Woman Rebel: Angry Rhetoric As a Collectivizing Moral Emotion." *Rhetoric and Public Affairs*, vol. 17, no. 3, 2014, pp. 381–420. doi:10.14321/rhetpublaffa.17.3.0381.

Zacharek, Stephanie, Eliana Dockterman, and Haley Sweetland Edwards. "The Silence Breakers." *TIME*, Dec. 2017, http://time.com/time-person-of-the-year-2017-silence-breakers/.

Zainab, Umara. "Hannah Gadsby's Nanette Is Feminist Rage Against Comedy." *Feminism in Media*, 27 June 2018, https://feminisminindia.com/2018/06/27/hannah-gadsby-nanette-review/. Accessed 15 Jan. 2019.

"Our Bodies Are Not *Terra Nullius*": Building a Decolonial Feminist Resistance to Gendered Violence

Ashley Noel Mack and Tiara R. Na'puti

ABSTRACT
Gendered violence is historically and presently a colonial tool that wields power over and against Indigenous peoples, attempting to destroy or erase their sovereignty and lives. Decolonization is necessary in movements addressing gendered violence in settler colonial nation-states. In this article, we forefront Indigenous organizing as a practice of survivance and decolonial feminist theory building. We argue that decolonial feminist critique deepens our understanding of complex iterations of gendered violence. By witnessing resistant Indigenous community responses to sexual violence, we can begin to imagine and build coalitional decolonial feminist possibilities. Witnessing, we argue, is a decolonial heuristic for engaging *with* resistant subjectivities at the colonial difference as embodied theory and praxis of decolonial feminism.

In an article in the *Washington Post* in November 2017, Me Too movement founder Tarana Burke lamented that dominant mediated representations of #MeToo took on a life of their own after going viral. Burke (2017) explained that mainstream #MeToo discourses often erased the experiences of women of color and obscured that the original purpose of the Me Too movement was to help survivors of sexual violence—particularly young women of color from low-wealth communities—emotionally heal. While the #MeToo moment in the Western digital public sphere represents for some a galvanizing and transformative mass resistance to systematic sexual violence, in this article we join Burke and others in problematizing #MeToo's public articulation (Crenshaw, 2018; Dougherty & Calafell, 2019; de la Garza, 2019; Onwuachi-Willig, 2018; Rowe, 2019; Tambe, 2018; Taylor, 2019; Turtle Talk, 2018). Specifically, we argue that a commitment to decolonization is necessary when addressing gendered violence within settler colonial nation-states and that feminist communication scholars should engage in decolonial feminist practices of critique. Such approaches are critical for rhetorical and cultural scholars who seek to understand the nuanced and multidimensional manifestations of sexual violence across racial, gender, and sexuality-based lines within the context of colonization and disenfranchisement.

Ubiquitous practices of colonial unknowing actively work to produce ignorance about "the histories and contemporary relations of colonialism" in North America and the Caribbean (Vimalassery, Pegues, & Goldstein, 2016, p. 1). Colonial unknowing renders unintelligible the effects of colonial relations of power and mark colonization and dispossession with a finality even though colonial violence is ongoing (Vimalassery et al., 2016; Vimalassery, Pegues, & Goldstein, 2017). A commitment to decolonization within analytical practice moves beyond merely marking violence from colonial legacies; it requires actively working to decolonize ongoing structures of power in settler colonial contexts. A decolonial feminist orientation understands gendered violence, such as sexual assault, as part of colonial violence and attends to the combined processes of racialization, gender dichotomization, and heterosexualism in modernity (Arvin, Tuck, & Morrill, 2013; Dougherty & Calafell, 2019; Lugones, 2007, 2010; Mack, Bershon, Laiche, & Navarro, 2018; Perry, 2018; Veronelli, 2016). Examining gendered violence from this orientation also requires resisting the reproduction of colonial logics by engaging with dissident ways of knowing and being (Ghabra & Calafell, 2019; Lugones, 2010, p. 748; Mack et al., 2018; Veronelli, 2016).

In this article, we choose not to directly address discourses of #MeToo, as its dominant mediated representations have already been criticized for reflecting colonial power relations by primarily centering the experiences of White Western women (Crenshaw, 2018; Dougherty & Calafell, 2019; de la Garza, 2019; Onwuachi-Willig, 2018); erasing the plurality of Black, Brown, Indigenous, Two-Spirit, and LGBTQQIA+ (Lesbian, Gay, Bisexual, Transgender, Queer, Questioning, Intersex, Asexual, plus) experience (Tambe, 2018; Taylor, 2019; Turtle Talk, 2018); reaffirming colonial epistemologies of dichotomous gender and colonial logics (Mack et al., 2018; Rowe, 2019); presuming White Western female subjectivity by emphasizing publicity through self-disclosure as the primary means of rhetorical agency (Burke, 2017); and celebrating increased state violence through calls for harsher carceral punishments for sexual violence (Mack & McCann, 2018). Instead, in an effort to engage intersubjectively with dissident epistemologies, we center two examples of Indigenous resistance to gendered violence that foreground decolonization. This is important because, as Native writer Sara Marie Ortiz explained in the aftermath of the #MeToo zeitgeist:

> We have a responsibility to create our own model… . We have old systems of restorative justice and different processes that have nothing to do with social media and have nothing to do with the often punitive, often repressive and dehumanizing thing that happens in courtrooms and in the court of public opinion in the U.S. (qtd. in Jones, 2018, para. 24)

Using collective language, Ortiz centers alternatives to the state and forefronts holistic and coalitional considerations that serve the Native community. Navigating publics in this way can be a fraught endeavor, particularly when the predominantly White U.S. public culture tends to erase or otherwise ignore Indigenous communities. Rather than seek justice from the legal and political systems of settler colonial nation-states, Indigenous activists often provide alternative approaches that privilege Indigenous forms of community building to confront gendered violence.

In the next section, we discuss the need for a decolonial feminism built through deep coalitions amongst those oppressed by and through colonial logics and structures, particularly in response to gendered violence (Ghabra & Calafell, 2019; Lugones, 2010; Veronelli, 2016). We encourage working toward a decolonial feminism that emphasizes learning "about each other as resisters to the coloniality of gender at the colonial difference, without necessarily being an insider to the worlds of meaning from which resistance to the coloniality arises" (Lugones, 2010, p. 753). We suggest that witnessing is one heuristic for approaching decolonial feminist critique that works to build deep coalitions by radically de-centering our voice as authors in favor of centering the voices of Indigenous communities. Such an approach illuminates colonial processes by engaging with Others at the colonial difference while enabling robust challenges to colonial violences by reasserting indigeneity (Byrd, 2011; Ghabra & Calafell, 2019; Kauanui, 2008; Na'puti & Rohrer, 2017; Rowe & Tuck, 2017; Trinh, 1989; Veronelli, 2016). Following this discussion, we reveal the curvatures of possible decolonial approaches to gendered violence by witnessing the resistance work done by two groups: Missing and Murdered Indigenous Women and the coalitional initiative Violence on the Land, Violence on Our Bodies. Both of these examples illustrate how gendered violence is opposed through resistant subjectivities in settler colonialism that actively work toward decolonization.

Decolonizing feminism and critiques of gendered violence

Decolonial scholars have called on communication scholarship to identify and critique colonial processes and structures more explicitly (Chakravartty, Kuo, Grubbs, & McIlwain, 2018; Ghabra & Calafell, 2019; Gutierrez-Perez, 2019; Rowe & Tuck, 2017; Sandoval, 2000; Shome, 2016; Trinh, 1989; Veronelli, 2016; Wanzer, 2012). Working toward decolonization necessitates reconsidering the methods and practices of knowledge production embodied in our scholarship without replicating colonial logics and relations (Ghabra & Calafell, 2019; Gutierrez-Perez, 2019; Sholock, 2012; Veronelli, 2016; Yep, 2010).

By reasserting White colonial logics and centering U.S. experiences, Western contemporary feminisms have been extensively critiqued for reinforcing racialization, gender dichotomization, and heteronormativity in theories or histories (Calafell, 2014; Chávez, 2015; Ghabra & Calafell, 2019; Lugones, 2010; Veronelli, 2016). Indeed, many Native and Indigenous peoples choose not to identify with the label "feminist" because of its long association with settler colonial Whiteness (Arvin et al., 2013; Goeman & Denetdale, 2009; Smith & Kauanui, 2008). The failure of Western feminists to recognize and actively engage in decentering Whiteness and colonial epistemologies in otherwise "progressive" feminist projects is what Trask (1996) calls the "feminist failure of vision." In Trask's account, White feminists tend to have "an outright insensibility to the vastness of the human world," so they often narrow their examination of its contents to be grounded solely in their perceptions of oppressive structures and then render those experiences universal or generalizable (p. 911). Considering that this "failure of vision" manifests in feminist writing and theorizing, it is not surprising that it also occurs when dominant feminist ethics and logics are mobilized in the U.S. public sphere to address social problems such as sexual assault.

For example, most feminist scholarship in communication studies has framed gendered violence as solely emerging from the binary gendered power relations sanctioned through systems of patriarchy (Hernández & De Los Santos-Upton, 2018; Mack et al., 2018). Such approaches privilege White Western feminist understandings of power structures and ignore decades of Indigenous, Black, Chicana, postcolonial, and decolonial feminist scholarship that argues gendered violence is a complex social problem that (often in seemingly contradictory ways and at various intersections) reinforces White supremacy, patriarchy, heteronormativity, binary Western epistemologies of gender, and capitalist logics (Crenshaw, 2018; Deer, 2015; Dougherty & Calafell, 2019; Goeman, 2017; Lugones, 2010; Mack et al., 2018). Given that Western feminist approaches have been critiqued for not investing in decolonization, we join these scholars in arguing for a decolonial feminist approach as a specific means of addressing gendered violence and ongoing colonialism and cisheteropatriarchy (DeLisle, 2015; Hall, 2009; Stewart-Harawira, 2007).

In moving toward decolonization, scholars studying gendered violence must more actively examine North American nation-states, such as the United States and Canada, as settler colonial nation-states that continue to enact violence against Native women and Two-Spirit individuals with impunity. So-called progression toward justice in U.S. national narratives tends to obscure ongoing institutional oppression toward Indigenous communities. Arvin and colleagues (2013) argue that, in both women's and ethnic studies, "too often the consideration of Indigenous peoples remains rooted in understanding colonialism (like state-sanctioned slavery) as an historical point in time away from which our society has progressed" (p. 9). If colonialism is catalogued as primarily "in the past," then it is not seriously considered as a structure that must be continuously confronted and challenged in the present.

Gendered violence as colonial violence

Gendered violence is one manifestation of ongoing U.S. settler colonialism (Deer, 2015, p. x; Mack et al., 2018). Rape, for example, is historically and presently a colonial tool that wields power over and against Indigenous peoples, attempting to destroy or erase their sovereignty and lives (Deer, 2015; Dougherty & Calafell, 2019). The "civilizing mission" of colonialism was a guise for "brutal access to people's bodies through unimaginable exploitation, violent sexual violation, control of reproduction, and systematic terror" (Lugones, 2010, p. 744). Drawing from Quijano's concept of "coloniality of power," Lugones (2007, 2010) argues that colonial epistemologies normalize colonial relations of power not just across racial and class-based lines but also in terms of gender and sexuality (p. 742). Gendered violence is/was used to violently impose gender on Indigenous bodies, and gender dichotomization is/was a central strategy of colonial conquest and control (Lugones, 2007). Deer (2015) argues that we can only build an honest anti-rape movement if it confronts colonial violence (p. xxiv) by addressing rape as a political construct and a product of colonialism, rather than associating rape with an epidemic like "a contagious disease" or framing it as a "short-term, isolated problem" (pp. ix–x).

National Crime Victimization Survey data indicate that Native women are raped at an average annual rate of 7.2 per 1,000 persons, while all other races compare at 1.9 per 1,000 persons (Deer, 2015, p. 4). More broadly, approximately 84% of Native women and 81.6% of Native men have experienced violence in their lives, and 56% of Native women have experienced some form of sexual violence (Rosay, 2016, p. 2). American Indian and Alaska Native women are 2.5 times more likely to experience sexual assault or rape than women in the United States in general (Amnesty International, 2007, p. 2), and 55% of Native women have experienced rape or violence from an intimate partner (Rosay, 2016).

Sexual violence against Native women in the United States is also mostly committed by non-Native men (Amnesty International, 2007, pp. 4–5), and these crimes remain largely unprosecuted (Deer, 2009; Rosay, 2016). Worse, federally imposed restrictions on the jurisdiction of tribal courts also significantly impedes Native communities from effectively addressing gendered/sexual violence perpetrated by non-Native men (Amnesty International, 2007, pp. 30–32). The U.S. nation-state's failure to recognize, respond to, or rectify sexual violence committed by non-Native men contributes to Indigenous peoples' widespread mistrust of the U.S. nation-state. It is also extremely difficult to separate widespread assault from individual experience because the violence is connected to "a history of forced removal, displacement, and destruction" (Deer, 2015, p. 12). Accordingly, self-determination and community-led coalitions are key components of Indigenous organizing around sexual violence because they do not involve the state.

Statistics about gendered violence, while staggering, do not reflect the full extent of sexual assault against Native peoples because many Indigenous people are reluctant to speak with representatives of the state who gather the data. Frequently, government agencies use reports of assault to justify coercive or violent enforcement and criminalization in their communities (Coomaraswamy, 2001, p. 3). These statistics therefore do not entirely convey the systemic reach and pervasive impacts of sexual and gendered violence on Indigenous communities. There are also no accurate data for the rates of sexual or gendered violence that occurs within and toward Two-Spirit and LGBTQQIA+ populations. Systemic marginalization of gender-nonconforming individuals has contributed to these populations being seemingly absent from extant data on gendered violence. This invisibility is exacerbated by the lack of statistical information regarding transgender, transsexual, and other gender-nonconforming people (National Collaborating Centre for Indigenous Health, 2016, p. 12). Gender-nonconforming people experience heightened levels of violence (Taylor, 2009), and the intersecting concerns of homophobic, racist, and transphobic violence may place two-spirited people in "triple jeopardy" as they experience systemic violence and discrimination by individuals in positions of power (Lehavot, Walters, & Simoni, 2009; National Collaborating Centre for Indigenous Health, 2016, p. 15). Although the available data do not accurately portray the full magnitude of gendered violence against Indigenous communities, they do highlight that Native populations are particularly at risk of sexual and gendered violence.

While it is an important factor, gendered violence cannot be considered only a result of colonization. Kuokkanen (2015) contends, "If gendered violence is recognized only as a consequence of the history of colonization of Indigenous peoples at large, analyses will overlook Indigenous women as victims of violence in their own right within their own communities" (p. 283). Rejecting the discourses of colonization "that externalize responsibility for gendered violence or construct male violence as a reflection of their own victimhood and loss of status" can also create dilemmas for Indigenous women that often lead them to not report gendered violence committed by men in their community (Kuokkanen, 2015, p. 272). Therefore, we must examine the "interconnectedness of surviving colonization and surviving rape" (Deer, 2015, p. xiv). This survivance hinges on sovereignty as both political and personal.

Decolonial feminist critique

In addition to highlighting the ways that gendered violence *is* colonial violence, a decolonial feminist approach also works to resist colonial logics by centering dissident epistemologies emerging from the embodied knowledge of resistant subjectivities at the colonial difference (Ghabra & Calafell, 2019; Lugones, 2010; Veronelli, 2016). For Lugones (2010), intersubjective coalitional engagement at the colonial difference is central to building a decolonial feminist project (see also Ghabra & Calafell, 2019; Veronelli, 2016).

"The process of colonization," Lugones (2010) writes, "invented the colonized and attempted a full reduction of them to less than human primitives, satanically possessed, infantile, aggressively sexual, and in need of transformation" (p. 747). The process of colonial subjectification (and dehumanization) is ongoing and constantly renewed, yet erased, obfuscated, and ignored in modernity (p. 748). But colonial subjectification "is met in the flesh over and over by oppositional responses grounded in a long history of oppositional responses and lived as sensical in alternative, resistant sociality at the colonial difference" (p. 748). Within the dynamism of the oppressing ↔ resisting relation is a fractured locus where the colonial difference enables resistant articulations of coloniality. Resistant subjectivities at the colonial difference are always in a process of fighting colonial subjectification; their embodiment serves to challenge normative colonial logics and presumptions (p. 748).

Working toward decolonial feminism requires engaging "subjects in intersubjective collaboration and conflict, fully informed as members of Native American or African societies, as they take up, respond, resist, and accommodate to hostile invaders who mean to dispossess and dehumanize them" (Lugones, 2010, p. 748). Lugones (2010) writes:

> What I am proposing in working toward a decolonial feminism is to learn about each other as resisters to the coloniality of gender at the colonial difference, without necessarily being an insider to the worlds of meaning from which resistance to the coloniality arises. That is, the decolonial feminist's task begins by her seeing the colonial difference, emphatically resisting her epistemological habit of erasing it. Seeing it, she sees the world anew, and then she requires herself to drop her enchantment with "woman," the universal, and begins to learn about other resisters at the colonial difference. (p. 753)

Lugones calls for a kind of intersubjective witnessing that might be undertaken as a way to build deep coalitions across those who are oppressed through, and who resist, coloniality. Engaging plurality in ways of knowing and being across lines of difference resists the pervasive logics of elimination in settler colonial contexts. In her earlier work, Lugones (2003) developed the concept of world-traveling as a heuristic for engaging in coalitional building across the plurality of difference. Women of color and Indigenous communities in the U.S. settler colonial nation-state are often forced to travel in and out of "worlds" as a strategy of survival. World-traveling, Lugones (2003) argued, is a source for women of color to engage in contingent coalitional building with one another. In this way, it is an enactment of survivance. She writes: "It is movement toward coalition that impels us to know each other as selves that are thick, in relation, in alternative socialities, and grounded in tense, creative inhabitations of the colonial difference" (Lugones, 2010, p. 748).

When engaging with the communicative practices at the colonial difference, we must engage in intersubjective relation *with*. Building a decolonial feminism rests on the production of deep coalitions among those who are oppressed at various fractured loci within the colonial difference. It also means acknowledging the colonial power relations that structure the relationship between us as outsiders-critics to the Indigenous communities we engage with in this article who may be considered as our "object of study." The type of engaged reading Lugones (2010) is suggesting resists

> the social-scientific objectifying reading, attempting rather to understand subjects, the active subjectivity emphasized as the reading looks for the fractured locus in resistance to the coloniality of gender as a coalitional starting point. In thinking of the starting point as coalitional because the fractured locus is in common, the histories of resistance at the colonial difference are where we need to *dwell*, learning about each other. (p. 753)

Because self-determination and sovereignty are primary components of decolonial Indigenous organizing, we are challenged as critics to consider the role of authorial voice and how practices of criticism and scholarship may function, even unintentionally, to invalidate Indigenous self-determination and sovereignty. As scholars, we selected movements to engage with and discourses to discuss, but from our positions we recognize our responsibility to avoid speaking *for* them and instead engage *with* them as resisters in a manner that forefronts their agency and active subjectivity in the production of knowledges that resist coloniality.

Informed by Lugones (2010), we argue for witnessing as a decolonial heuristic for engaging *with* resistant subjectivities at the colonial difference as embodied theory and praxis of decolonial feminism. Building deep coalitions around a common interest in decolonization (Mohanty, 2003) or experiences at the colonial difference (Lugones, 2010) is crucial for building (contingent) coalitional resistance at the colonial difference (Tuck & Yang 2012, p. 35; Ghabra & Calafell, 2019; Veronelli, 2016). Rather than embodying a traditional position as authoritative critics of the communicative practices of Indigenous movements, we attempt throughout this article (admittedly imperfectly) to orient ourselves as *resisters with* and witnesses to how these specific Indigenous organizations envision and practice decolonial resistance to gendered violence. Their resistance is a praxis of theory building, and our article is an attempt to learn *with* each other as resisters to settler colonialism and the gendered violence that enables and is enabled by it. The heuristic of witnessing forefronts the agentive subjectivity and survivance of Indigenous bodies at the colonial difference.

In the analysis that follows, we seek to embody witnessing as an intersubjective heuristic to understand how decolonial feminist resistance to gendered violence is enacted in these specific Indigenous communities. We attempt to do so by weaving together the words, as well as descriptions of actions and approaches, of their various coalitional responses to gendered violence. Rather than paraphrasing or heavily translating the work of these Indigenous coalitions, we offer extended quotations and detailed descriptions of their organizing efforts and practices. By beginning from their words, stories, and practices, we select and emplace their discourses as fully as we can within their context, recognizing and respecting their presence and sovereignty over their narratives and stories.

We perform interpretive work that focuses on building connections between the various practices of decolonial resistance across the coalitions and contexts to look for "the fractured locus in resistance to the coloniality of gender as a coalitional starting point" (Lugones, 2010, p. 753). This includes seeking understanding of their active subjectivity and modes of survivance as they assert their presence, resist and defy logics of coloniality, and address various social and political issues within settler colonial contexts as dynamically relational and interconnected struggles. We structure our next section around the various overlapping strategies for how survivance, sovereignty, and self-determination are embodied in how these specific coalitions organize resistance to gendered violence.

We must recognize and reflect on our respective positionalities as we write in relation from a position of uncertainty about one another and these Indigenous communities working towards decolonization. As a White queer person raised in the continental United States, I—Ashley—am an outsider to the Indigenous communities and movements we forefront in our analysis. Yet as a non-conforming sexual and gendered subject, I question how epistemologies and frameworks for studying and resisting gendered violence rest on colonial logics and structures that replicate gender-dichotomization, racialization, and heterosexualism. And as a Chamoru, my position as an Indigenous woman does afford me access with my own community and many others. In this work I—Tiara—am an outsider to the movements we engage with in this article. From our positions as scholars and resisters, there is a witnessing relationship that occurs between us as authors and between each of us and the communities we engage with. In addition, as you will see within the following section of this article, several of the organizations also perform a kind of witnessing as an approach for building deep coalitions within their own communities through engagement as resisters with humility and respect.

While we are arguing for a commitment to decolonization in feminist critique and organizing around gendered violence, we recognize the various ways our approach can fail and how our engagement herein can unintentionally reinforce colonial relations. Given the deeply entrenched colonial ways of knowing that we—Ashley and Tiara—both inhabit and embody through our respective positionalities, aspects of our respective colonial difference as well as the groups we engage are fundamentally unintelligible and inaccessible to us. We center these movements in an attempt to give space and amplify their voices on their own terms, but because we are outsiders we do not have access to or the ability to understand or fully articulate their perspectives. We recognize it is impossible to completely represent the complexities of these movements in an article reliant solely upon their public communications via their Web sites and digital materials. Some of our decolonial feminist practice is also inaccessible to you as readers, as it occurred between the authors in engagement with each other across our difference through undocumentable conversations on the phone and in text messages while writing and constructing this article.

We are also conscious of how, in its most perverse and misunderstood manifestation, the call for feminist communication scholars to witness colonial difference may be misinterpreted as an invitation to go forth and consume the Other (Veronelli, 2016). Rendering Indigenous knowledges visible can occlude their oppositional and decolonial possibilities through appropriation (Barker, 2014), and we do not wish for this project to provide a generic template of decolonial feminist organizing that could be easily co-opted by primarily White Western movements to end sexual violence. The approaches used by these movements should also not be taken as representative of all Indigenous or decolonial feminist approaches to resisting gendered violence. Enacting witnessing as a mode of learning and resisting *with* cannot include appropriating Indigenous movement tactics and applying them to Western feminist movements in the U.S. settler colonial context (Morgensen, 2011). This would be an act of "loving, knowing ignorance" (Ortega, 2006) and arrogant perception (Frye, 1983; Lugones, 2003, p. 78). The colonial translation into a dominant Western movement would reenact colonial power relations by erasing indigeneity and with it the fractured locus of the colonial difference that enables a resistant articulation of coloniality through witnessing (Morgensen, 2011).

Doing decolonial feminist work requires embracing plurality at the colonial difference and accepting inaccessibility and incomprehensibility as we work toward decolonization (Veronelli, 2016). In the next section, we detail commonplace communicative practices across selected exemplars that seek to eradicate gendered violence through decolonization. We describe these decolonial approaches on their own terms—recognizing their specificity and locality—to provide examples of oppositional logics and embodied knowledges that address gendered violence as part of broader critiques of colonial violence and movements towards self-determination.

"It Starts With Us"

In consideration with Indigenous communities and peoples affected, we proceed here with a discussion of two groups—Missing and Murdered Indigenous Women (MMIW) and "Violence on the Land, Violence on our Bodies: Building an Indigenous Response to Environmental Violence" (VLVB)—as examples of decolonial feminist projects that center Indigenous culture, voice, experience, and knowledge. As the Web site for the Canadian MMIW coalitions acknowledges, coalitional community-based organizing between families and Indigenous peoples has been done for decades as a way of addressing missing and murdered Indigenous women ("It Starts With Us," n.d.). The issue of missing and murdered Indigenous women is not confined to single nation-states, but is a pervasive phenomenon in settler colonial locales. Bodily sovereignty and self-determination are central principles of MMIW organizing because missing and murdered Indigenous people are often ignored and forgotten by state agencies and dehumanized through media coverage (Brady, 2016). Organizing among themselves "when police and governments have failed to acknowledge, listen, or act despite Indigenous women, Two-Spirit and Trans people that have continued to disappear or be murdered," they articulate that "It Starts With Us" ("It Starts With Us," n.d.).

Since the 2000s, MMIW movements have mobilized more expansively through online exchanges among Indigenous communities in the United States and Canada (although we recognize that not all of the work of MMIW is accessible or documented in online archives). MMIW-USA formally formed in 2015 to address the problem of missing and murdered Indigenous women in the United States and maintains an active presence on Facebook where they publicize bulletins and organize events geared at engaging young women and girls, such as the Staying Sacred Protection Camp (MMIW-USA, 2019). MMIW in Canada and MMIW-USA both provide analyses of sexual and gendered violence as an expression of colonialism and emphasize the complex ways such violence contributes to precarity for Indigenous women, Two-Spirit, and trans people. Foregrounding sovereignty, their work resists colonial narratives that erase violence against Native peoples.

As a coalitional project, LandBodyDefense.org was launched in 2014 by the Women's Earth Alliance (WEA) and the Native Youth Sexual Health Network (NYSHN). The Web site houses VLVB, the coalition's primary initiative; it also includes an extensive report and activist toolkit to address gendered violence. The project is part of a multiyear initiative to document the ways that the sexual and reproductive health of Indigenous women, Two-Spirit individuals, and young people in North America are impacted by extractive industries (Landbodydefense.org, n.d.). The group is "also aimed to support their leadership in resisting environmental violence in their communities" (Landbodydefense.org, n.d.) As we witness its works and words, we respect that the activist toolkit exists primarily for Indigenous communities to organize themselves around environmental and gendered violence and is not designed for use by non-Native organizers or movements. However, we can learn with them as resisters of gendered violence at the colonial difference. Moving forward, we consider how MMIW and VLVB assert self-determination while negotiating modernity through a holistic and coalitional analysis of gendered violence that emphasizes sovereign bodies and sovereign stories. These negotiated dimensions are interconnected and mutually reinforcing, and we examine how the collective decolonial approaches of these grassroots organizations deepen coalitional opportunities and actions to address gendered violence in their communities.

Sovereignty and self-determination

Simpson (2015) explains sovereignty as "not just about land; it is also a spiritual and emotional, and intellectual space that spans back seven generations and that spans forward seven generations" (p. 19). Sovereignty is an embodied and collective concept that refers to self-determination of Indigenous peoples' "political cultures and non-hierarchical systems of governance" by maintaining relationships "through balance, care, and nurturing rather than coercion" (p. 19). In other words, sovereignty is the ability to make decisions about land, body, and mind. In this regard, the concept of embodied sovereignty in Indigenous communities is drastically different from how sovereignty is understood or deployed by settler colonial nation-states. Indigenous scholars have worked for their knowledge, ideas, and practices to be understood as theoretical on their own terms. This scholarship emphasizes embodied sovereignty and demonstrates how we might productively engage Indigenous theory as a decolonizing practice. Our witnessing emphasizes Indigenous scholars' own knowledge and praxis in conceptualizing embodied sovereignty as a practice of decolonization.

The Web site "It Starts With Us" serves as a hub for Canadian coalitions of the MMIW movement ("It Starts With Us," n.d.). Its name, "It Starts With Us," conveys an intentional starting point rather than an ending point for Indigenous communities and their orientation to gendered violence. As a community-led initiative, the coalition promotes "core values and beliefs about engaging in organizing around violence against Indigenous women." The Web site outlines the specific value of "Alternatives to the State," describing how its community "work is not funded by state-based agencies or in collaboration with law enforcement." The organization also recognizes that sometimes the police may be the "only option available to families or individuals" ("It Starts With Us," n.d.). Here, it admits the ambiguity of state relations and the reality of settler colonial contexts where communities are confronted by a problematic state apparatus that is also sometimes their only option for redress—where agency is present and also absent. VLVB acknowledges that police and state solutions are critical tools for addressing sexual and domestic violence, and it takes great care to articulate the various legal resources available. VLVB provides information on human trafficking policies, the Violence Against Women Act (VAWA) of 2013, and treaty rights, while also addressing the possible harms of such tools (Konsmo & Pacheco, 2016, pp. 83–84).

Throughout its Web site, the organization emphasizes sovereignty "over our bodies and stories" and asserts that Indigenous people are "capable of making decisions about their bodies, safety, and lives" ("It Starts With Us," n.d.). It also underscores ceremony and healing as acts of self-determination. For example, the Web site circulates community-defined narratives of the missing and murdered to practice communal healing and resist dominant mainstream media framings. "Public Mourning," the Web site explains, is "a political act that flies in the face of societal indifference and complicity" ("It Starts With Us," n.d.). The coalition's active pursuit of alternatives to the state shifts conceptions of sovereignty away from juridical state politics and onto healing, self-determination, and community-based public ceremony and stories that begin "with us." Its work illustrates collective embodied practices of sovereignty.

Its community database—created and run by a coalition of community groups—documents violent deaths of Indigenous women, Two-Spirit people, and trans people. The database specifically responds to the need for solutions that are outside of North American nation-state frameworks. As the Web site explains, "It's time for community to build our own structures independent of government and institutional funding" ("It Starts With Us," n.d.). The database is a "public" resource with a relatively private and autonomous community-based structure for decision making. Through community work that begins "with us," the database's purpose is "to honour our women and provide family members with a way to document their loved ones passing" ("It Starts With Us," n.d.). The first priority in their purpose statement illustrates responsibility to "our women" in a community-oriented perspective toward the missing and/or murdered. The project's second priority focuses on "family members" who may offer a means of documenting the passing of a loved one. In both elements of the database's publicly stated purpose, the project is explicitly turned inward to their common, holistic community. Through their expressed ownership of "our women," "family members," and "loved ones"—rather than nameless victims—their database ensures that Indigenous people are not only or exclusively labeled as "missing and murdered." The words anchor the importance of centering and recognizing indigeneity, rather than erasing or ignoring their names or their personhood.

VLVB also emphasizes alternatives to state-based or legal solutions by supporting self-determination and community-based organizing. VLVB argues that carceral and state-based solutions can often be circular responses to violence because "in their attempt to alleviate harm, [they] end up causing more harm" (Konsmo & Pacheco, 2016, p. 52). As their report explains:

> We also see the solutions to violence as coming from a resurgence of self-determination and consent for people over their bodies and the lands of which they are a part. This framework is an alternative to mainstream responses that often see the bodily impacts of environmental destruction as being solved by increased policing or criminalization, rather than community-based solutions developed by those most often impacted. This framework seeks to move beyond a carceral approach to the violence resulting from environmental destruction. It calls on us to meet communities with humility, respect, and a commitment to deep listening. We understand that each community is unique and may have different needs and struggles. We also recognize that gender-based violence (including environmental violence) disproportionately affects Indigenous women, youth and people who are part of the Two-Spirit, LGBTTIQQAiii community and those who are gender non-conforming (GNC) and non-binary. (Konsmo & Pacheco, 2016, p. 6)

The report foregrounds how multiple systems function together to create violence within colonialism and the U.S. settler state. In addition, by calling for "a commitment to deep listening" to various communities with humility and respect, they perform an ethical orientation toward coalitional building at the colonial difference that reflects the principles of witnessing.

The VLVB toolkit and report foreground the production of self and community through "transformative resurgence"—the process of offering more options for justice to Indigenous communities through community-based organizing. Their report explains that "this resurgence recognizes original teachings and cultural knowledge as spaces for transforming how Indigenous communities respond to violence (including state and environmental violence), while also supporting peer-led initiatives" (Konsmo & Pacheco, 2016, p. 52). Transformative resurgence emphasizes traditional healing practices and ceremony as crucial to responding to violence. The report adds that "while local, federal, and international laws and policies serve as critical tools [for addressing violence], Indigenous peoples are also designing more immediate solutions to reducing harm, which are culturally-safe and community-based" (Konsmo & Pacheco, 2016, p. 3).

Through their respective projects, both MMIW and VLVB demonstrate values and practices of self-determination that operate outside of state-based frameworks. Simultaneously, they acknowledge the necessity of utilizing state-based systems when there are no other options. Their work challenges settler colonialism and its associated violence that impacts Indigenous lands and lives; their Web sites and practices highlight that these processes are unsuccessful and are always resisted. Thus, their work is a diligent reminder that despite centuries of violence, the continued presence of Indigenous peoples proves that the structural project of colonialism has not worked completely (Simpson 2014, p. 12).

Sovereign bodies

Sovereignty is inextricably linked to the body. Indigenous women, LGBTQQIA+, and Two-Spirit people have continuously organized around the concept of "sovereign bodies" to address resistance to the biopolitics of settler colonialism (Morgensen, 2011). Sovereign bodies enact self-determination by making decisions about how to keep their bodies safe from violence, defining and identifying relationships and sexualities, and making decisions about their land, resources, and lives (Simpson, 2015, p. 20). Grounding sovereignty as embodied agency reframes community efforts toward governance and nation building and challenges heteropatriarchal elements of colonial power such as sexual violence.

Deer (2009) astutely explains that perpetrators of sexual assault and colonization both thrive on control and power over their victims and "sexual assault mimics the worst traits of colonization in its attack on the body, invasion of physical boundaries, and disregard for humanity" (p. 150). This link is made clearer when considering that "a survivor of sexual assault may experience many of the same symptoms—self-blame, loss of identity, and long-term depression and despair—as a people surviving colonization" (p. 150). Such impacts are further complicated by the U.S. federal government's jurisdiction over sexual assault cases on most American Indian reservations, which Deer (2009) explains as an act of "usurping governments, spirituality, and identity" (p. 150). State-based intervention, as indicated, is woefully inadequate at challenging colonial power structures or providing effective responses to violence against Indigenous peoples.

In contrast, organizations like VLVB convey that sovereign bodies must have self-determination over land, heart, mind, and body. VLVB frames different types of systemic violence, including environmental and gendered violence, as interconnected and mutually conditioning forms of settler colonialism (Konsmo & Pacheco, 2016, p. 60). VLVB's extensive report details what it witnessed from community-based Indigenous organizing taking place across Canada and the United States. Worth quoting at length, the first paragraph of the VLVB report details:

> For Indigenous communities in North America, the links between land and body create a powerful intersection—one that, when overlooked or discounted, can threaten their very existence. Extractive industries have drilled, mined, and fracked on lands on or near resource-rich Indigenous territories for decades. Although the economic gains have been a boon to transnational corporations and the economies of the U.S. and Canada, they come at a significant cost to Indigenous communities, particularly women and young people. Many of these communities are sites of chemical manufacturing and waste dumping, while others have seen an introduction of large encampments of men ("man camps") to work for the gas and oil industry. The devastating impacts of the environmental violence this causes ranges from sexual and domestic violence, drugs and alcohol, murders and disappearances, reproductive illnesses and toxic exposure, threats to culture and Indigenous lifeways, crime, and other social stressors. (Konsmo & Pacheco, 2016, p. 2)

VLVB directly opens its report by bringing to the forefront that "man camps," comprising often thousands of non-Native male workers, arrive to the land in order to profit from unsustainable extractive industries. They mark the "devastating impacts of the environmental violence" committed by the influx of these workers as deeply interwoven with acts of gendered violence committed against populations in these areas that often have little legal recourse. Given the interconnected relationship between environmental and gendered violence, VLVB advocates for "an Indigenous reproductive justice framework—examining issues of land and body as intimately connected" (Konsmo & Pacheco, 2016, p. 6). In fact, the final words concluding the report are in

Figure 1. "Our Bodies Are Not Terra Nullius" by Erin Marie Konsmo (from Konsmo & Pacheco, 2016).

bold: **"Everything connected to the land is connected to our bodies"** (Konsmo & Pacheco, 2016, p. 60).

VLVB's report also explores the connections between violence on land and body through Indigenous art and photography. For example, the report and toolkit feature artwork by the author of the toolkit, Erin Marie Konsmo (Figure 1). Her painting features the heading "Our Bodies Are Not Terra Nullius," written in a black banner running over the top of a torso wearing what appears to be a red tank top. As VLVB explains, *terra nullius* is "a Latin expression meaning 'nobody's land,' which was a legal concept used as justification that lands were empty and therefore open for colonization, conquering and resources extraction. This legal concept has also been used as justification that Indigenous bodies are empty and open for conquering" (Konsmo & Pacheco, 2016, p. 81). *Terra nullius* is a prefigured fantasy, which has worked simultaneously with the disavowal of Indigenous sovereignty in order to narrate and construct the nation-state. Behind the figure with the red tank top, there is a yellow background with ordered columns featuring symbols of fire, drilling lines, skull and crossbones, and biohazards. The figure's arms and hands are pointing down over and onto its stomach, with its fingers connecting in the middle to point toward the pelvic area.

The artwork also depicts a colonial ship positioned across the torso with the subject's hands creating a barrier between the ship and the pelvis. Drawn horizontally across the pelvis are images depicting extractive industries (smokestacks, industrial buildings, drilling rigs) and covering the subject's dark brown legs are oil barrels—as if buried in the body and also within the earth. The colonial ship and its charter course are depicted as a parallel to the imagery of extractive industry. In VLVB's activist toolkit, an activity encourages organizers to engage this art by asking workshop participants to explore the ways in which "Indigenous territories (water and land)" and Indigenous bodies "are considered to be empty" (Konsmo & Pacheco, 2016, p. 81). The concept of *terra nullius* is used in the toolkit to suture the struggles of body and land and to critique the processes of colonization that treat both land and body as empty and open for occupation. It is important to examine these relations of the terrain as they contribute to an understanding of how the disavowal of Indigenous sovereignty shapes nationalism and colonial violence, including gendered violence and environmental violence.

VLVB certainly makes efforts to publicize its initiative and uses images to illustrate the concept of *terra nullius* as part of its outreach with Indigenous activists who seek strategies for resistance within their own communities. For example, leading up to the inaugural week of action and the accompanying conference, VLVB invited people to take pictures of themselves touching the land directly with their hands and then share the photographs "on social media with a personal statement on the connection between our lands and bodies, or with the sample language below. Tag #LandBodyDefense and link to landbodydefense.org" (LandBodyDefense.org, 2016). The hashtag #LandBodyDefense embodies a dynamic relationality with community knowledge circulating through posts that emphasize connections between struggles.

Individuals engaged with the hashtag #LandBodyDefense and art from the toolkit on platforms such as Twitter and Instagram. For example, the NYSHN retweeted a photograph depicting four midwives at Standing Rock holding fists in the air with the caption "Midwives for Standing Rock!" (NativeYouthSexHealth, 2016). The retweet comments, "Shout out to @changingwomanin & the midwives at Standing Rock! Environmental Justice is #ReproJustice #NoDAPL #LandBodyDefense" (NativeYouthSexHealth, 2016). This post makes important connections among coalitional resistance to colonial relations that are normalized. Such connections consider how environmental injustice reproduces subjugation that is tied to racialized knowledges and investments in heteropatriarchal White sovereignty. While VLVB encouraged social media engagement, it is not stating that these online performances replace or stand in for embodied resistance. The coalition calls for solutions that are rooted in community/self-determination—at once enacting sovereignty over its bodies, lands, and lives. The posts provide messages of sovereign bodies circulating their own stories.

Sovereign stories

Indigenous movements that address gendered violence enact decolonization through the production of sovereign stories that engage oppositional knowledges and histories. These efforts challenge dominant public narratives of sexual violence that often dehumanize or erase Indigenous victims or reassert settler colonial structures. As a coalitional project that documents work from other Indigenous community-based organizers, VLVB centers the knowledge and experiences of those working on the ground to address environmental and gendered violence impacting their communities (Konsmo & Pacheco, 2016, p. 3). The very beginning of the report provides a map of North America that indicates the "sites of impact" or "the communities and territories of the people who shares their stories with this initiative" (Konsmo & Pacheco, 2016, p. ii).

Their report spotlights individuals or organizations working within their communities to eradicate violence on lands and bodies. It is in this way that the report is written as an intersubjective collaboration with various communities as *resisters with* in working toward decolonization. For example, the report highlights, among others, community organizer and Indigenous rights advocate Melina Laboucan-Massimo of the Lubicon Cree Nation in Little Buffalo, Alberta, Canada (Konsmo & Pacheco, 2016, p. 31). Much of her work has been to resist the "tar sands extraction and expansion in Alberta," but during that time she "has seen the impact" extractive industry "has had on the sexual health and safety of women" (Konsmo & Pacheco, 2016, p. 31). VLVB forefronts stories and practices of community organizers on the ground, and its efforts highlight sovereign stories that rearticulate the rights of Indigenous people through self-determination and self-government. Laboucan-Massimo explained to VLVB:

> The industrial system of resource extraction in Canada is predicated on systems of power and domination. This system is based on the raping and pillaging of Mother Earth as well as violence against women. The two are inextricably linked. With the expansion of extractive industries, not only do we see desecration of the land, we see an increase in violence against women. Rampant sexual violence against women and a variety of social ills result from the influx of transient workers in and around workers' camps. (qtd. in Konsmo & Pacheco, 2016, p. 31)

Reinforcing the relationship between environmental violence and gendered violence, the coalitions continuously focus on stories as more expansive means of enacting survivance and sovereignty.

The coalitional storytelling across the "It Starts With Us" Web site also resists narratives that foreclose on Indigenous sovereignty by engaging resistant subjectivities at the colonial difference. For example, the core values and beliefs section of "It Starts With Us" clearly articulates a desire to decolonize gender and sexuality through "unlearning homophobia and transphobia, supporting Two-Spirit, Trans, and gender non-conforming people" ("It Starts With Us," n.d.). By prioritizing the decolonization of gender/sexuality, the section shifts narratives surrounding gender-nonconforming individuals impacted by gendered violence. Such shifts reframe the coalition's sovereign stories to challenge the symbolic constitution of victimhood as only impacting women.

No More Silence (NMS), in partnership with NYSHN and Families of Sisters in Spirit (FSIS), works to maintain a community-led database of MMIW. The "It Starts With Us" Web site houses the database, and its coalitional approach reinforces the "understanding that no one can own this work" ("It Starts With Us," par. 2). The community-led database also highlights the need to "change the story" regarding MMIW by "resisting and shifting victim blaming approaches, languages and narratives about who can or does go missing or face violence" ("It Starts With Us," n.d.). Together, NMS,

FSIS, and NYSHN address reproductive and sexual health, rights, and justice in Canada and the United States. The expansive scope of their work also shares responsibility:

> We hope to be as transparent as possible—gathering information directly from family members who are open and consent to sharing, by searching and collaborating with existing regional lists created by community members who give consent to share their work, as well as digging through media reports and anecdotal evidence. ("It Starts With Us," n.d.)

This commitment to transparency and consent facilitates family involvement while also engaging communities to craft public approaches and negotiate publicity through their connections and work.

The "It Starts With Us" Web site also includes a Tributes section that provides space for families to "honour the lives of their loved ones through personal stories, photos or other important aspects of someone's life. We [MMIW] hope this will balance the death related details the media tends to over focus on" ("It Starts With Us," n.d.). The Tributes section of the database is maintained by FSIS and offers a space for families to write about their family members and reminding visitors that community can be built through the telling of "our stories." As FSIS explained:

> This is a chance to share how important your loved one was to you, and only you can do that, your contribution to the database is essential. Something that you can share with the world. This can be about witnessing our own history, family stories and creating oral history through storytelling even if that means learning about family history through the loss of loved ones. ("It Starts With Us," n.d.)

This description engages values of sovereignty over and capacity of stories to support one another in this work. The database and its framing embody intersubjective witnessing as a means of building coalitions among those impacted by violence.

The Tributes section includes clickable thumbnail images of particular family members and short descriptions that include facts such as the individuals' dates of birth, descriptions of their personalities and interests, and recent updates about their cases. At the bottom of the descriptions are "Read More" buttons that can be used to access additional resources, such as embedded videos and photographs provided by families and friends, and Web site links to media coverage about the individuals' murders or disappearances. The Tributes page also highlights a family member explaining the significance of these stories on the Web site:

> We don't want the media to speak about our family members. They always focus on facts and details about the bodies. We don't want the media using inaccurate and harsh language about our family members. We should be the ones creating the messages and language. We need to have a place to remember our family members and how we experienced them. Having a tribute section allows people to see who these people were, and that they were loved and valued. We can talk about how beautiful and special our family members were to us, whereas mainstream media can't, or won't do that. This is why families need this space to humanize our loved ones in ways that honours their stories and is accessible to families. (qtd. from "It Starts With Us," n.d.)

This family member asserts the need for self-determination over "creating the messages and language" used to "humanize our loved ones" and tell their stories on their own terms. This enactment of sovereignty over their stories reflects a decolonial approach to remembering the lives of family members. These tributes enable families to share memories and sovereign stories rather than only focusing on disappearance, death, or statistics that overwhelmingly disavow the bodies and lives of their family members. We witness and listen to the tellings of this family by paying close attention to the language and the ways in which the discourse ensures that Indigenous lives continue to be remembered on their own terms. The very existence of these stories is what makes them so important, as they are written responses to colonization that enact survivance by reimagining and reinforcing a presence of their loved ones instead of an absence. We reflect on how these stories hold the power to remake the world ("whereas, mainstream media can't, or won't"). Sovereign stories construct transformative possibilities for family members and loved ones who carry them on.

These tributes defy hierarchical and heteropatriarchal aspects of colonial control, as the family member clearly argues, through the telling of stories that challenge Indigenous erasure. Indeed, they exercise sovereignty over both the mechanisms of control that structure storytelling (by housing these archives on their own Web site) and the articulation of stories (by centering family narratives and language). By carving out a public space that is dynamic, interactive, and community led, the Tributes section of the Web site maintains a collective embodiment of self-determination and seriously "honouring the fact that Indigenous peoples are so much more than statistics" ("It Starts With Us," n.d.). In this way, the various MMIW organizations involved in "It Starts With Us" also act as *resisters with* and intersubjective witnesses to expansive notions of sovereignty practiced across coalitions.

Conclusion

In this article, we have argued that a commitment to decolonization is necessary when addressing gendered violence within settler colonial nation-states and that feminist communication scholars should engage in practices of critique that build toward a decolonial feminism sutured through deep coalitions with resisters at the colonial difference. Such an approach is critical for communication scholars who seek to understand the vexed manifestations of sexual violence within the context of colonization, White supremacy, and cisheteropatriarchy. We have centered the communicative practices of MMIW and VLVB as Indigenous movements that emphasize decolonization in addressing gendered violence as a coalitional starting point.

Without risking uncritical appropriation of these movements' methods and approaches, we offer several considerations for feminist communication scholars invested in decolonization: First, decolonial feminist approaches that address sovereignty are necessary, especially in the context of analysis and/or resistance to gendered violence. Second, our charge of taking decolonial feminism seriously provides cogent challenges to White Eurocentric critical approaches and methodologies in communication studies.

We have argued that challenging colonial logics is necessary to resist gendered violence in modernity. Both MMIW and VLVB demonstrate the necessity of decolonial feminist critique by treating colonialism as an ongoing process of structural violence and providing a holistic analysis of gendered violence at the intersections. For example, mainstream feminist organizing against sexual violence often relies on precarious claims for state protection (i.e., increased prosecution of rape or domestic violence). This type of organizing often justifies increased state violence and juridical control to maintain and regulate bodies, which is particularly complicated for Indigenous communities. In contrast, MMIW and VLVB balance an orientation of teaching and advocating to dismantle the colonial state while maintaining focus on community and self as a means of public and internal healing and organizing. The decolonial critique emerging from these coalitions deepens our understanding of the complexities of challenging settler colonial nation-states while also not relying entirely on state recognition or jurisdiction as the primary means of constituting liberation and social change (e.g., MMIW's community-led database; #LandBodyDefense). We witness how both movements encourage intrapolitical liberation through practices that center internal community solutions rather than seek change exclusively through state processes or legal frameworks (e.g., LandBodyDefense.org, 2016). MMIW and VLVB also emphasize the importance of decolonizing gender dichotomization and heteronormativity, providing alternatives to the state as a means of avoiding circular responses to violence, and enacting a decolonial politics of self-determination rooted in bodily sovereignty.

An important element of our decolonial approach in this article is also our embodiment of witnessing. Witnessing, we have argued, is a decolonial heuristic for engaging with resistant subjectivities at the colonial difference as embodied theory and praxis of decolonial feminism. Critical protocols for producing scholarship often demand the adoption of an authoritative critic voice, and in producing this article we continuously struggled with these expectations while prioritizing how we could embody an ethical relation between us as critics and the Indigenous communities and organizations we engage with in our writing. Such considerations challenge communication scholars to consider the role of authorial voice in critical practice as we work to build deep coalitions. We wanted to find approaches to discussing Indigenous organizers as agentive subjects whom we see ourselves as *resisters with* in the fight towards decolonization, not objects that we extract knowledge from or speak authoritatively for or about. In line with this commitment, we worked to radically de-center our voices as critics and center Indigenous knowledge about resisting gendered violence in settler colonial nation-states. Our witnessing privileges these groups' own calls that "It Starts With Us." This enactment of witnessing is the coalitional starting point for building a decolonial feminist resistance against gendered violence.

But in conversations while writing this article and responding to feedback from the editor and anonymous reviewers, we have reflected together on the impossibility of writing as outsiders to these Indigenous communities without performing a kind of extraction, appropriation, or erasure that replicates colonization. We asked ourselves: In practicing witnessing are we reenacting colonial relations of power as outsider-critics? What does it mean to form contingent coalitions and emerge as resisters with Indigenous communities in moving toward decolonization? As we worked throughout this process, we realized that asking and engaging these questions is a fundamental aspect of the process of building deep coalitions in decolonial feminist work. Enacting a politics of colonial resistance is understanding that our work sometimes is to unlearn, shift, and reframe what we have accepted as common sense when it is actually colonial imposition. This work entails challenging disciplinary norms, approaches, and methodologies.

It also means learning *with* resistant subjectivities at the colonial difference that there are dissident ways of knowing and being. As the authors of this article, we navigated our relation to MMIW and VLVB by challenging our critical practices as scholars, resisters, and active subjects at differing loci of colonial difference. We have tried, as Lugones (2010) suggests, to dwell and learn—from each other and from the work of MMIW and VLVB (p. 753).

I, Tiara, remember dwelling on this special issue call for papers on "The #MeToo Moment: A Rhetorical Zeitgeist" and thinking specifically about Indigenous/Native feminisms. I thought about how a zeitgeist is marked temporally, while settler colonialism is an ongoing structure, eschewing periodization. I considered how I navigate my positionality as an Indigenous feminist academic, working at an institution where campus statistics indicate that I am one of only eight Native American or Pacific Islander faculty. I have long worked and written with my Chamoru community, yet my commitments are also enriched by engaging with other communities that have similar and distinct struggles, such as MMIW and VLVB.

I, Ashley, remember coming to decolonial work through listening to friends and colleagues, including Tiara. Even now, I reflect and question whether I should write about Indigenous communities as a non-Native person, because the reproduction of colonial relations feels inevitable. But choosing to avoid doing the work of engaging *with* (no matter how imperfect) also feels like a copout—an easy way to circumvent the uncomfortable reality that I am implicated.

In various processes of coming to and writing this project, we have both felt disturbed and overwhelmed by the realization of settler colonial violence that persists—and no doubt will continue well after this article's publication.

Our analysis has been constructed in conversation with each other, as colleagues that embraced this article as part of a much larger process of collaboration and coalition to help us understand ways to address erasure, gendered violence, and settler colonialism that is also often alive and well in our discipline and in feminist spaces. Though it can be difficult to realize this, we considered how to *resist with* as a means of navigating these complexities, our own positions—Tiara's as an Indigenous academic and Ashley's as a queer White academic—living in distinct territories, with privileged jobs within the academy, and working and supporting struggles for decolonization.

Non-Natives can also *resist with* Indigenous populations, in part by listening and learning how to recognize practices of survivance, and by deepening a commitment to decolonization (Powell, 2002). The continuation of Indigenous practices in the coalitional efforts of MMIW and VLVB offers insight into a decolonial feminism that cuts against heteropatriarchy. This work communicates the names/lands/memories/lives of Native women and Two-Spirit, LGBTQQIA+ people to ensure that they are not merely labeled "missing and murdered," otherwise disappeared, or made into a statistic, if referenced at all. Through engaging in organizing that emphasizes bodily sovereignty and oppositional knowledges, these Indigenous groups enact a decolonial project deeply invested in caring for land, body, and subjectivity. Building a decolonial feminist resistance to gendered violence that understands bodies as anything but *terra nullius* begins with the articulation and witnessing of sovereignty and self-determination.

Acknowledgements

We wish to recognize the labor and autonomy of the Indigenous organizations and individuals we engage with in this article. We are grateful to learn with and from them in the fight to end colonization and gendered violence. We would also like to thank Lisa Flores, Logan Rae Gomez, Judy Rohrer, Kristen Hoerl, and the anonymous reviewers whose guidance and support was vital in developing this project.

ORCID

Ashley Noel Mack ⓘ http://orcid.org/0000-0002-4947-4288
Tiara R. Na'puti ⓘ http://orcid.org/0000-0002-7984-8308

References

Amnesty International. (2007). *Maze of injustice: The failure to protect indigenous women from sexual violence in the USA*. Retrieved from https://www.amnestyusa.org/pdfs/mazeofinjustice.pdf

Arvin, M., Tuck, E., & Morrill, A. (2013). Decolonizing feminism: Challenging connections between settler colonialism and heteropatriarchy. *Feminist Formations*, 25(1), 8–34. doi:10.1353/ff.2013.0006

Barker, J. (2014). The specters of recognition. In A. Goldstein (Ed.), *Formations of United States colonialism* (pp. 33–56). Durham, NC: Duke University Press.

Brady, M. J. (2016). Gender and state violence: Films that do justice to the issue of missing and murdered Indigenous people in Canada. *Feminist Media Studies*, 16(5), 918–922. doi:10.1080/14680777.2016.1213573

Burke, T. (2017, November 9). #MeToo was started for Black and Brown women and girls. They are still being ignored. *Washington Post*. Retrieved from https://www.washingtonpost.com/news/

Byrd, J. A. (2011). *The transit of empire: Indigenous critiques of colonialism*. Minneapolis: University of Minnesota Press.

Calafell, B. M. (2014). The future of feminist scholarship: Beyond a politics of inclusion. *Women's Studies in Communication*, 37(3), 266–270. doi:10.1080/07491409.2014.955436

Chakravartty, P., Kuo, R., Grubbs, V., & McIlwain, C. (2018). #CommunicationSoWhite. *Journal of Communication*, 68(2), 254–266. doi:10.1093/joc/jqy003

Chávez, K. R. (2015). Beyond inclusion: Rethinking rhetoric's historical narrative. *Quarterly Journal of Speech*, 101(1), 162–172. doi:10.1080/00335630.2015.994908

Coomaraswamy, R. (2001, July 27). *Review of reports, studies, and other documentation for the Preparatory Committee and the World Conference against racism, racial discrimination, xenophobia and related intolerance: Note by the Secretary-General* (A/CONF.189/PC.3/5). Retrieved from https://digitallibrary.un.org/record/446563/files/A_CONF.189_PC.3_5-EN.pdf

Crenshaw, K. (2018). Demarginalizing the intersection of race and sex: A Black feminist critique of antidiscrimination doctrine, feminist theory, and antiracist politics. *University of Chicago Legal Forum*, 1989(1), 139–167. Retrieved from https://chicagounbound.uchicago.edu/uclf/vol1989/iss1/8

de la Garza, S. A. (2019). No more magic mirrors: Confronting reflections of privileged feminisms in #MeToo. *Women and Language*, 42(1), 175–181. doi:10.34036/WL.2019.020

Deer, S. (2009). Decolonizing rape law: A native feminist synthesis of safety and sovereignty. *Wicazo Sa Review*, 24(2), 149–167. doi:10.1353/wic.0.0037

Deer, S. (2015). *The beginning and end of rape: Confronting sexual violence in Native America*. Minneapolis: University of Minnesota Press.

DeLisle, C. T. (2015). A history of Chamorro nurse-midwives in Guam and a "placental politics" for indigenous feminism. *Intersections: Gender and Sexuality in Asia and the Pacific*, 37. Retrieved from http://intersections.anu.edu.au/issue37/delisle.htm

Dougherty, C., & Calafell, B. M. (2019). Before and beyond #MeToo and #TimesUp: Rape as a colonial and racist project. *Women and Language*, *42*(1), 213–218. doi:10.34036/WL.2019.021

Frye, M. (1983). *The politics of reality: Essays in feminist theory*. New York, NY: Crossing Press.

Ghabra, H. S., & Calafell, B. M. (2019). Intersectional reflexivity and decolonial rhetorics: From Palestine to Aztlán. In R. García & D. Baca (Eds.), *Rhetorics elsewhere and otherwise: Contested modernities and decolonial visions* (pp. 62–84). Urbana, IL: National Council of Teachers of English.

Goeman, M. (2017). Ongoing storms and struggles: Gendered violence and resource exploitation. In J. Barker (Ed.), *Critically sovereign: Indigenous gender, sexuality, and feminist studies* (pp. 99–126). Durham, NC: Duke University Press.

Goeman, M. R., & Denetdale, J. N. (2009). Native feminisms: Legacies, interventions, and indigenous sovereignties. *Wicazo Sa Review*, *24*(2), 9–13. doi:10.1353/wic.0.0035

Gutierrez-Perez, R. (2019). Theories in the flesh and flights of the imagination: Embracing the soul and spirit of critical performative writing in communication research. *Women's Studies in Communication*, *41*(2), 404–415. doi:10.1080/07491409.2018.1551695

Hall, L. K. (2009). Navigating our own "sea of islands": Remapping a theoretical space for Hawaiian women and indigenous feminism. *Wicazo Sa Review*, *24*(2), 15–38. doi:10.1353/wic.0.0038

Hernández, L. H., & De Los Santos-Upton, S. (2018). *Challenging reproductive control and gendered violence in the Américas: Intersectionality, power, and struggles for rights*. Lanham, MD: Rowman & Littlefield.

"It Starts With Us." (n.d.). *Honouring the lives of missing and murdered indigenous women, girls, trans, and two-spirits*. Retrieved from http://itstartswithus-mmiw.com/

Jones, L. (2018, March 6). *What these women couldn't say publicly about Sherman Alexie until now*. Retrieved from http://www.kuow.org/post/what-these-women-couldn-t-say-publicly-about-sherman-alexie-until-now

Kauanui, J. K. (2008). *Hawaiian blood: Colonialism and the politics of sovereignty and indigeneity*. Durham, NC: Duke University Press.

Konsmo, E. M., & Pacheco, A. M. K. (2016). *Violence on the land, violence on our bodies: Building an indigenous response to environmental violence*. Toronto, Canada: Land Body Defense. Retrieved from http://landbodydefense.org/uploads/files/VLVBReportToolkit2016.pdf

Kuokkanen, R. (2015). Gendered violence and politics in indigenous communities: The cases of the aboriginal people in Canada and the Sámi in Scandinavia. *International Journal of Feminist Politics*, *17*(2), 271–288. doi:10.1080/14616742.2014.901816

LandBodyDefense.org. (2016). *Launch and Week of Action kit: Violence on the land, violence on our bodies: Building an indigenous response to environmental violence*. Retrieved from http://landbodydefense.org/uploads/files/VLVB%20Week%20of%20Action%20Kit%202016.pdf

LandBodyDefense.org. (n.d.). *For land and body*. Retrieved from http://landbodydefense.org/home

Lehavot, K., Walters, K. L., & Simoni, J. M. (2009). Abuse, mastery, and health among lesbian, bisexual, and two-spirit American Indian and Alaska Native women. *Cultural Diversity and Ethnic Minority Psychology*, *15*(3), 275–284. doi:10.1037/a0013458

Lugones, M. (2003). *Pilgrimages/peregrinajes: Theorizing coalition against multiple oppressions*. New York: Rowman & Littlefield.

Lugones, M. (2007). Heterosexualism and the colonial/modern gender system. *Hypatia*, *22*(1), 186–209. doi:10.1111/j.1527-2001.2007.tb01156.x

Lugones, M. (2010). Toward a decolonial feminism. *Hypatia*, *25*(4), 742–759. doi:10.1111/j.1527-2001.2010.01137.x

Mack, A. N., Bershon, C., Laiche, D. D., & Navarro, M. (2018). Between bodies and institutions: Gendered violence as co-constitutive. *Women's Studies in Communication*, *41*(2), 95–99. doi:10.1080/07491409.2018.1463765

Mack, A. N., & McCann, B. J. (2018). Critiquing state and gendered violence in the age of #MeToo. *Quarterly Journal of Speech*, *104*(3), 329–344. doi:10.1080/00335630.2018.1479144

Missing and Murdered Indigenous Women USA. (2019). Retrieved from https://www.facebook.com/mmiwusa/

Mohanty, C. T. (2003). *Feminism without borders: Decolonizing theory, practicing solidarity.* Durham, NC: Duke University Press.

Morgensen, S. L. (2011). *Spaces between us: Queer settler colonialism and indigenous decolonization.* Minneapolis: University of Minnesota Press.

Na'puti, T. R., & Rohrer, J. (2017). Pacific moves beyond colonialism: A conversation from Hawai'i and Guåhan. *Feminist Studies, 43*(3), 537–547. doi:10.15767/feministstudies.43.3.0537

National Collaborating Centre for Indigenous Health. (2016, May). *An introduction to the health of two-spirit people: Historical, contemporary, and emergent issues.* Retrieved from https://www.nccih.ca/495/An_Introduction_to_the_Health_of_Two-Spirit_People__Historical,_contemporary_and_emergent_issues.nccah?id=156

NativeYouthSexHealth. (2016, October 12). Shout out to @changingwomanin & the midwives at Standing Rock! Environmental Justice is #ReproJustice #NoDAPL #LandBodyDefense [Tweet]. Retrieved from https://twitter.com/NYSHN/status/786201252401147905

Onwuachi-Willig, A. (2018). What about #UsToo? The invisibility of race in the #MeToo movement. *Yale Law Journal Forum, 128,* 105–120. Retrieved from https://www.yalelawjournal.org/forum/what-about-ustoo

Ortega, M. (2006). Being lovingly, knowingly ignorant: White feminism and women of color. *Hypatia, 21*(3), 56–74. doi:10.1111/j.1527-2001.2006.tb01113.x

Perry, I. (2018). *Vexy thing: On gender and liberation.* Durham, NC: Duke University Press.

Powell, M. (2002). Rhetorics of survivance: How American Indians use writing. *College Composition and Communication, 53*(3), 396–434. doi:10.2307/1512132

Rosay, A. B. (2016, May). *Violence against American Indian and Alaska Native women and men: 2010 findings from the National Intimate Partner and Sexual Violence Survey* (Research report). Washington, DC: National Institute of Justice. Retrieved from https://www.ncjrs.gov/pdffiles1/nij/249736.pdf

Rowe, A. C. (2019). A long walk home: Decolonizing #MeToo. *Women and Language, 42*(1), 169–174. doi:10.34036/WL.2019.019

Rowe, A. C., & Tuck, E. (2017). Settler colonialism and cultural studies: Ongoing settlement, cultural production, and resistance. *Cultural Studies ↔ Critical Methodologies, 17*(1), 3–13. doi:10.1177/1532708616653693

Sandoval, C. (2000). *Methodology of the oppressed.* Minneapolis: University of Minnesota Press.

Sholock, A. (2012). Methodology of the privileged: White anti-racist feminism, systematic ignorance, and epistemic uncertainty. *Hypatia, 27*(4), 701–714. doi:10.1111/j.1527-2001.2012.01275.x

Shome, R. (2016). Gender, nation, and colonialism: Twenty-first century connections. *Cultural Studies ↔ Critical Methodologies, 16*(4), 347–350. doi:10.1177/1532708616640007

Simpson, L. B. (2015). The place where we all live and work together: A gendered analysis of "sovereignty." In S. N. Teves, A. Smith, & M. H. Raheja (Eds.), *Native studies keywords* (pp. 18–24). Tucson: University of Arizona Press.

Smith, A., & Kauanui, J. K. (2008). Native feminisms and the nation-state. *American Quarterly, 60,* 241–249. doi:10.1353/aq.0.0001

Stewart-Harawira, M. (2007). Practicing indigenous feminism: Resistance to imperialism. In J. Green (Ed.), *Making space for Aboriginal feminism* (pp. 124–139). London, United Kingdom: Zed Books.

Tambe, A. (2018). Reckoning with the silences of #MeToo. *Feminist Studies, 44*(1), 197–203. doi:10.15767/feministstudies.44.1.0197

Taylor, C. (2009). Health and safety issues for Aboriginal transgender/two spirit people in Manitoba. *Canadian Journal of Aboriginal Community-Based HIV/AIDS Research, 2,* 63–84. Retrieved from https://caan.ca/wp-content/uploads/2012/05/Health-and-Safety-Issues-for-Aboriginal-TransgenderTwo-Spirit-People-in-Manitoba.pdf

Taylor, T. L. (2019). Dear nice White ladies: A womanist response to intersectional feminism and sexual violence. *Women and Language, 42*(1), 187–190. doi:10.34036/WL.2019.022

Trask, H. (1996). Feminism and indigenous Hawaiian nationalism. *Signs, 21*(4), 906–916. doi:10.1086/495125

Trinh, T. M. (1989). *Woman, native, other: Writing postcoloniality and feminism*. Bloomington: Indiana University Press.

Tuck, E., & Yang, K. W. (2012). Decolonization is not a metaphor. *Decolonization: Indigeneity, Education, and Society, 1*(1), 1–40. Retrieved from https://jps.library.utoronto.ca/index.php/des/article/view/18630

Turtle Talk. (2018, September 26). #MeToo in Indian Country: A short and incomplete collection of news stories [Blog post]. Retrieved from https://turtletalk.wordpress.com/2018/09/26/metoo-in-indian-country-a-short-and-incomplete-collection-of-news-stories/

Veronelli, G. (2016). A coalitional approach to theorizing decolonial communication. *Hypatia, 31*(2), 404–420. doi:10.1111/hypa.12238

Vimalassery, M., & Pegues, J. H., & Goldstein, A. (2016). Introduction: On colonial unknowing. *Theory and Event, 19*(4). Retrieved from muse.jhu.edu/article/633283.

Vimalassery, M., Pegues, J. H., & Goldstein, A. (2017). Colonial unknowing and relations of study. *Theory and Event, 20*(4), 1042–1054. Retrieved from https://muse.jhu.edu/article/675631

Wanzer, D. A. (2012). Delinking rhetoric, or revisiting McGee's fragmentation thesis through decoloniality. *Rhetoric and Public Affairs, 15*(4), 647–657. Retrieved from muse.jhu.edu/article/490122

Yep, G. A. (2010). Toward the de-subjugation of racially marked knowledges in communication. *Southern Communication Journal, 75*(2), 171–175. doi:10.1080/10417941003613263

Isolating Structures of Sexual Harassment in Crowdsourced Data on Higher Education

Tiffany A. Dykstra-DeVette and Carlos Tarin

ABSTRACT
This analysis of Karen Kelsky's (founder of a blog called *The Professor Is In*) crowdsourced data on sexual harassment in higher education describes the communication processes involved in the widespread isolation and "chilling effect" of inadequate structural responses to sexual harassment. Through the lens of structuration theory, the data demonstrate how communicative processes of isolation are appropriated throughout higher education. The analysis highlights two themes in the data that demonstrate the role of (1) networks and professionalization and (2) the structural estrangement from agency in the (re)production of isolation and organizational exit. Finally, the analysis identifies resignification and participation in the crowdsourced survey as potentially empowering acts of resistance.

On December 1, 2017, Karen Kelsky launched "A Crowdsourced Survey of Sexual Harassment in the Academy" as a way of documenting the frequency and severity of sexual misconduct in higher education. Kelsky, a former professor and founder of a blog titled *The Professor Is In*, explained that the goal of the survey was to "allow victims to find a safe way to anonymously report their experience of sexual harassment … [and] for the academy as a whole to begin to grasp the true scope and scale of this problem in academic settings" (2017, para. 4). The survey instrument, a simple Google form, asked respondents to provide information such as status of the perpetrator, the institutional response, the impact of the harassment on health, career, and life choices. Beyond asking about "what happened and when," the survey focused on immediate and long-term consequences. The survey became a viral sensation; within days, Kelsky's survey had amassed several hundred responses with many pointing to systemic and institutional failures. At the time of this writing, the survey has been completed by nearly 2,400 respondents ($n = 2,386$). In this article, we take up the responses to Kelsky's crowdsourced survey as a way of understanding the organizational dynamics that undergird sexual harassment and misconduct in academia. As movements like #MeToo and #TimesUp continue to gain traction and expose the commonality and pervasiveness of sexual harassment, we contend that Kelsky's survey is an invaluable resource that can critically transform institutional responses.

Sexual harassment in higher education is a widespread and pernicious phenomenon. In fact, a recent report by the National Academies of Sciences, Engineering, and Medicine (2018) found that only the military outpaces higher education as the employment sector with a higher rate of reported sexual harassment incidents. Harassment is decidedly a concern for communication scholars. Beyond the harrowing accounts of harassment by communication scholars like Carol Stabile (2017) and Annie Hill (2018), who described their personal experiences at the University of Pittsburgh and University of Minnesota, respectively, sexual harassment constitutes one facet of what some have termed "the dark side of communication" (see Lutgen-Sandvik & Sypher, 2010; Griffin & O'Leary-Kelly, 2004; Spitzberg & Cupach, 2007). Sexual harassment is a structural problem (re)produced by toxic workplace culture and a failure of organizational policy to adequately curtail harmful behaviors.

Given these realities, our focus in this article is on the institutional and organizational dynamics that enable and constrain responses to sexual harassment in academia. We draw on structuration theory (Giddens, 1984) to make sense of how rules and resources in higher education work to communicatively constitute the relational dynamic of sexual harassment and, more specifically, how these system elements work to silence survivors and reinforce normalization of misconduct in the workplace, resulting in isolation and organizational exit. Kelsky's survey (2017) has provided a salient source of data for interrogating structurating communication patterns given that respondents were able to articulate their own experiences, including how institutional mechanisms limited possible recourse and tacitly reproduced oppressive structures. This work extends research on the normalization of sexual harassment in higher education (Strine, 1992; Clair, 1993a; Dougherty & Smythe, 2004) by providing a structurational account of routinized and distanciated communication practices that reinforce norms and practices surrounding networking and professionalism, estrangement from agency, and resignification.

Our argument in this article is twofold. First, we contend that organizational and institutional structures obfuscate the reality and commonality of sexual harassment in academia, isolating targets from resources and alienating them from their own agency, thereby re-entrenching the widespread, tacit acceptance of these problematic behaviors. Second, we argue that projects like Kelsky's survey point to transformative possibilities for intervention by challenging institutional norms and creating communities that legitimize survivors' voices through shared commonality and public acknowledgment. While merely providing an outlet for shared experiences will not transform social and institutional structures that enable misconduct, the data give us reason to be hopeful that crowdsourced projects like Kelsky's can contribute to the dismantling of widespread communication processes that enable sexual misconduct to proliferate in settings like higher education.

In analyzing the responses, we begin by situating this work within the context of structuration theory and related research on the rules and resources that enable sexual harassment. Next, we detail the methods used to identify consistent themes and patterns in the survey responses. We identify several salient structurating processes that (re)produce harassment via *networking and professionalization* and *estrangement from agency*, which draw on resources, rules and norms, and agency in particular ways. Finally, we conclude by discussing the practical and theoretical implications for approaching sexual harassment in higher education contexts.

Structuration theory

Structuration theory (ST) is a broad social theory derived primarily from the work of Giddens (1984). The theory is often used to describe the complex interplay between social systems and individual agency as a way of recursively organizing and sustaining social processes. ST has been used extensively in organizational communication since the 1980s and, as McPhee, Poole, and Iverson (2013) discussed, structurational approaches have been used to study a variety of communicative phenomena, such as identity and identification, organizational climate and culture, decision making, and institutional impacts on organizations (p. 75). At its core, ST is interested in explaining how routine interactions in social systems persist across space and time in order to communicatively constitute organizational life. As Canary and Tarin (2017) clarified, "ST centralizes communicative interaction as the defining element of social institutions and organizations insofar as these social systems are constitutively and perpetually (re)created through discourse and meaning" (p. 2282). Despite widespread use of the theory in contemporary organizational communication scholarship, ST has not yet been used as an analytic framework for interpreting the contours of sexual harassment. Following Canary (2010), we draw on the structuration approach as a way of understanding emergent contradictions as productive sites of meaning where policy, knowledge, discourse, and human experience intersect.

A central concept of ST that is useful for our analytic aims in this article is the duality of structure. According to Giddens (1984), the duality of structure assumes that the "constitution of agents and structures are not two independently given sets of phenomena, a dualism, but represent a duality ... [that is,] the structural properties of social systems are both medium and outcome of the practices they recursively organize" (p. 25). Unlike other social theories that place an overemphasis on either structural properties or human agency, the duality of structure posits that the production and reproduction of structures is an interactional accomplishment by which human agents draw on or are constrained by system elements such as rules and resources (Canary & Tarin, 2017). Within ST, rules are understood as principles or routines that guide behavior and activity. By contrast, resources are anything that facilitates activity or interaction and can be either material (such as budgets) or nonmaterial (such as knowledge shared within the social system). As McPhee et al. (2013) demonstrated, "As actors draw on rules and resources to participate in a system, they enact and sustain these structures as part of the ongoing organization of the system, thereby reproducing these structures" (p. 76). In the context of sexual harassment, the duality of structure can be meaningfully used to explain how system elements constrain possibilities for action, thereby reproducing and normalizing problematic activities or behaviors. For instance, widespread cultural beliefs (i.e., constraining resources) in organizations may dissuade survivors from seeking recourse (i.e., through system rules such as policy), thereby perpetuating tacit acceptance of a culture of silence.

Given that structures are (re)produced by (inter)action in complex social systems, ST places a significant emphasis on agency. Giddens (1984) defined agency as concerning the "events of which an individual is the perpetrator, in the sense that the individual could, at any phase in a given sequence of conduct, have acted differently" (p. 9). Following Foucault, Giddens asserted that all actors in a social system have some degree of agency and power, although the ability to act is often constrained by rules and resources. Moreover, ST posits that actors rarely resist social structures because they are engaged in a constant process of reflexive monitoring that "is a chronic feature of everyday action and involves conduct not just of the individual but also of others" (Giddens, 1984, p. 5). Put differently, agency is typically used to recursively perpetuate system features because routinization provides a sense of ontological security, thereby rendering the possibility of acting against structures to be a particularly risky endeavor. Agents can develop a sense of practical consciousness that enables them to act purposefully, however.

The expansive view of agency articulated in ST is crucial for understanding how sexual harassment becomes institutionalized and routinized in day-to-day practice. While all survivors may have the ability speak out against perpetrators in theory, their ability to act may be constrained by rules and resources acting against them in social systems. Moreover, given the hierarchical nature of most contemporary organizations, resisting the durée of day-to-day life may have unintended consequences that "systematically feedback to be the unacknowledged conditions of further acts" (Giddens, 1984, p. 8).

We proceed with the view that Kelsky's survey is significant precisely because it highlights how rules, resources, agential constraints, and practical consciousness typically work concertedly to limit action. In providing a crowdsourced mechanism for speaking about individual experiences, the survey illuminates structurational features while also providing a unique platform for resistance that is informed by the social milieu in the era of the #MeToo movement. In the next section, we situate Kelsky's project within the larger scholarly conversation about the theorization of sexual harassment as a communicative phenomenon.

Structurating sexual harassment

Sexual harassment and gender discrimination have become embedded in the symbolic resources and communication practices that constitute organizations. Consequently, we use *structurating* to describe the dynamic and ongoing process of organizing around and amidst sexual harassment. Approaching sexual harassment as a discursive practice exposes the ways that "micro-level exchanges support the macro-level system and the macro-level system legitimates acts of sexual harassment against individuals" (Mumby & Clair, 1997, p. 195). This approach understands the practice, meaning, and constitutive force of sexual harassment as arising through discourse and as always playing an explicitly political role (Wood, 1992). Communication research addressing workplace sexual harassment is diverse, employing feminist standpoint theory (Dougherty, 1999; Quinn, 1993), ideology critique (Scarduzio & Geist-Martin, 2010), linguistic and conversational analysis (Keyton & Menzie, 2007), organizational culture and sensemaking approaches (Dougherty & Smythe, 2004), and intersectional and critical race theory (Forbes, 2009; Chen, 1997). For the purposes of this article, the following review assembles research addressing the ways that sexual harassment is entrenched in organizational structures through persistent, enduring communication patterns surrounding policies, positions of authority, and agency.

Policies

The expectation that targets follow "procedure" and report harassment is common. However, this is complicated by research suggesting communication practices preclude the use and effectiveness of organizational policy (Kirby & Krone, 2002; Dougherty & Goldstein Hode, 2016). Policy interpretations are culturally specific, and their application can contradict organizational norms (Dougherty & Goldstein Hode, 2016). Reporting may threaten the interests of the target or may be discouragingly inaccessible and ineffective. Policy and procedural discourse of "not pressing charges" perpetuate the myth that men cannot be harassed and that women who report later are either lying or exaggerating the severity of the situation (Scarduzio & Geist-Martin, 2010). In this way, discourse structures the availability and utility of organizational policies, determining who is able to access them and at what cost (Kirby & Krone, 2002; Buzzanell & Liu, 2005; Cowan, 2011).

Further, norms that reproduce structures of sexual harassment include oppressive rhetorical and discursive patterns. For instance, framing devices are "rhetorical or discursive practices that define or assign interpretation to the social event by the actor or actors" (Clair, 1993b, p. 118). These framing devices can sequester narratives of sexual harassment or reinforce dominant gender ideology, or they can challenge and resist hegemonic systems of power. Frames can de/limit or recontextualize the experiences of harassment through the universalization of dominant interests, characterizations of the harassment as a misunderstanding, reification or normalization, trivialization, denotative hesitancy or lack of knowledge, through public/private framing; and referencing the mystification of sexual harassment by relegating it to the interpersonal level (Clair, 1993a, p. 121). While it may often be attributed to "a few, dirty old men" (Hickson, Grierson, & Linder, 1991, p. 112), this construction of sexual harassment in higher education abdicates the organization of its role and responsibility to address it while concealing the legal and financial stakes.

Positional power

The authority derived from a harasser's or a target's position within the organization or disciplinary network impacts the likelihood of reporting and the ability to resist or challenge harassment (Forbes, 2009). Kroløkke's (1998) research on communication strategies in response to sexual harassment found that success and safety, often in the form of tenure, predict more assertive responses. Conversely, when the harasser is outside of the chain of organizational command, such as when nurses are harassed by patients, there are fewer organizational mechanisms for discipline (McGuire, Dougherty, & Atkinson, 2006). Disciplinary networks may provide positions of power to harassers that exist beyond the authority of their own universities. In this way, grievance processes that treat single offenses through informal resolution fail to punish repeat offenders for cumulative offenses (Kihnley, 2000). In the same way that sexual harassment is experienced as both a personal injustice and an organizational failure (Scarduzio & Geist-Martin, 2010), meso-level networks may also be held accountable for their role in (re)producing structures of harassment.

Finally, it is clear that norms and organizational culture play an important role in perpetuating sexual harassment. An "organizational conspiracy of silence" effectively condones harassment (Conrad & Taylor, 1994, p. 4; Gardner, 2009), while sexualized work environments can make it more difficult to identify sexual harassment (Keyton & Rhodes, 1999). Forbes (2002) described how the "lack of organizational scrutiny of this phenomenon potentially leads to the unconscious construction of a more hegemonic patriarchal system to which both women and men contribute" (p. 270). Silencing through normalization and a lack of scrutiny constrains possibilities for resistance. On the other hand, silence can also be a way of drawing on one's agency to influence the situation by choosing not to engage harassers (Forbes, 2009). In this way, not reporting or responding can challenge and/or perpetuate sexual harassment, depending on positional power.

Methods

We began with a research question: How does communication embed structures of sexual harassment within institutions of higher education? After initial readings and discussions of the data, ST continued to be a useful sensitizing concept throughout the process and thus guided the researchers at every stage of the analysis. The study proceeded in three steps: First, we negotiated access to the data set. Then we engaged in first-level, descriptive coding. Finally, we conducted analytical coding that connected first-level codes and memos with key tenets of ST. While the qualitative approach taken in this study focuses less on frequency and categories of harassment, it does attempt to identify the "interplay among elements that contribute to defining and to describing sexual harassment" (Keyton & Menzie, 2007, p. 101). This study takes seriously the detailed descriptions of the events, responses, and impacts as recalled by the survivors, while referring back to the original research questions to focus the analysis on ways that communication creates and perpetuates structures that enable and constrain sexual harassment.

Data collection and sampling

The data were collected via Kelsky's wide network sample (Lindlof & Taylor, 2017). As the founder and president of the advice Web site *The Professor Is In*, Kelsky has a significant presence online through her blog, Twitter, Facebook, and other social media platforms. She has granted personal permission to use the publicly available data for research purposes. Along with the link to the survey and results, the accompanying message explains that Kelsky wished to provide people in higher education who have experienced sexual harassment a safe place to report in the hopes that "the academy as a whole [can] begin to grasp the true scope and scale of this problem in academic settings" Kelsky, 2017, para. 4). All participants were warned in bold letters before the link that the data would be public and that they might not wish to use identifying information.

Crowdsourcing has both limitations and advantages. Narrative reports of sexual harassment are not often collected in an interactive or dialogic format (Keyton & Menzie,

2007). This data set is unique for a few reasons. First, Kelsky challenged nondialogic norms by selectively replying to entries, offering her time and resources. Second, the open crowdsourced format allowed the survey to be linked and shared through various social media platforms, amassing a large number of responses and providing users with the option of reviewing other stories on the Web site after the survey was completed. While anonymous crowdsourced data prevented clarification and private follow-up conversations, such data may also make naming and otherwise private information more easily accessible by mitigating the risk of retaliation.

Data analysis

The research question directed us to look for enduring organizational features that could account for sexual harassment across the diverse higher education environments described in the data. While we approached the data with ST as a sensitizing concept, we remained open to emergent explanations. Early memos reflected themes such as capability constraints, resources, norms, and power. It was during initial readings and memoing that ST was chosen as a useful theoretical lens. Data analysis proceeded in three phases: (1) thorough, close reads of the data, (2) first-cycle, descriptive-level coding, and (3) second-cycle, analytical coding (Saldaña, 2013). During the initial stage, we engaged in memo writing and conferencing to tease out analytic themes of structuration and sexual harassment. Upon completion of data collection and before we began the second phase of data analysis, we discussed the memos, familiarized ourselves with emergent themes and observations, and clarified any uncertainty in the meaning of the data. During the second and third phases of analysis, data were organized and coded in Excel. Data were broken into natural responses resulting from each questionnaire response to ensure the fidelity of the interpretation (Charmaz, 2006). First-cycle, descriptive-level coding identified major "structures and processes" of sexual harassment in higher education, while second-cycle, analytical coding reflected on their "causes and consequences," which in this case was their "embeddedness" in institutional processes (Saldaña, 2013, p. 15). At this point a codebook was established, listing key codes, definitions, and examples to serve as a reference for code checking and to keep both researchers in agreement (Tracy, 2013). In the final phase of data analysis, second-cycle coding processes engaged in hierarchical coding to link and group patterns in the first-cycle codes (Charmaz, 2006; Tracy, 2013). Hierarchical coding involves "systematically grouping together various codes under a hierarchical umbrella category" (Tracy, 2013, p. 195). In this case, these umbrella codes were networking and professionalization, estrangement, and resignification. Smaller themes like normalization and mistrust were then connected to broader structurating processes.

Structural isolation

Building on research addressing the normalization and narratives of sexual harassment in higher education (Strine, 1992; Clair, 1993a; Wood, 1992; Dougherty & Smythe, 2004; Clair, Chapman, & Kunkel, 1996), responses reflected a chorus of voices (Clair et al., 1996, p. 243) describing the isolation and alienation they experienced, with comments such as, "I felt very lonely during this process"; "[I] felt isolated from [the] department and cohort"; "I felt like an outsider in my department"; and "I isolated myself. I doubt my ability." The results reflect themes that were salient in their repetition and heuristic significance, reflecting "institutionalized features of social systems" (Giddens, 1984, p. 86) that are continually reconstituted across space and time throughout higher education. This analysis explores how isolation results from structurating communication processes, including (1) cordoning off networks and professional resources and (2) estranging survivors from their own agency by fostering uncertainty, such as the "imposter syndrome" routinely mentioned by respondents. Normative practices, rules, and ideas about sexual harassment structure the isolation of survivors by precluding or obstructing access to both collective (professional networks, mentoring, letters of recommendation) and individual (loss of employment, imposter syndrome) resources. These processes become routinized and appropriated across activities and disciplines (Giddens, 1984).

The first section addresses the rules, norms, and resources involved in networking and professionalization that function to regulate and constitute isolating social practices through the reorganization of networks, personal rules stemming from mistrust (e.g., "Don't work with men"), and the normalization of sexual harassment. The second section identifies the ways that targets are estranged from their own agency through a loss of employment, the threat of retaliation, uncertainty and the feeling of inadequacy, or "imposter syndrome" (Fotaki, 2013, p. 1267).

The Appendix details the frequency of these thematic categories in the crowdsourced survey. The final section describes the way that respondents directly challenged their loss of agency through resignification by drawing on their experiences to construct themselves as resources for other survivors.

Networking and professionalization

One of the major consequences of sexual harassment and misconduct is isolation through communication practices regarding networking and professionalization. In this section, we focus on structurating processes within networks and professionalization practices. In all, 38% of respondents in the survey ($n = 907$) reported some loss of resources as a result of their experiences. We argue that isolation is a structurating process in which the deployment of rules and resources recursively organizes practice(s) so as to normalize and enable sexual misconduct in higher education. Being cordoned off from networks and professional resources was the most prevalent theme expressed by respondents in Kelsky's survey. In particular, we identified three overarching regulatory features: reorganization of networks, (self-imposed) personal rules stemming from mistrust, and the discursive normalization of sexual harassment that reified the alienation and isolation through a loss of professional opportunity.

Reorganizing networks

Many of the respondents in the survey indicated their experiences shaped their decision to work with (or discontinue working with) certain professors, withdraw from departments or professional associations, and eliminate or pursue opportunities for research. One person replied, "I've seen women in academia change institutions to get away from the male dominance of power; which in some instances involved changing into disciplines that are more female-driven." Sometimes organizations will intervene to reorganize networks in an attempt to address gender disparity with unintended consequences: "[T]his was in a physics department with very few female students, and it seemed the department had organized it so the female students were evenly distributed among the TA groups. They probably meant well by this but it meant I was the only woman around most of the time." Women may be experiencing well-intentioned structures as isolating systems that reorganize their networks in disadvantageous ways.

Conferences and professional events further structurate isolation even after survivors leave that particular place by cordoning off networks that could be more familiar, more receptive, and more trusting of new professional relationships. As one respondent stated, "I want to be more active in my field but I don't want to interact with him at conferences, and he is reasonably well-known in my field now and continuing to grow in prominence." Another respondent recalled a story about when her "graduate advisor (another older male) wore speedos to seduce women in a hot tub at a conference." One reported that at their largest disciplinary conference, "I was unable to network with anyone because he was trying to interfere with me the entire time. I had to avoid my own diss[ertation] director's session. I ended up avoiding him by hiding off in a corner with a couple and their toddler during the final reception." In one example of this theme, a respondent described having to "start a new PhD and make new networks from scratch, I think twice when I go to conferences where this man might be (when I really shouldn't have to), I worry about when I meet people who might collaborate with this man if they also subscribe to the manner in which he treats women, or tolerate that behavior." Relatedly, isolation occurs from the loss of access to professional resources, withdrawal from conference spaces, and changing advisors and reorganizing networks.

Reorganization of networks following incidents of sexual harassment and misconduct does not involve only professional affiliations or associations; isolation also frequently occurs when targets are cut out of (in)formal social networks. Social dynamics in these academic spaces are often shaped by rumors or perceptions that are shared through gossip. For instance, one respondent explained, "I lost relationships with other professors in the department and other students who are still in his web because I can't stand to see them enable him and sing his praises as if it's not known that he's a creep and not at all the 'ally' he would like us to think he is." Fear of gossip or rumors can be a motivating factor that compels many targets to isolate themselves from colleagues. By choosing to disengage from these (in)formal social networks, survivors recursively organize alienation to prevent further victimization.

One respondent confessed, "I fear rumors will persist as I am still within the academic community alongside several of my harassers. I feel like I have to be the perfect student and the perfect colleague lest anyone in my current graduate program ever catch wind of old rumors and the cycle of harassment begins again." Others reported losing friends or colleagues after going public with their complaints. One respondent noted that even though a formal complaint was never filed, discussions about the harassment incident politicized interactions in the graduate program. This respondent revealed how supporting a friend's decision not to report harassment created divisions and "vendettas" among students, so that students turned on one another:

> Though the events were never pursued through any formal complaint or through any public forum, they continued to structure a great deal of graduate student life in and around the department.... Departmental politicking ensued in which two camps appeared, both of which mirrored the "sides" that had formed in response to the prior year's harassment.... [I]t strikes me that the scenario is a textbook case of projection, in which the female student/harasser accused me of carrying out a vendetta against her through departmental politics as an explicit justification for her vendetta against me.

Collectively, the reorganization of networks is a structurating process that reifies the isolating and alienating effects of sexual harassment. Survivors must make deliberate choices about whether to discontinue working with mentors and colleagues, but they also must negotiate the loss of professional development opportunities that occur when disengaging from formal (e.g., professional associations) and informal (e.g., graduate cohorts) networks.

Rules stemming from mistrust

Although institutional failures abound when responding to reports of sexual harassment, many survivors also self-impose rules or modify behaviors that effectually isolate them from their academic community. Isolation may occur because survivors are cut off from institutional resources, such as network opportunities or working with mentors, as noted, but they also occur because of a general sense of mistrust following incidents of sexual harassment or assault. Many respondents in Kelsky's study indicated they no longer feel comfortable working with male colleagues or being alone in spaces with men. For instance, one respondent mentioned, "I never really trusted male heterosexual professors after that, even years after the incident. I was always waiting for the other shoe to drop even with men rumored to be 'gentlemen.'" Another respondent told the story of reporting her sexual assault as a student, only to be preyed upon by a professor who repeatedly harassed her and others. Not only did she "feel wary about going to meetings with male professors alone," but she also found herself "over-analyzing everything they say. I feel he has deprived me of access to resources (such as networking) and support that I could have if I did not have these anxieties." Isolation from networks and professional resources is dependent on norms that encourage women to avoid men and to recognize sexual harassment as a widely accepted practice.

Following Giddens (1984), we consider this unease and mistrust to be a form of knowledgeability or "everything which actors know (believe) about the circumstances of their action and that of others, drawn upon in the production and reproduction of that action, including tacit as well as discursively available knowledge" (p. 375). Many respondents highlighted knowledge of perpetrators and their common networks, departmental history, strategies of dressing, and whisper networks as points of knowledgeability that helped them avoid or mitigate the effects sexual harassment through personal action, sometimes at great cost to themselves. As one respondent reported, "I've learned to be so distrusting of people that it's hard to connect. I had become really distant (because of further harassment) and aloof to protect myself." Another respondent can "no longer trust the institution I work for (also because of insistent protection of harassers of students, and willingness to destroy students' careers in order to achieve that protection)." One respondent acknowledged, "I have never trusted another professor fully. If anything, this incident is only proven to me over and over again that I should not trust professors." This sense of mistrust socially isolates targets of harassment and, consequently, harms opportunities for personal and professional growth.

Normalization of sexual harassment

The data suggest that attitudes toward harassment function to recursively sustain the practice through normalization. Although policies and rules may formally condemn sexual misconduct, targets are discouraged from pursuing formal complaints or investigations, thereby perpetuating institutional isolation. Clair's (1993a) critique of managerial discourse on sexual harassment is complemented by this analysis of self-report data from survivors with personal experiences in higher education. Here, the privatization of sexual harassment (Clair, 1993a) is materialized through norms that center on individual stereotypes and "shrug off" ineffective organizational responses. We argue that sexual harassment is distanciated through discourse(s) that effectually normalize the practice and limit opportunities for intervention.

Respondents to Kelsky's survey frequently reported how their harassment evinced a widespread pattern that, despite being extremely problematic, was not altogether unsurprising. For instance, one respondent, who was harassed by a male colleague during her first year on the tenure track, explained:

> The experience really burst my bubble. I honestly believed that the trope of the "old creepy male professor" was a thing of the past. I never in my life expected that I would come face to face with the cold reality that this still takes place. It has tarnished what should have been the most exciting part of my career up to this point.

Remarks like these function to recursively construct the tacit acceptance of sexual harassment insofar as they invoke tropes and stereotypes that have become normalized in both academia and popular culture. In this case, the "old creepy male professor" stereotype is affirmed and individually centered explanations of harassment are normalized. The centering of sexual harassment as primarily an individual propensity and not also located in broader systems of communication neglects the enduring, structurating dimensions of this persistent phenomenon. Sexual harassment is normalized and enabled at both micro- and macrolevels (Clair, 1993a, p. 124); if not, the stereotype would fail to persist as a "cold reality" in higher education.

Many respondents mentioned that they quickly had to learn to "shrug off" harassment because it has become so normalized. Although the #MeToo movement has done much to bring instances of sexual misconduct into the mainstream, these comments highlight how the structural-symbolic foundation of sexual harassment in higher education is still largely predicated on normalization and acceptance. For example, the sentiment summed up by one respondent—"[I]t pays to be part of the boys club"—was repeated throughout the data. Another discussed her feeling of hopelessness, that "men will always protect each other and I'll be the whiny female for complaining." Despite knowledge of sexual harassment, one respondent reported that the "the old boys' club protected its own and junior and female faculty never seemed to survive past a couple of years." The "boys' club" norm generated gendered expectations that silenced or ostracized others.

Furthermore, a willingness to accept or overlook instances of sexual harassment creates norms of complicity that discourage reporting. Respondents frequently mentioned their realization that this "was not the first time" and recognized that repeated institutional failures indicated a larger and more systematic problem. As a result, many were inclined *not* to report their harassment because they believed little would actually be done. As one respondent remarked, "The chair at the time was utterly spineless and I knew that talking to him would be pointless." Another respondent declared, "The non-results of the inquiry influenced me to never approach [human resources] about a serious harassment situation in my career because of the proof that they would never take me seriously. This cost me another academic job I held after this incident." These comments illustrate how repeated failures can contribute to norms about formal reporting.

Unsurprisingly, many respondents did not formally report their harassment. However, the data show evidence of how mishandling or failing to address complaints in a satisfactory way has lasting effects on the way those resources are viewed and utilized in the future by others. One respondent stated, "There was nothing I could do about it, and was reminded of that lesson when the [university] faculty association said it could do nothing about the man who was harassing me. It was a powerful lesson about not really belonging in the academy." One respondent recounted that it "made me wary of my male professors, and now colleagues." These norms get routinized in practice and contribute to the widespread belief that reporting may be a futile exercise, thereby reinforcing isolation and alienation.

Estrangement from agency

The second most prevalent way that sexual harassment has become embedded in institutions is by alienating or estranging victims from their sense of agency. Our analysis revealed that many respondents directly and indirectly invoked agential constraints when making sense of their experiences with sexual harassment as they lost employment, experienced retaliation, and lost confidence in themselves. A total of 40% of respondents ($n = 955$) discussed leaving or actually quit their jobs. We argue that discursive practices surrounding sexual harassment limit agency through material and symbolic resource constraints, effectually reinforcing the isolating implications of misconduct. Targets are estranged from their agency in at least three ways: discouragement from reporting ("the chilling effect"), losing faith and exiting academia, and uncertainty or the imposter syndrome.

The chilling effect

One of the most common responses regarding the consequences that harassment had had on the perpetrator's life was "none," with comments explaining that the perpetrator was "clearly bulletproof somehow," still "beloved" in the field, had "married a graduate student," or had been "given a warning and tenure." Other comments indicated the perpetrator had not suffered consequences or was now retired. Consequences seemed to mitigate risk at best. One respondent noted the result of a formal complaint was that "he was required to stop hosting a monthly happy hour in a bar near campus." Ultimately, the responses suggest that silence is structurated and embedded in higher education. Multiple respondents used the phrase "chilling effect" to describe the impact of harassment on their careers, while others described this in more detail. In the words of one respondent, the harassment "made me decide that I was going to have to keep my mouth shut about this kind of stuff, sadly." Many survivors reported being unable or unwilling to file formal complaints against their harassers. This is not surprising because, as Kirby and Krone (2002) suggest, "micro-level interactions rooted in policy can have macro-level implications" (p. 71). That is, given the widespread acceptance and normalization of sexual harassment in higher education, survivors may feel that their agency is constrained, as they are not able to access macrolevel structures, such as institutional policies that could offer recourse.

More problematically, however, several respondents noted that when they did report sexual misconduct claims, they suffered professional consequences that entrenched their willingness not to pursue action in the future. As one respondent disclosed:

> Right after this point my two bosses began to try to pin various fire-able or reprimand-worthy offenses on me (not dressing appropriately was a huge one, despite the fact that I wear the same clothes I've always worn to work). They intentionally change their expectations constantly so I'm always wondering when I'll be in trouble next, and if/when I'll be fired, and I'm afraid to speak up about this as well as other things they've done.

Although this trend was less common in the survey responses, it highlights the precarious subject position of targets in institutional contexts. The perceived threat of retribution creates a chilling effect that presents a no-win scenario for targets of sexual harassment: Either do nothing or come forward and risk the consequences. In both cases, isolation and alienation are structurating processes that normalize sexual misconduct and limit agency.

Losing faith and exiting the academy

Targets of sexual harassment are also estranged from their agency when confronted with the bleak reality that sexual violence is commonplace and most reporting processes are entirely ineffectual. Many respondents frequently disclosed that they had lost faith in academia and were unsure whether they wanted to continue to pursue careers in higher education after being harassed. Notably, graduate students were the most frequent targets of sexual harassment (often with tenured full professors as the harassers). Many respondents described having thought academia was different from other industries or fields but quickly becoming disillusioned after realizing the prevalence. One respondent revealed, "I will never again even think of a career in academia, it is a blanket protecting predators and power freaks. My dream was always to teach and be a researcher. No more." Another respondent described her attempt to intervene that caused her to question how sexual misconduct is ingrained in academic culture: "If—even in my tenured position—I can't do anything to stop such blatant harassment … how much worse is it for the young generation still … and so what's the point of contributing to this primal patriarchal form of science?!?" Nearly 20% of respondents in

Kelsky's survey reported some sense of disillusionment, loss of confidence in academic institutions, or a lack of faith that policies will be able to address sexual violence.

Uncertainty or imposter syndrome

A sense of uncertainty about one's abilities, sometimes explicitly referred to as the "imposter syndrome," contributes to isolation and organizational exit. Almost 20% of respondents recounted feeling unsure of themselves. For example, one respondent considered that others saw her "as a piece of ass, not an emerging scholar." Another remarked that it "nearly broke my intellectual esteem, made me feel like people would never value me for anything other than wanting to have sex with me. Made me distrust praise and encouragement." And another reflected, "[H]e made me doubt my own talents and abilities—are all male professors complimenting me only because they want to sleep with me?" Self-doubt was described as a direct consequence of sexualization, objectification, and harassment.

Finally, the loss of faith in one's chosen field of study following harassment incidents leads to several outcomes that reify the isolating effects of sexual misconduct. First, on a symbolic level, as survivors lose faith in these institutions, they implicitly reify the widespread acceptance of a culture of sexual violence. For instance, one respondent said, "I feel like I did everything right (reporting, waiting for the process) and it didn't matter. If it didn't matter for me (he's got a tenure track job somewhere now), I don't trust anyone to be safe." When the institutional processes that are designed to protect targets fail, survivors are less likely to attempt to utilize these mechanisms in any case. In addition, and far more problematically, the loss of faith in academia compels many survivors to exit higher education entirely. This effect is a compounding one; when more and more women are forced out of academia, the toxic culture of higher education proliferates due to the lack of collective power by/from survivors to resist. In disciplines where women are already traditionally underrepresented (such as science, technology, engineering, and math [STEM] fields), sexual harassment propagates not only the culture of sexual violence but also gender disparities. Disillusionment is, thus, a recursive process that structurates alienation.

Resignification

To this point, our analysis has focused on the structurating mechanisms that contribute to a sense of isolation following sexual harassment incidents. However, speaking out on personal experiences with sexual harassment can expose problems and also give survivors a sense of liberation (Clair et al., 1996). Although the vast majority of respondents in Kelsky's survey detailed negative experiences that had profound impacts on their professional development and life trajectory, 90 respondents also noted that their experiences provided an opportunity for productive inflection. In this section, we turn our attention to these survivors and how their experiences (re)structured how they enact agency within institutional contexts. Specifically, we argue that some were able to resignify their harassment as a turning point that manifests resistance in the form of resource enactment.

Resignification understands agency as an act of radical transformation or an opening of new contexts and meanings (Medina, 2006). This is characterized by a transgression of boundaries between infelicitous and felicitous interpretations (Medina, 2006), in this case what it means to be a target of sexual harassment. Responses like "I rebelled" and "I stuck my spurs in" challenge constructs of victimhood and helplessness. A significant theme in the data showed that harassment was reconstructed as a learning experience, a turning point from which one operated differently, if not necessarily qualitatively better. One respondent commented, "[W]hat doesn't kill you makes you stronger? I did start to protect myself and begin to document any difficulties that came up at work." These responses suggest that reconstructing sexual harassment in terms that empower survivors by describing their actions and articulating their own strengths can resignify meaning in empowering ways.

Resignification can coincide with a seemingly joyful exit from the academy, as in the case of one woman who remarked, "I am now a much stronger and confident person! I like being free of the fear, pain and horror of being in academia!" For others, that exit was less liberating. Reclaiming the meaning of sexual harassment and defining it on individual terms can be a significant act of resignification and agency, but it is also a long and difficult process enabled through connections and support networks as well as access to positions of power, through employment, financial security, and authority (tenure). For instance, one tenured faculty member described how her harassment incident compelled her to become an advocate and resource for others at her institution:

> I am a work-a-holic, and once I got tenure I became a fierce protector and defender of others in the academy who are subject to sexual harassment. I do not allow anyone to feel isolated and alone as I did. Every new woman who enters our University is welcomed by me, and I open up channels for conversation as they navigate their experiences. Each new colleague I mentor in this way eventually shares her own story of harassment with me. Not one has been free of it. NOT ONE.... I am quite successful at fighting though, so I continue, and I try to learn how to gather around me the life resources I need to support my work on behalf of others.... I'm not sure I'll ever be free from this plague.

In response to what she described as a plague, an ever-present disease, this respondent positioned herself as a resource for support and resistance to sexual harassment by welcoming women and starting conversation. In addition, many respondents indicated that support networks and relationships that they formed following their harassment were "invaluable" for coping with the stress and anxiety induced by the trauma. In pivoting to become a resource for others, survivors resignified the meaning of their harassment and effectually became a resource for others. Thus, while many experienced an overwhelming sense of isolation and alienation, others were able to use their experiences to create a sense of commonality and social support. Enactments of the self-as-resource are powerful and provide targets with symbolic resources when institutional mechanisms and resources are cordoned off.

Finally, we contend that participation in Kelsky's survey is itself a critical intervention that challenges the normalization of sexual harassment in higher education. Participants in the survey became symbolic resources for one another and for those who have not come forward with their harassment by demonstrating the commonality of experience. One respondent reported:

Since the #MeToo campaign started I have been looking for an outlet to share the story of what happened to me and other women who worked for this person. Thank you so much for providing space to me and others who have experienced harassment in academia. It's comforting to know that I am not alone.

Kelsky's survey presents an invitation for targets of harassment to publicly name their experience and share in a collective, freely available log of information about sexual harassment in higher education. In this way, online, public records and communities can be a form of "emancipatory discourse" that "open[s] dialogue rather than close[s] it" (Clair, 1993a, p. 149). While recounting past trauma can be painful, participating in the survey is one way of participating in a larger movement for social change.

Discussion

This study renders a picture of the isolating mechanics in higher education sustained by structurating communication processes. Isolating structures of sexual harassment are distanciated through rules and resources regarding networking and professionalization, estrangement, and resignification. These experiences have a profound impact on survivors' health and careers, as well as broader implications for higher education. In this section, we address the theoretical and practical contributions of this analysis and future directions of research, the role of critical reflexivity in this project, and limitations and conclusions.

Implications

We identify two key contributions: First, this study uses self-reports to describe the communication processes surrounding networking and professionalization and the estrangement from agency that structurate and embed conditions of isolation in higher education environments. Second, the analysis identifies resignification and crowdsourcing as important potential avenues for the constitution of communities and networks of survivors, potential targets, and allies.

Foremost, respondents described communicative processes of isolation and the "chilling effect" of inadequate structural responses to sexual harassment. While it is undoubtedly not the only issue, sexual harassment may compound problems, including the dismal ratio of women to men in STEM and other fields with disproportionate representation. Women are less likely to receive tenure than men and are more likely to be instructors and hold non–tenure track positions (National Center for Education Statistics, 2016). Women of color and women with children are particularly underrepresented in tenure track positions, while men still outearn women in tenured positions (American Association of University Professors, 2017; National Center for Education Statistics, 2016; Mason, 2013.) The data indicate that sexual harassment and related communication practices, including loss of professional resources, mistrust, and uncertainty, systematically isolate survivors and create the conditions for organizational or disciplinary exit. The "boys' club" influences norms in higher education that incentivize siding with powerful networkers and edging out targets of harassment. One respondent commented that "with his power, there's nothing left for those of us who speak out or don't put out. I've given up on the field." Exit is a reasonable response to persistent and unaddressed harassment; unfortunately, it only compounds existing problems. Sexual harassment can create extra, unpaid communication labor for survivors working in the same universities and professional networks as their harassers. It is clear that appropriate solutions to sexual harassment in higher education and the workplace cannot be as simple as punishing perpetrators and leaving survivors unsupported.

Further, this analysis describes the ways that structures of isolation are distanciated and institutionalized through resources, rules, norms, and agency that are continually reconstituting (and sometimes resignifying) hostile environments in higher education. The data substantiate Forbes's (2009) findings on isolation in Black women's experiences with sexual harassment in the workplace that have an alienating effect on these women due to the lack of informal networks, mentorships, and interpersonal friendships at work, leading many to quit their positions. From this view, it is not difficult to see how organizations become increasingly more homogenous, potentially hostile, and sexual as they drain members who might challenge permissive structures. Potential change agents, including survivors of sexual harassment, are likely to leave their positions if they are not already being forced out.

In recognizing the need for more critical reflexivity and the difficulty of implementing effective interventions to prevent or respond to sexual misconduct, we follow Keyton and colleagues (2018) and contend that more emphasis must be placed on bystander interventions that distribute accountability in materially impactful ways. Bystander intervention programs such as Green Dot and Step Up provide one measure of accountability by encouraging individuals to take action when they recognize that sexual harassment or misconduct is occurring. Unfortunately, as Clair explained, "Situations may not always be so straightforward and the intervention may not always go as smoothly as planned" (quoted in Keyton et al., 2018, p. 670), and this is especially true in academia, where complex power dynamics, career precarity, and other issues may prevent survivors or witnesses from coming forward.

Indeed, Kelsky's survey suggests that the alienating nature of sexual harassment is, perhaps, goaded by the complicity of those unwilling to disrupt practices and discourses that have become normalized in academia. In arguing against bystander complicity, Mack (2018) suggested that real self-reflection would require reorienting the #MeToo movement so that "abusers, enablers, rape-apologists—and those who are not sure— looked ourselves in the mirror and acknowledged #ItWasMe" (para. 28). Drawing on a phrase from recovery culture, Mack argued that those who are committed to ending the culture of sexual violence should take a "sexual inventory" that encourages reflection on "how you might have acted selfishly, coercively, inappropriately, or abusively regarding sex or how you have enabled the harassment and abuse of others" (para. 25). As members of the higher education community, we must be attentive to the power dynamics that shape the reality faced by survivors of sexual misconduct in academia. Undertaking a critical self-assessment might serve as a starting point for recognizing how we may be unknowingly complicit in the systems that perpetuate the toxic culture of sexual violence.

Theoretically, this data set responds to demands from feminist scholars to study the "particularities of harassment experiences" to break down "monolithic categorizations" and better understand the frequency and nature of harassment in higher education

(Quinn, 1993, p. 24). Understanding the particularities of experience in the context of social and institutional structures helps illuminate how both are mutually implicative. A structurational approach to sexual harassment offers one way to understand how power vacillates between the microlevel of human experience and the macrolevel of institutional structures. Like Giddens (1984), we are weary of social theories that overestimate structural components and, instead, have articulated a cogent representation of sexual harassment that attends to the particularities of individual experiences as they manifest within the larger domains of policy, organizational knowledge, and practice. Given the opportunity to choose how their experiences were framed, some respondents engaged in resignification, seizing the power to frame their responses in ways that celebrated their resilience and the proactive changes they made to help others and challenge "victim" stereotypes.

Finally, the crowdsourced data suggest the importance of constructing communities and networks of support when those in existence have failed us. While research suggests crowdsourcing is a way to address resistance to admitting the extent of sexual harassment (Dougherty, 1999), this study indicates crowdsourcing might provide additional affordances and opportunities for change. Two key considerations from this study suggest that (1) large-scale crowdsourcing may better address the preferences of those who disclose stigmatized and threatening accounts of experiences like sexual harassment and (2) open crowdsourcing can play an important role in community building and collaboration.

First, respondents may prefer to be able to directly interact with the data and read other accounts of sexual harassment. They are situated within a chorus of stories that resist and challenge alienation anonymously. This study adds to research on policy-making suggesting that crowdsourcing can encourage more participation, making it especially useful in generating social movement momentum (Hildebrand, Ahumada, & Watson, 2013). Collective stories can make people feel less alone in their experiences and more able to promote social change. In this case, the very act of adding to the public database on harassment was an empowering one for many respondents. One respondent thanked Kelsky for the space to "offload" and "become more aware of the toxicity of work in academia." Still, narratives of sexual harassment can illustrate covert forms of resistance while simultaneously reinforcing the conditions that maintain sexual harassment (Dougherty, 1999). Although narratives can certainly play a "consciousness raising function" (Clair et al., 1996), further research focused on crowdsourcing and community building is needed.

Finally, this study suggests a need to better understand the meaning and the significance of crowdsourcing methods. Kelsky's survey constitutes a radical act of resistance in breaking norms of keeping complaints "in house" by submitting them to public scrutiny (Quinn, 1993). Reading through the responses as a register of "unofficial" accounts can be more telling about the failure to retain women and people of color than numbers and categorizations of diversity. The online survey database acted as a running compilation of thousands of personal experiences that might otherwise be wrongly described as isolated incidents. Open and public knowledge of widespread harassment circumvented organizational norms of anti-transparency. Scrolling through the number of responses demonstrates the excess labor levied upon survivors who may be limited in their ability to respond to harassment. In this way, the online survey can be thought of as a "public" whisper network, acting as a resource for connection, protection, and establishing a sense of community based on shared experience.

Reflexivity

Moreover, Kelsky's work highlights the need to be critically reflexive of the institutional practices that undergird problematic discourses and behaviors surrounding sexual misconduct in higher education. As junior faculty at research institutions, we are both attentive to our social positions and recognize that we are, at least tacitly, a part of the institutional machinery that has enabled such widespread misconduct. We assert that our roles—as critical scholars, as feminists, as educators, as members of the higher education community—must facilitate critical reflexivity that can enable prompt organizational transformation. In this regard, we situate this project not merely as research but as a reflexive interpretation aimed at addressing the pernicious consequences of sexual harassment. As Harris and Fortney (2017) suggested, "When reflexivity is interactive rather than purely confessional, some scholars are able to highlight how macro and political processes—not just individual psychological processes—influence scholarship" (p. 22).

Yet connecting isolated incidents to the structural features that we experience on a daily basis is itself an emotionally laborious process. As we worked through the data and read the accounts of sexual harassment, the burden of this problem felt like a weight being placed on our shoulders. During our numerous conference calls, we often expressed frustration and exasperation about the commonality of these experiences and the lack of sufficient institutional response. This project, though difficult, allowed us to methodologically participate in reflexive caring (Harris & Fortney, 2017) and critically interrogate how our social locations, experiences, and perceptions of academe are enmeshed with larger commitments for social justice. This project, then, is not merely a structurational account of sexual harassment; it is our intention that it also functions as a disruption to the dominant, business-as-usual environment of higher education that has reified and normalized toxic behaviors.

Limitations and conclusions

Although Kelsky's survey is an important resource for understanding experiences of sexual harassment in higher education, a few limitations of this analysis must be noted. First, the survey itself is focused on a relatively homogenous set of experiences (English-speaking academics, primarily located in the United States) and does not fully account for members of the higher education community who may be precluded by the survey's focus. The majority of respondents are graduate students and professors; other members of the broader higher education community (such as administrative assistants and nonacademic administrators) are largely absent from the survey responses and may also be targets of harassment. Moreover, the survey does not ask respondents to provide any demographic data beyond professional status at the time of harassment, type of institution, and field/discipline. However, as Harris (2017) noted, experience with sexual misconduct in higher education is often complicated by factors such as race, gender, and sexual orientation. Without a broader intersectional understanding and awareness of sexual harassment, it becomes difficult to more deeply interrogate the intricacies of inequity as they play out in this context. Given that Black women face sexualization and harassment in the workplace in particularly violent ways (Forbes, 2009), identities beyond gender play an important role in influencing individual experiences.

In sum, the systematic isolation of survivors is in part a product of structurating communication processes regarding sexual harassment that render networks and professional resources inaccessible, threaten the loss of career and income, and limit individuals' sense of agency and empowerment. Indeed, organizations may participate in sustaining a violent system of meaning that uses individual conceptualizations of harassment to conceal organizational accountability (Harris, 2013). With this in mind, our study situates communication structures as central components in the embeddedness and institutionalization of sexual harassment. Networks and professional associations can be a haven for sexual predators or they can be resources that support survivors and actively challenge the norms surrounding harassment. From this perspective, the #MeToo movement's successes extend far beyond the removal of predators from positions of power. An important goal is the continual (re)construction of discursive communities of supporters and survivors who might serve as resources in dismantling the isolating structures of sexual harassment.

Acknowledgments

The authors would like to thank the anonymous reviewers for their insightful criticisms and contributions, as well as Danielle Biss for her timely assistance on this project.

ORCID

Tiffany A. Dykstra-DeVette http://orcid.org/0000-0001-7737-2660
Carlos Tarin http://orcid.org/0000-0002-5818-7942

References

American Association of University Professors. (2017, March–April). *Visualizing change: The annual report on the economic status of the profession, 2016–17*. Retrieved from https://www.aaup.org/report/visualizing-change-annual-report-economic-status-profession-2016-17

Buzzanell, P. M., & Liu, M. (2005). Struggling with maternity leave policies and practices: A poststructuralist feminist analysis of gendered organizing. *Journal of Applied Communication Research*, *33*(1), 1–25. doi:10.1080/00909880420000318495

Canary, H. C. (2010). Constructing policy knowledge: Contradictions, communication, and knowledge frames. *Communication Monographs*, *77*(2), 181–206. doi:10.1080/03637751003758185

Canary, H. C., & Tarin, C. A. (2017). Structuration theory. In C. R. Scott & L. Lewis (Eds.), *The international encyclopedia of organizational communication* (pp. 2281–2296). Oxford, United Kingdom: John Wiley & Sons.

Charmaz, K. (2006). *Constructing grounded theory: A practical guide through qualitative analysis*. Thousand Oaks, CA: Sage.

Chen, E. (1997). Sexual harassment from the perspective of Asian-American women. In C. R. Ronai, B. A. Zsembik, and J. R. Feagin (Eds.), *Everyday sexism* (pp. 51–62). New York, NY: Routledge.

Clair, R. P. (1993a). The bureaucratization, commodification, and privatization of sexual harassment through institutional discourse: A study of the "big ten" universities. *Management Communication Quarterly, 7*(2), 123–157. doi:10.1177/0893318993007002001

Clair, R. P. (1993b). The use of framing devices to sequester organizational narratives: Hegemony and harassment. *Communication Monographs, 60*(2), 113–136. doi:10.1080/03637759309376304

Clair, R. P., Chapman, P. A., & Kunkel, A. W. (1996). Narrative approaches to raising consciousness about sexual harassment: From research to pedagogy and back again. *Journal of Applied Communication Research, 24*(4), 241–259. doi:10.1080/00909889609365455

Conrad, C., & Taylor, B. (1994). The context(s) of sexual harassment: Power, silences, and academe. In S. G. Bingham (Ed.), *Conceptualizing sexual harassment as discursive practice* (pp. 45–58). Westport, CT: Praeger.

Cowan, R. L. (2011). "Yes, we have an anti-bullying policy, but … ": HR professionals' understandings and experiences with workplace bullying policy. *Communication Studies, 62*(3), 307–327. doi:10.1080/10510974.2011.553763

Dougherty, D. (1999). Dialogue through standpoint: Understanding women's and men's standpoints of sexual harassment. *Management Communication Quarterly, 12*(3), 436–468. doi:10.1177/0893318999123003

Dougherty, D., & Goldstein Hode, M. (2016). Binary logics and the discursive interpretation of organizational policy: Making meaning of sexual harassment policy. *Human Relations, 69*(8), 1729–1755. doi:10.1177/0018726715624956

Dougherty, D., & Smythe, M. (2004). Sensemaking, organizational culture, and sexual harassment. *Journal of Applied Communication Research, 32*(4), 293–317. doi:10.1080/0090988042000275998

Forbes, D. (2002). Internalized masculinity and women's discourse: A critical analysis of the (re)production of masculinity in organizations. *Communication Quarterly, 50*(3/4), 269–291. doi:10.1080/01463370209385664

Forbes, D. (2009). Commodification and co-modification: Explicating Black female sexuality in organizations. *Management Quarterly Communication, 22*(4), 577–613. doi:10.1177/0893318908331322

Fotaki, M. (2013). No woman is like a man (in academia): The masculine symbolic order and the unwanted female body. *Organization Studies, 34*(9), 1251–1275. doi:10.1177/0170840613483658

Gardner, S. (2009). Coming out of the sexual harassment closet: One woman's story of politics and change in higher education. *NWSA Journal, 21*(2), 171–195.

Giddens, A. (1984). *The constitution of society*. Berkeley: University of California Press.

Griffin, R. W., & O'Leary-Kelly, A. (Eds.). (2004). *The dark side of organizational behavior*. San Francisco, CA: John Wiley & Sons.

Harris, K. L. (2013). Show them a good time: Organizing the intersections of sexual violence. *Management Communication Quarterly, 27*(4), 568–595. doi:10.1177/0893318913506519

Harris, K. L. (2017). Re-situating organizational knowledge: Violence, intersectionality, and the privilege of partial perspective. *Human Relations, 70*(3), 263–285. doi:10.1177/0018726716654745

Harris, K. L., & Fortney, J. M. (2017). Performing reflexive caring: Rethinking reflexivity through trauma and disability. *Text and Performance Quarterly, 37*(1), 20–34. doi:10.1080/10462937.2016.1273543

Hickson, M., Grierson, R. D., & Linder, B. C. (1991). A communication perspective on sexual harassment: Affiliative nonverbal behaviors in asynchronous relationships. *Communication Quarterly, 39*(2), 111–118. doi:10.1080/01463379109369789

Hildebrand, M., Ahumada, C., & Watson, S. (2013). CrowdOutAIDS: Crowdsourcing youth perspectives for action. *Reproductive Health Matters, 21*(41), 57–68. doi:10.1016/S0968-8080(13)41687-7

Hill, A. (2018, July 19). Reporting sexual harassment: Toward accountability and action. *The Gender Policy Report*. Retrieved from http://genderpolicyreport.umn.edu/reporting-sexual-harassment-towards-accountability-and-action/

Kelsky, K. (2017, December 1). A crowdsourced survey of sexual harassment in the academy. Retrieved from https://theprofessorisin.com/2017/12/01/a-crowdsourced-survey-of-sexual-harassment-in-the-academy/

Keyton, J., & Menzie, K. (2007). Sexually harassing messages: Decoding workplace conversation. *Communication Studies, 58*(1), 87–103. doi:10.1080/10510970601168756

Keyton, J., & Rhodes, S. C. (1999). Organizational sexual harassment: Translating research into application. *Journal of Applied Communication Research, 27*(2), 158–173. doi:10.1080/00909889909365532

Keyton, J., Clair, R., Compton, C. A., Dougherty, D. S., Forbes Berthoud, D., Manning, J., & Scarduzio, J. (2018). Addressing sexual harassment in a sexually charged national culture: A Journal of Applied Communication Research forum. *Journal of Applied Communication Research, 46*(6), 665–683. doi:10.1080/00909882.2018.1546472

Kihnley, J. (2000). Unraveling the ivory fabric: Institutional obstacles to the handling of sexual harassment complaints. *Law and Social Inquiry, 25*(1), 69–90.

Kirby, E., & Krone, K. J. (2002). "The policy exists but you can't really use it": Communication and structuration of work–family policies. *Journal of Applied Communication Research, 30*(1), 50–77. doi:10.1080/00909880216577

Kroløkke, C. (1998). Women professors' assertive-empathic and non-assertive communication in sexual harassment situations. *Women's Studies in Communication, 21*(1), 91–103. doi:10.1080/07491409.1998.10162415

Lindlof, T., & Taylor, B. (2017). *Qualitative communication research methods*. Thousand Oaks, CA: Sage.

Lutgen-Sandvik, P., & Sypher, B. D. (2010). *Destructive organizational communication: Processes, consequences, and productive ways of organizing*. New York, NY: Routledge.

Mack, A. (2018, October 27). #ItWasMe: For monsters, rapists, abusers, enablers, rape-apologists, and those who aren't sure. Retrieved from https://medium.com/@ashleymack_25236/itwasme-for-monsters-rapists-abusers-enablers-rape-apologists-and-those-who-arent-sure-100de312cc29

Mason, M. A. (2013, August 5). The baby penalty. *Chronicle of Higher Education*. Retrieved from https://www.chronicle.com/article/The-Baby-Penalty/140813

McGuire, T., Dougherty, B. S., & Atkinson, J. (2006). "Paradoxing the dialectic": The impact of patients' sexual harassment in the discursive construction of nurses' caregiving roles. *Management Communication Quarterly, 19*(3), 416–450. doi:10.1177/0893318905280879

McPhee, R. D., Poole, M. S., & Iverson, J. (2013). Structuration theory. In L. L. Putnam & D. K. Mumby (Eds.), *The Sage handbook of organizational communication: Advances in theory, research, and methods* (pp. 75–99). Thousand Oaks, CA: Sage.

Medina, J. (2006). *Speaking from elsewhere: A new contextualist perspective on meaning, identity, and discursive agency*. Albany: State University of New York Press.

Mumby, D. K., & Clair, R. P. (1997). Organizational discourse. In T. Van Dijk (Ed.), *Discourse as social interaction* (pp. 181–205). Thousand Oaks, CA: Sage.

National Academies of Sciences, Engineering, and Medicine. (2018). *Sexual harassment of women: Climate, cultures, and consequences in academic sciences, engineering, and medicine*. Washington, DC: National Academies Press.

National Center for Education Statistics. (2016). Full-time instructional staff, by faculty and tenure status, academic rank, rank/ethnicity, and gender (degree-granting institutions): Fall 2015. Retrieved from https://nces.ed.gov/ipeds/use-the-data

Quinn, R. L. (1993). "I should learn to see the truth as great men have seen it": Male mentoring, seduction, and sexual harassment in higher education. *Feminist Teacher, 7*(2), 20–25.

Saldaña, J. (2013). *The coding manual for qualitative researchers*. Thousand Oaks, CA: Sage.

Scarduzio, J. A., & Geist-Martin, P. (2010). Accounting for victimization: Male professors' ideological positioning in stories of sexual harassment. *Management Communication Quarterly, 24*(3), 419–445. doi:10.1177/0893318909358746

Spitzberg, B. H., & Cupach, W. R. (2007). *The dark side of interpersonal communication* (2nd ed.). New York, NY: Routledge.

Stabile, C. (2017, December 3). Confronting sexual harassment and hostile climates in higher education. *Ms. Magazine Blog.* Retrieved from http://msmagazine.com/blog/2017/12/13/confronting-sexual-harassment-hostile-climates-higher-education/

Strine, M. (1992). Understanding "how things work": Sexual harassment and academic culture. *Journal of Applied Communication Research*, 20(4), 391–400. doi:10.1080/00909889209365345

Tracy, S. (2013). *Qualitative research methods: Collecting evidence, crafting analysis, communicating impact.* Malden, MA: Wiley-Blackwell.

Wood, J. (1992). Telling our stories: Narratives as a basis for theorizing sexual harassment. *Journal of Applied Communication Research*, 20(4), 349–362. doi:10.1080/00909889209365343

Appendix: Table of Themes and Frequency

Themes and Subthemes	Frequency	Example
Networking and professionalization		
Loss of resources (e.g., mentors, networking, positions of authority)	907 (38%)	"I wanted to go to graduate school. I'm 3 years out of college and still haven't applied. I don't want to have to revisit that time in my life, ask for references, etc." "I moved offices to another building and stepped down from the position I held at a director's level."
Reorganizing network	701 (29%)	"Lack of trust for that national society, and that individual. We are few, because we are minorities, and it makes it harder for me to go to that community as a resource." "At my request, I was removed from collaborations with my accuser so I would not have to work with him. This drastically limited the scope of my research from what I had originally intended to do."
Mistrust	290 (12%)	"It definitely makes me wary about engaging with male colleagues."
Normalization	407 (17%)	"The academic industry is the worst I've ever worked in for the kind of pervasive 'bro' culture that overlooks if not directly encourages rape culture."
Estrangement from agency		
Nothing (no impact, did not report)	327 (13%)	"None—never reported." "I was experienced enough to know that keeping my mouth shut and dodging the gropers & perverts was the best way to get thru school safely and keep on progress to my own career goals."
Disillusionment and exit	955 (40%)	"I left the area as the management of the area did not care about this behaviour, and treated it as part of the boys club way of doing things. 3 women left the group and the managers were shocked, they are now actively recruiting women to the area and wondering why nobody wants to work there."
Uncertainty and imposter syndrome	473 (19%)	"I have major imposter syndrome, thinking that all of my accomplishments were only because of our relationship. I fear forming relationships with men in my field due to the power they may have over me or that my accomplishments may be diminished under them."
Resignification	90 (3%)	"It's made me a more empathetic professor who listens when students report things." "The only positive part is that this has made me a fierce protector of and advocate for other young women in ecology."

Index

administrative violence analysis 19
"African American Women in Defense of Ourselves" 75
agency, defined 110–11
aggregation/ dispersion 69
Alexander, Marissa 14, 15, 17
Alexander, Michelle 13, 14
American cultural interpretation 46
amplification/diminishment 69
anger 66–8
"Angry Black Women" 69
Ansari, A. 45–6
anti-black racism 52
anti-LGBTQ violence 72
anti-queer violence 8
anti-trans violence 8
Arceneaux, M. 31
Archila, Ana Maria 19, 20
Arvin, M. 87
The Atlantic 47, 76, 77

Banks, Antoine J. 68
Barrymore, Drew 72
Bennett, Jessica 11
Betsy DeVos's Department of Education 2
Bierria, Alisa 12
Black children 35
Black male victims 25
Black male vulnerability 34, 36–9
"the borderlands of nonrecognition" 13
Bose, Adrija 48
Brownmiller, S. 32–3
Bryant, Gerard 6, 7
Burke, Tarana 10, 26, 27, 31–6, 70, 75–6, 84

Canary, H. C. 110
carceral punishment 7
Carlin, Shannon 71
Carmon, Irin 19
Center for Media Justice 12
The Centers for Disease Control and Prevention (CDC) 26
Central High School (1957) 2
"character assassination" 73
Charlton Law 16

child physical abuse 34–5
child sexual abuse 34–5
chilling effect 119–20
cisheteropatriarchy 87
Clair, R. P. 118, 124
CNN cameras 19
Cohen, C. 32
"coloniality of power" concept 87
colonial violence 87–9
colonization process 89
community-led coalitions 88
Compton, C. A. 124
consent 2
Cooper, Anna Julia 11
Cooper, Brittney 68
Corey, Angela 14
Cosby, Bill 11
Crenshaw, Kimberlé 11
Crews, Terry 24–31
criminal legal system 13
"A Crowdsourced Survey of Sexual Harassment in the Academy" 108
crowdsourcing 113–14
cultural anticipation 58
"culture of brutality" 6
Currah, Paisley 9
Curry, Tommy 3
Curry, T. J. 35

Damon, Matt 64
"the dark side of communication" 109
data analysis 114
data collection and sampling 113–14
Davé, Shilpa 52
decolonial feminist practices 84, 85, 89–92
Deer, S. 87, 96
defense campaigns 18
dehumanization of women 31
deindustrialization 9
"Demarginalizing the Intersection of Race and Sex" 11
Department of Justice 33
deposit systems 75
Desi masculinity 3, 49–59
Desi masculinity and performing funny cute 46–7

Dingo, Rebecca 9
disciplinary networks 112
discriminatory voter ID laws 19
disenfranchisement 84
Dockterman, Eliana 10
dominant emotionological standards 68
Dougherty, D. S. 124
drowning, energetic snag 76
Dykstra-DeVette, Tiffany 3–4

Edwards, Haley Sweetland 10
effeminacy 52
Emancipation Proclamation 29
Eng, David 51
The Expendables 28

fear converge 37
felony disenfranchisement 19
female objectification 30
female victimization 27
"feminist failure of vision" 8
feminist responses 47–9
Ferracuti, F. 32–3
flagrant gerrymandering 19
Flake, Jeff 20
Flanagan, Caitlin 47–8
Flores, Lisa A. 78
Forbes Berthoud, D. 113, 124
Ford, Blasey 19, 20, 64
"former office assistant" 10
Fortney, J. M. 126
framing devices 112
Freedom Overground 16–17
"The Free Ky Project" 16
Fricker, Miranda 67

Gadsby, Hannah 72–4
Gallagher, Maria 19
"gender based" approach 11
gender dichotomization 85
gender discrimination 111–13
Gender Equity 27
gender-nonconforming individuals 88
gender violence 17, 87–9
Giddens, A. 110, 125
Goodale, Greg 71
Good and Mad: The Revolutionary Power of Women's Anger 65

Harold and Kumar (movie) 52
Harris, K. L. 126–7
hashtag, "storytelling device" 75
Haverford, Tom 45, 50, 53, 55
health care services 2
hermeneutical marginalization 67
heterosexualism in modernity 85
hierarchical coding 114
Hill, Annie 109
Hoerl, Kristen 1
"How The Treatment of Indigenous Women in the U.S. Compares to Canada" 1

Hsu, Jo 3
hypermasculinity 37
hypersexuality 37

Immigration and Customs Enforcement (ICE) 15–16
Indian diasporic/international audience 51
intersectional feminism 8
Iverson, J. 110
"I Went on a Date With Aziz Ansari. It Turned Into the Worst Night of My Life" 45

Jim Crow segregation 37

Kai, Maiysha 65
Kaur, Harnidh 50
Kavanaugh, Brett 2, 18, 64, 77
Kelsky, K. 108, 109, 118, 124, 126
Keyton, J. 124
King, Aliya S. 49
Kirby, E. 120
Klee, M. 27
"knowing resistant anger" 69
knowledge practices 67
Konsmo, Erin Marie 97
Koss, M. P. 31
Krishnaswamy, Revathi 52
Krølokke, C. 112
Krone, K. J. 120
Krugman, Paul 65
Kuokkanen, R. 88

Laboucan-Massimo, Melina 99
large-scale crowdsourcing 125
The Late Show with Stephen Colbert 72
LGBTQ folx 2
"LGBTQ" politics 8
losing faith and academy 120–1
"Love and Protect" (L&P) organization 12
Lugones, M. 87, 89–90

Mack, A. 3, 124
MacKinnon, C. A. 31
macro-level system 111
made-to-penetrate violence 26
"male as perpetrator" paradigm 25, 27
male privilege 25
Male Rape Is a Feminist Issue: Feminism, Governmentality, and Male Rape 32
male victimization 25
male victims 1
mandatory minimums 15
Manning, J. 124
Maroney's perspective 77–8
masculinity 30, 47
Master of None (drama) 45, 52
The Mating Mind 55
McCullers, Tynesha 77
McPhee, R. D. 110
#MeToo assemblages 59–61
Meyer, I. 32

INDEX

micro-level system 111
Milano, Alyssa 1, 9, 18
Miller, Geoffrey F. 55
Missing and Murdered Indigenous Women (MMIW) 92–3
mistrust 117–18
Modern Romance: An Investigation (book) 45
Moore, Lisa Jean 9
Morrill, A. 87
Mount, Steve 16

Na, Ali 3
Nan-Hui Jo 15
Na'puti, Tiara 3
National Academies of Sciences, Engineering, and Medicine (2018) 109
National Collaborating Centre for Indigenous Health 88
National Crime Victimization Survey (NCVS) 26, 87
National Football League 24
National Intimate Partner and Sexual Violence Survey (NISVS) 26
National Women's Studies Association 67, 68
Native American reservations 10
Native dispossession 10–11
Native Youth Sexual Health Network (NYSHN) 93
Negrophilic and Negrophobic relations 38–9
networking arguments 9
networking and professionalization 115
"Networking the Macro and Micro" 9
"New Jersey 4," young lesbians 15
The New Jim Crow 14
New York Magazine 19
90th annual Person of the Year 7
No More Silence (NMS) 99
normalization of sexual harassment 118–19
norms and organizational culture, role of 113
Norton, P. 27

Ono, Kent 51
open crowdsourcing 125
"An Open Letter on Diversity in the Communication Discipline" 3
Ortiz, Sara Marie 85
The Oxford English Dictionary 69

Parks and Recreation (television satire) 45, 50, 56
patriarchy 25, 30
Penn, Kal 52
period of incarceration 16
Perry, D. M. 31
Peterson, Ky 16, 20
Petrusich, Amanda 76
Pham, Vincent 51
policies 112
Poole, M. S. 110
positional power 112–13
power functions 59
The Professor Is In 108
"Public Mourning" (Web site) 94

"race based" approach 11
racial inequities 7
racialization process 85
racialized criminalization 17
Ramirez, Deborah 18
reflexivity 126
reorganizing networks 115–17
resignification 121–3
respondents 119, 125
Rodriguez, Marcela 15
The Root 30

Sanger, Margaret 67
"Sapphire," treacherous Black woman 14, 69
Saturday Night Live (SNL) 64
Scarduzio, J. 124
Schroeder, J. 32
Secure Communities 15
self-determination 88, 90, 93–6
self-determination of survivors 17
Senate Judiciary Committee 64
sexual assault 27–8, 39, 85
sexual coercion 34–5
sexual harassment 1, 109, 111–13, 118
sexual victimization 31–6
sexual violence 1, 7, 25, 30, 31, 34, 36–9
Shankar, Shalini 46–7
sidestepping normative assessment 48
"The Silence Breakers" 1, 7, 10–12, 70
Silva, Kumarini 53
Simpson, L. B. 93
"single axis" politics 11
South Asian model minority 52–3
sovereign bodies 95–9
sovereign stories 98–101
sovereignty 90, 91, 93–6
Stabile, Carol 109
statutory rape 34–5
Stemple, L. 32, 34
structural isolation 114–15
structuration theory (ST) 110–11
Stryker, Susan 9
The Subculture of Violence 33
#SurvivedAndPunished (guidebook) 8, 12–18
"Survived and Punished" (S&P) organization 12
Survivors' Bill of Rights Act 24, 28
Swetnick, Julie 18
Sydney Opera House 73

Tarin, C. A. 3–4, 110
technological advancement 9
Terra nullius, prefigured fantasy 97–8
Thangaraj, Stanley I. 50
themes and frequency 130
Thomas, Clarence 75
"thought provoking" 30
Thurman, Uma 71
Till, Emmett 2
TIME magazine 7, 70
toxic masculinity 25, 30
transformative justice movements 8

transformative resurgence 95
trans/gender-nonconforming/queer organizations 18
transgender prisoners 6
transgender theory 8
transitional terms and transformative justice 12–18
trans lives 20
trans people experience 7
trans/transgender, defined 9
The Tributes section 100
"triple jeopardy" 88
"Trust Women" (slogan) 2
Tuck, E. 87

uncertainty or imposter syndrome 121
Uniform Crime Reporting (UCR) programs 33, 34
U.S. Bureau of Justice Statistics (BJS) 26
U.S. prison system 9
Utley, E. 35

Van Wilder (movie) 52
Venit, Adam 24, 25, 28
"Violence Against the Transgender Community in 2019" 1
Violence Against Women Act (VAWA) 94

Violence on the Land, Violence on our Bodies (VLVB) 92, 95, 99
vitiated testimonial dynamics 67
vocabulary of criminalization 7
volume aggregation process 74–6
volume amplification 70–1
volume diminishment 71–2

War on Drugs 15
Washington Post (2017) 84
Watch What Happens Live 38
Weinstein, Harvey 1, 24
We Real Cool: Black Men and Masculinity 33
Western contemporary feminisms 86
William Morris Endeavor (WME) Entertainment 28
Winderman, Emily 3
Wolfgang, M. 32–3
Women's Earth Alliance (WEA) 93
The work of justice 18–20

Young black males 33
Young, Damon 30

Zacharek, Stephanie 10
Zimmerman, George 14